THE BATTLE OF THE BULGE
December 16, 1944 . . .

Before dawn, roaring cannons along an eighty mile front served notice on startled American troops that a German attack had begun. German infantry could be seen moving forward in the early-morning dark. Behind them followed tanks, ready to race through the camps cleared by the infantry.

By nightfall, the situation was chaotic. Whole regiments had been overwhelmed or cut off and the victorious Panzer columns were sweeping on toward Antwerp.

The surprise had been complete. Not until weeks later was it known that Hitler had launched his last offensive in the West—seventeen divisions and 200,000 men in a desperate do-or-die gamble to win the war!

THE BATTLE OF THE BULGE is the amazing true story of World War II's most important battle, written by the former chief of the Army Historical Division in the Ardennes and based on all available information from German and Allied sources.

THE BATTLE OF THE BULGE

(Abridged version of
DARK DECEMBER,
originally published by
Ziff-Davis Publishing Company)

Robert E. Merriam

BALLANTINE BOOKS · NEW YORK
An Intext Publisher

SBN 345-02525-3-125

PAPERBOUND EDITION
FIRST PRINTING: JANUARY, 1957
Published: February, 1957
SECOND PRINTING: MARCH, 1957
THIRD PRINTING: MAY, 1957
FOURTH PRINTING: JUNE, 1957
FIFTH PRINTING: FEBRUARY, 1963
SIXTH PRINTING: DECEMBER, 1965
SEVENTH PRINTING: DECEMBER, 1965
EIGHTH PRINTING: MARCH, 1966
NINTH PRINTING: MARCH, 1966
TENTH PRINTING: JANUARY, 1972

Printed in the United States of America

Photo courtesy of Photo World

Ballantine Books, Inc.
101 Fifth Avenue • New York, N.Y. 10003

CONTENTS

MAPS

Dedicated to the memory of the men who fought and died in those dark December days, in the hope that the lessons learned through their sacrifice will be well remembered.

Foreword

THE ORIGIN OF THIS BOOK TRACES BACK TO THE EARLY DAYS
of the war when a group of farsighted historians, recognizing
the inevitable weaknesses of official military reports, convinced
the Chief of Staff of our Army, General Marshall, that some
attempt should be made to capture, for posterity, the accurate
story of our then-pending military operations. Out of that
meeting came a new historical section of the War Department,
charged with the responsibility of recording, insofar as possible, the complete history of our military operations. Faced
everywhere with suspicion and lack of understanding, the historians struggled against overwhelming odds to convince Army
commanders, high and low, of the importance of their mission.
The effort was most successful in Europe, where each field
army had an historical team attached to it. I was a member of
such a team in the Ninth Army, and in the course of my duties,
I spent much of my time with the 7th Armored Division. Free
to wander where I pleased, to sit in on such conferences as I
could find out about, to interview whomever I desired, I was
able to gather considerable material about this Division's fights.
Always viewed with suspicion by the soldiers who were being
interviewed, I was faced with a constant fight to convince them
they should tell the true story, to show them that I was pre-
serving the facts for posterity, and not for the dreaded Inspector
General. Those of us who were intrusted with this strange task
soon discovered the inevitable tendency to cover up mistakes,
to warp facts, to convey the impression that all went according
to plan. But the historians found that, despite these obstacles,
they could piece together adequate accounts of the operations
if they persisted in their searching.

About six o'clock on the evening of December 16, 1944, I
was sitting in the office of the 7th Armored Division's Intelligence Officer, speculating with some of his assistants about the
meaning of a recent 12th Army Group Intelligence report
which said that the crust of German defenses was thinner than
ever before. As we were talking, the assistant operations officer
dashed in to say that the division was alerted for immediate

movement to First Army where they were to fight a small counterattack somewhere in Belgium. Inasmuch as the division was going to another army, I returned to Ninth Army headquarters for new orders, unaware of the harrowing week which lay ahead for the division. When I rejoined them six days later, the men of the division were many years older; they were just withdrawing from a pocket in which they almost had been caught by the Germans. Over half the equipment and nearly one-third of the men were missing, as units of the division straggled back through friendly lines. In the meantime, I had been wandering from army to corps headquarters, listening, noting, and talking with men who were attempting to stem this sudden German tide. This was the beginning of my book.

During the next thirty days I interviewed more than one hundred members of the 7th Armored Division, examined all battle records, went over the ground where the fighting had taken place, and finally pieced together the story of those six days. Later, I returned to Paris, where I became a member, and then Chief, of the Ardennes section of the Historical Division, European Theater of Operations, writing the official history of this great battle. We spent eight long months poring over the records from all units mixed up in the battle; we analyzed the reports of various historical officers; we interviewed again, in written or oral questioning, most of the Allied commanders; and several of us spent weeks going through Germany, interviewing German commanders who had led and planned this attack. Out of it all came five long, detailed volumes describing the Battle of the Bulge. From my notes, through access to these volumes which are available in the War Department, from other unclassified documents now available, and from papers which I had collected during this work, the factual basis of this story is gathered. My interviews with Generals Eisenhower, Bradley, and Hodges in the summer of 1946, when as a civilian I could more freely question them, rounded out the factual analysis. The interpretations are, of course, my own.

ROBERT E. MERRIAM

CHAPTER I

Wacht am Rhein : The German Plan

PRELUDE

IT ALL BEGAN ON JULY 20, 1944, FORTY-FIVE DAYS AFTER THE first Allied soldiers waded ashore through the carnage on the Normandy beaches. Shortly after noon on that day, Count Felix von Stauffenberg, Chief of Staff of the Replacement Army, and an intimate of high Nazis, sauntered into a barracks in a wood near Rastenburg in East Prussia to meet with *Der Fuehrer*, his military aides, Field Marshal Keitel, Colonel General Jodl, and eight other high ranking German officials. Nobody thought it strange that Count Stauffenberg placed a huge brief case against the leg of the conference table and shortly thereafter left the room. About ten minutes later, the room erupted into fire as the bomb in Stauffenberg's brief case exploded in the most serious attempt against the Hitler regime in its twelve years in power. *Der Fuehrer* escaped with only arm and ear injuries, thanks to a flimsy building which absorbed the force of the explosion, but he was ordered to bed, where he personally hatched the famed German attack called the Battle of the Bulge.

The aftermath of the bomb incident bordered on the comic opera. Stauffenberg watched in silent glee from a safe distance as the bomb blew the roof off the barracks. Certain that Hitler was dead, Stauffenberg hastened to the nearby airport to fly to Berlin, where his accomplices awaited the word that was to start a carefully planned uprising which would seize control of the government. But right there, things began to go wrong. Stauffenberg, methodical military planner, impatiently paced the airfield near Berlin for an hour, waiting for a car he had forgotten to order. Meanwhile, in Berlin itself, events were not running smoothly. An obscure major named Remer, who was in command of Hitler's personal *Wachtbatallion,* was called in by the conspirators and told that Hitler was dead, that he was to surround the *Bendlerblock* (government buildings) to prevent anyone from either entering or leaving. Remer was not brilliant, but even he smelled a rat; his doubts were further stirred by one of his lieutenants who went to see a confidant of Goeb-

1

bels to relate the information. The result was an order for Remer to confer immediately with Goebbels.

Picture if you can, an obscure major dashing breathlessly into Goebbels' office, and demanding of the "Mouthpiece" if he were loyal to *Der Fuehrer*. But that is exactly what Remer demanded of an indignant Goebbels. Remer hastily blurted out the facts as he knew them, mainly that there was something strange going on which he did not thoroughly understand. Goebbels picked up the private phone connecting him with Rastenberg and after some minutes delay found himself connected with a much-shaken, but very much alive, *Fuehrer*. "Let me speak with Remer," demanded Hitler. "Now we have the criminals and saboteurs of the Eastern Front; only a few officers are involved, and we will eliminate them from the root," Hitler told Remer. "You are placed in a historic position. It is your responsibility to use your head. You are under my direct command until Himmler arrives to take over the Replacement Army. Do you understand me?" And so Remer became a German hero.

The rest is now ancient history. The insurrection was put down; most of the ringleaders captured or killed. Hitler was bedridden with lacerated thighs, bruised elbows, cut hands, and a broken eardrum; but, though seriously hurt, he was not permanently incapacitated. A ruthless purge of the army was then conducted—even Rommel, the desert giant, killed himself in a hospital, contrary to popular rumors of a peaceful death while recuperating from effects of wounds received in an Allied strafing.* We thought the attempt on Hitler's life was good, but it gave *Der Fuehrer* time to think.

AN IDEA IS BORN

During the last days of July and the month of August, Hitler lay bedridden, recovering from the shock of the bomb attempt of July 20th. Although unable to carry on with the many details to which he ordinarily devoted his time, he was able to concentrate on the higher strategy and to worry about his greatest problem: how to regain the initiative lost since the Anglo-American landings in Normandy two months before. There is no doubt that the attack in the Ardennes was Hitler's idea.

---

* Both Rommel's wife and General Jodl's aide confirmed the fact that Rommel was connected with the putsch attempt and had killed himself when confronted with the choice of suicide or liquidation.

The first plan for a gigantic attack to regain the offensive was developed during the height of the greatest American gains through France, when we were fast approaching the German West Wall. In mid-August, General Blaskowitz was recalled from Italy. In early September, as American forces raced across France toward the German border in a northeasterly trend, Hitler called in his General Staff and ordered immediate preparations for an attack from the German border on the rear of General Patton's Third Army. Two crack German units, *3* and *15 Panzer Grenadier Divisions*,** were hastily assembled and moved from Italy to the Western Front. They hoped to cut off the rear of Patton's army and drive a German wedge across the eastern portion of France, in front of Metz, to the Belgian border. They proposed to cut off the American lines of communication, and then to pinch off the armored and mechanized infantry spearheads of the American forces just meeting their first resistance in the German West Wall. But the plan was never carried out. The bridgehead west of the Moselle River was too weak and the available troops too few. The idea of an attack, however, was not forgotten. In early September, Hitler called in Jodl and Keitel to tell them bluntly, "We must regain the initiative. *Der Fuehrer* has spoken."

WHITHER NOW

Once having determined that only by sensational counterattack could Germany expect to regain the initiative and stave off inevitable defeat, it remained for Hitler and his military henchmen, Field Marshal Keitel, Chief, *Oberkommando der Wehrmacht*, equivalent to Minister of War, and Colonel General Jodl, Chief, *Wehrmacht Fuehrungs Stat*, the Armed Forces Operation Staff, to analyze the situation on various fronts completely and to determine exactly the right place to strike with the comparatively limited resources available to Germany. The abortive attack planned against Patton's southern flank was hastily thrown together; the new attack was to be carefully considered and craftily planned.

Turning first to the Russian Front, Hitler found himself confronted with a serious situation created by the withdrawal of Rumania from the war and the collapse of *Army Group South*. However, he hoped to stabilize the front by the use of counter measures, among them being the increased employment of

---

** To avoid confusion with American Army units, German Army units have been set in italics throughout the book.

Hungarian troops in the front lines. It was hoped that a new line could be erected in the Carpathian Mountains. The center of the Russian Front had been stabilized by mid-September in a line running, roughly, along the Vistula and Narew Rivers and then the East Prussian border. A serious Russian bridgehead across the Vistula River at Baranow had been considerably narrowed by German counterattacks. *Army Group North* was cut off in Courland, but the front had been stabilized there also, and strong Russian forces were employed in containing the German troops, which prevented the Russians from employing these sorely needed reinforcements on the East Prussian front. The general impression by mid-September was that the Russian summer offensive had died down and that, with the possible exception of the southern group of armies, a quiet period could be expected. Hitler was confident the Reds would not be ready for a sustained offensive until sometime in February.

By mid-September, the gasolineless Americans were sputtering to a halt along most of the Western Front as the supply lines, long taut, gave way. For once, Hitler could boast of a continuous front line in the west which, although thin and a little worn in spots, was amply backed up by the West Wall and other natural obstacles. Hastily mobilized fortress troops had been moved into the West Wall, and for the first time since the Allied invasion, Hitler was afforded a breathing spell. It gave him time to reorganize and refit his legions, which had been sorely battered by the Anglo-American teams.

Turning to the Southern Front, Hitler and his grand strategists were not at all displeased, because there they found that the *Army Group* in Italy had managed to build another stable front after its retreat from middle Italy, a front still in advance of the Apennines positions. Thus, time was available to construct the main fortified lines, and to reorganize and recuperate the troops.

In the Balkans, Hitler's legions were in retreat to Croatia. Sudden withdrawal of the Rumanian troops from the war forced a hasty readjustment of the line to close this gap between the Balkan front and the Eastern front. Treacherous mountainous terrain and harassing partisan activities were delaying the withdrawal, but despite these obstacles *Der Fuehrer* and his staff were agreed that the situation was well in hand, as long as the Allies did not land troops on the Dalmatian coast behind the German withdrawal.

Even the home front gave Hitler cause for optimism. Swarms

of probing secret agents found that the attempt on his life and regime had not aroused strong popular support. On the contrary, the imminent invasion of the sacred soil of the homeland from two directions rallied the people behind the Nazis, as the most ruthless purges and pogroms had failed to do. The German people, still unconvinced that they were defeated, were ready to rally to the last great stand.

Most startling to Americans, who had overestimated the effect of our air raids, was the continued vitality of German industry. Despite ceaseless war in the air, Germany succeeded in maintaining production levels in many industries, and even increasing it in the absolutely vital fields of artillery, airplanes, and tanks. This remarkable achievement was brought about largely through the transfer of important facilities underground. Further cause for optimism on the production front was offered Hitler by the prospect of stabilizing the air war in several months, through use of the new *Duesen* (jet-propelled) plane, which he knew would be superior to anything the Allies would be able to offer for some time. With stability in the air achieved, he would be able to expand production still further.

These were the considerations which led Hitler to believe that he would be able to take the initiative on at least one front, to destroy considerable enemy troops, and to influence the course of the war. But where to attack? And with how many divisions?

"*Mein Fuehrer,* give me between twenty and thirty divisions, and I will launch an attack," blustering Field Marshal Keitel opined. But the Germans could no longer pick up such a number of divisions at a moment's notice because they had been fighting for five long years. Where would such a force come from? First, by scraping the manpower barrel for the last time, a whole new series of divisions called the *Volksgrenadiers,* were to be formed—infantry divisions shorn of all but essential units, largely horsedrawn rather than motorized. Into the *Volksgrenadiers,* not to be confused in any way with the *Volkssturm* (the People's Army), were to be poured new draftees, young men barely old enough to fight and older men who had fought out the war on the production front. These men were to be fitted around a core of regular army officers and noncommissioned officers, and the divisions were to be filled out with *ersatz* infantrymen—pilots without planes, ground crews without fields, sailors without ships—all of whom were to be given guns and told how to shoot and fight. Next, the divisions which had been battered in the Battle of France were to be reconstituted and refitted as they lay in readiness behind the West Wall. And finally, the *coup de grâce* would be administered by a completely new army, the core of which would be four of the élite SS panzer divisions, which were to be completely refitted and retrained deep in the heart of Germany. Christened the *Sixth Panzer Army*, this group was given top priority of men, equipment, and officers, and selected to head it was Hitler's old friend and fanatic follower, Josef "Sepp" Dietrich, loyal Nazi since the beerhall days in Munich. Here, then, were the makings of the attack force; if more divisions were needed, Hitler was prepared to strip all his other fronts. This was to be an all-out gamble.

But where to attack? The Russian Front? No, the resources would be wasted in an attack which would have no decisive influence on the course of the war. The plotters agreed that even a highly successful operation in the east could, at most, eliminate only twenty or thirty Russian divisions. While serious, such a loss would be only a drop in the huge Russian manpower barrel. Nor were there any grand strategic objectives which could probably be attained with such a striking force. Likewise, in Italy, supply, terrain, and weather precluded the possibility of a large-scale attack in this theater, and again the strategic objectives were minor.

In the west conditions appeared more favorable. The Germans were well aware of the limited nature of our troop concentrations. We had won the French campaign with a minimum of troops, thanks to our complete superiority in the air and our almost complete mechanization. Despite this smashing victory, our forces were still weak—under fifty divisions. Other considerations entered German thinking: German troops, holding out in the channel ports, had forced the Allies to supply themselves through a few conquered ports, plus the beaches in Normandy. Antwerp was still blocked by mines, and German troops covered the sea approaches to the port. Already, our armies had slowed down because of supply difficulties. Our airborne assault at Arnhem had met with only partial success, and the Germans had successfully driven back our most forward penetrations across the Rhine River. Finally, the German High Command, correctly estimating our intentions, expected our main effort would be in the area of Aachen, where we would attempt to break through to the Rhine River, and, eventually, the Ruhr industrial area just east of the Rhine.

Here then, on the Western Front, were the ingredients for a successful offensive: a sudden attack which would trap twenty to thirty divisions would change the entire situation on the Western Front. Such a success would allow, at the least, respite to refit many divisions, which then could be transferred to the Russian front. Even with only partial success, such an attack would so disrupt all Anglo-American plans that it would be weeks or months before the Allies could recover. German morale would thus shoot up many hundredfold. Finally, Hitler in his most optimistic moments hoped the Americans and British might even be driven from the war by this severe setback, which would dull what he thought was the feeble democratic will to win.

The risks were great. It would be necessary to weaken all fronts to ready the attack formations. The *Volksgrenadier* divisions would be held back at a time when they were imperatively needed on all fronts for reinforcement of exhausted troops. The re-equipment of these divisions would claim a large part of the new production and would mean, especially for the Eastern Front, a sharp reduction in new tanks and gasoline, all desperately needed. And finally, there was always the acute danger that the Allies would go over to the offensive while the preparations were in progress and force their way through the German defenses. In addition, Allied air superiority on the Western Front would force the Germans to pick a period of bad weather to allow comparative quiet as the troops and supplies were being assembled. Lastly, the experience of the 1943 German summer offensive in Russia was a bitter lesson: frontal attack against a deep, well-manned enemy line would be doomed to failure. In that attack, after two weeks the German formations were still pushing through deep Russian defenses; they became exhausted, and the attack was called off. Thus, a new factor must be injected—surprise in a weakly held zone. But at last, Hitler felt he had the ingredients for a successful attack: surprise, a quick break-through in a weak enemy position, and a quick thrust to the rear areas, all during a period of unfavorable air weather. This would give him the offensive. The possibilities were limitless: destruction of large Allied forces; capture or destruction of large quantities of supplies; possible end to the war in the west. The risks were great, but the stakes high.

THE FINGER POINTS

It was during these deliberations, on a bright summer day in mid-September, that Colonel General Jodl stalked into Hitler's room, followed by his aide, Major Herbert Buechs, who was carrying the large map of Europe on which, twice daily, progress of the fighting was recorded for *Der Fuehrer*. As General Jodl ran his stubby finger up the line representing the Western Front, he pointed to the forests of Belgium and Luxembourg, where four American divisions held a total of eighty miles. Hitler sat up in bed, propped himself on his elbows, and asked Jodl to point out that area again. Still later in the briefing, Hitler again asked about the sector where the Americans were so few. The seed had been planted, and from it the German attack in the Ardennes forests was to burst forth on December 16 to shock the Allied world.

On September 25th, Hitler summoned Jodl and Keitel. This time he was prepared to attack. He was still a sick man, but he was also a desperate, determined man. "I am," he cried, "determined to hold fast to the execution of this operation, regardless of any risk, even if the enemy offensives on both sides of Metz and the imminent attack on the Rhine territory lead to great terrain and town losses." The die had been cast; Jodl was ordered to prepare for the detailed plan for submission at the earliest possible date. *Der Fuehrer's* outline was bold and simple: a quick thrust toward Antwerp to cut off the rear installations of the Allies and crush twenty to thirty divisions in the trap north of Antwerp. And a fanatic Hitler hoped that this would turn the tide of battle on the Western Front.

A FATEFUL DAY

Hitler, once determined on one last desperate course of violence on the Western Front, arrayed his pieces in the gigantic game of chess, preparing for the final moment. Up to the famous military library at Liegnitz went one of his aides; by dint of several hard nights poring over the now dusty books, he returned in a few days with reams of papers outlining the German plans and actions in the forests of Luxembourg and Belgium in the campaign of 1940. Jodl, working long, wearying hours with his aide, Major Herbert Buechs, consulted with a few carefully selected high officers, finally drew up the first preliminary plan for the attack. Gradually a pattern emerged from this research and from almost daily discussion with Hitler: the brunt of the attack would be carried by two panzer armies; infantry divisions supported by heavy formations of antitank and antiaircraft weapons would block to the north and south to protect the flanks of the attacking armor; the

Luftwaffe would be unwrapped for a "dying gasp" support of the attacking forces. The surprise attack would be preceded by a short, but powerful, artillery concentration. Bridgeheads across the Meuse River were to be secured the second day of the attack. Following this, armored divisions of the second wave would reinforce the attacking divisions while they reprovisioned. Then both waves were to strike hard through disorganized and demoralized Allied resistance toward Antwerp. The panzer units were not to waver in their single determination to reach the Meuse River; all pockets of opposition were to be left for following infantry units, and all flank attacks were to be dealt with by the supporting troops. As Model later said, "Onward to the Maas" (Meuse).

It was a lovely fall day October 8, 1944, when Colonel General Jodl walked into Hitler's office bearing with him the first fateful plan to rewin the war in the west. It is no wonder that Hitler broadly smiled at Buechs, Jodl's aide, even winked and joked a bit, as details of the ingenious plan were unfolded to him. *Der Fuehrer* could not imagine that six months later he would be dead, alongside his wife, and Colonel General Jodl would be apologizing for his actions before an Allied court. Those were thoughts as unreal to the plotters as was the possibility of a German attack in the minds of the Allied High Command. It is almost inconceivable: on October 8, when the bitter struggle for Aachen, first major German city to be attacked, was underway, Hitler, Jodl, Keitel, and Buechs, calmly sat in Berlin, planning the destruction of half the Allied troops on the continent. On October 8, two weeks after the combined Allied Chiefs of Staff had met with Roosevelt and Churchill in Quebec, three Germans were issuing the first orders which would culminate in the concentration of twenty-nine German divisions, in the largest single pitched battle of the war on the Western Front. On October 8, five days after another new American army, the Ninth, had assumed its place in the line ironically enough in the forests of the Ardennes region of Belgium and Luxembourg, Hitler was receiving reports outlining the strategy of the German attack through this very area in 1940, and planning a new campaign to destroy our new army. Not many of us who drove and walked along those roads on October 8th, as I did, were even thinking of the German attack of 1940—none of us in the wildest nightmare dreamed that this would be repeated.

Unbelievable as it may seem, on October 8th, General Jodl presented a favorable picture: four panzer divisions in the

Sixth Panzer Army, two panzer divisions in the *Fifth Panzer Army*, six additional panzer divisions which could be rested near the front lines—total twelve panzer divisions which could be made available for the attack. By November 20, sixteen of the new *Volksgrenadier* divisions would be ready for action, and by December 10, four more; two parachute divisions could be made available; twelve artillery corps, fourteen army artillery battalions, seven rocket brigades, thirteen antitank battalions, all to be available for action by November 15. Hitler gleefully rubbed his hands, made tentative assignments of divisions to armies: nine divisions to the *Sixth Panzer Army* led by erratic, fanatic, but loyal, "Sepp" Dietrich; seven divisions to trusty and crafty Manteuffel in the center with his *Fifth Panzer Army;* and seven divisions to Brandenberger on the south. The plan? While Brandenberger swung to the south to hold off attempted reinforcement by Patton's Third Army and Dietrich employed an infantry corps, borrowed from the *Fifteenth Army* to the north, with the same mission, the main panzer forces of Dietrich and Manteuffel were to plunge through the center in the mad dash for the Meuse River, which the optimistic High Command hoped to reach on the second day, and then onward toward Brussels and Antwerp. When these objectives were reached, the other fronts would be drained to provide the additional troops necessary to liquidate the Americans and British isolated by this swift knockout blow. Command of the three armies was to rest with Field Marshal Model, commander of *Army Group B*, working under the direction of the old master, von Rundstedt, Commander in Chief of all forces in the west. "It was a gamble," said Jodl, "but we were in a desperate situation, and the only way to save it was by a desperate decision—we had to stake everything."

Jodl continued his discussion with Hitler. The attack, said Hitler, would go to the north toward Antwerp, rather than south because there was no *Schwerpunkt* (limiting pole) to the south, no anchor on which to hinge a halt. The distance to be travelled was 125 miles to Antwerp, 60 miles to the Meuse River at the nearest point. Jodl made certain that Hitler recognized the obstacles to be met, the physical obstacles having nothing to do with the state of German industry, manpower and transportation systems. There were narrow unpaved roads, diagonally running rivers offering numerous opportunities for demolitions which could delay the advance, many hills, possible mud. All this only strengthened the determination to reach the Meuse River quickly. West of the Meuse to Antwerp was good tank terrain; and then, too, although the land on the flanks east of the Meuse was rugged, once obtained it was superb for defensive purposes.

Three days later, a second conference was held with Hitler. This time *Der Fuehrer* had some counterproposals: "Broaden the attack base," he said, "carefully plan artillery positions to achieve maximum fire power, especially prepare plans to protect the northern flank where the heaviest attacks will occur. Issue orders that under no circumstances will Liége be attacked. Give up the idea of using parachute units to capture the Meuse River bridges—the *Luftwaffe* could not be counted on to get them through. Base plans on target date of November 25, as this is the new moon period, good for attack because the nights will be dark, and this will aid us in night movements; but above all else, surprise is our keynote—secrecy must prevail."

ON PAIN OF DEATH

Even Hitler recognized that 1944 was a far cry from Poland in 1939, the Lowlands in 1940, Jugoslavia and Russia in 1941. This time it was a weakened Germany, with many of her best men already dead (a million and a quarter according to Jodl), with her industries still running, but hard-pressed by incessant Allied "terror raids." A supposedly alert Allied army was already on Germany's doorstep, waiting only the right moment to make the final kill. With a fixed front, the only way to achieve the mobile conditions of blitz warfare was by surprise, complete surprise, and an attack at a weak point where the Germans could get a running start before the Allies could react.

Anyone who has been with an army in the field knows the difficulties which beset a commander attempting to maintain secrecy while planning a huge offensive. Add to that the suspicions heaped up through twelve years of dictatorship and absolute rule, top it off with a recent attempt on the dictator's life by numerous leaders previously considered friendly by him, and then just to emphasize your point, kill off your top commander in the west because he wants to surrender to the enemy, and you have the situation in Germany as confident Hitler, cocky Keitel, and cunning Jodl plotted the new attack in the Ardennes.

All of these thoughts must have flashed through Hitler's mind on October 12, 1944, as he conferred with his key advis-

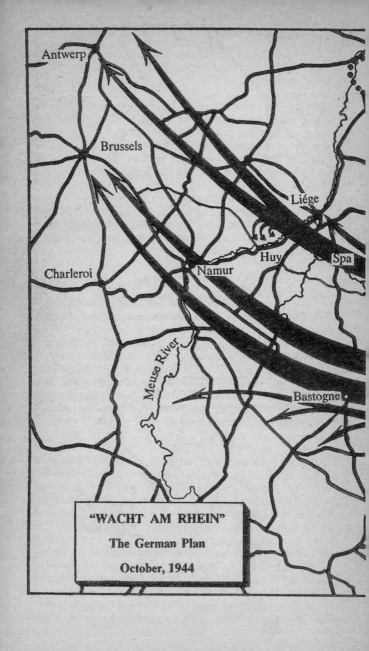

"WACHT AM RHEIN"

The German Plan

October, 1944

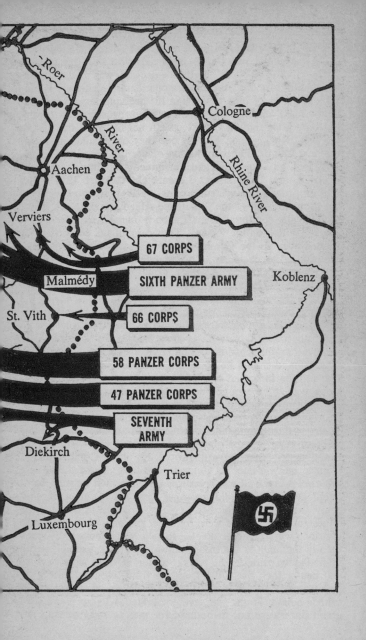

ors. Could he trust Goering? Press Chief Dietrich? Rundstedt?
Model? even Himmler and Goebbels? Who were his friends?
How could he be sure? Finally the decision was made: at first,
he would trust only the closest confidants, Keitel, Jodl, and
a small group of high officials in his headquarters. Gradually,
as the need arose, and only then, others would be informed,
but only after signing a written oath not to reveal the plan at
the risk of being shot. One by one they were called in during
the next month: Fegelein, liaison officer to Himmler; General
Burgdorf, aide to Hitler and Personnel Adjutant; Press Chief
Dietrich, and his assistant Lorenz. On October 12th Hitler
sent an order to Rundstedt, saying that new reserves were being grouped to meet the threatened Allied attack to the Rhine
River by a counterattack. The code name was *Wacht Am
Rhein* (Watch on the Rhine). Thus camouflage deception was
carried even to the Commander in Chief in the West. Hitler
was taking no chances; he decreed that Rundstedt would be
kept in the dark until he, Hitler, gave the word. There was no
trust in Germany.

These secrecy regulations were strictly adhered to during the
entire planning period for the German attack. Almost to the
very end, those who were informed of the attack plans were
painfully forced to sign the secrecy pledge. Hitler himself laid
down a careful schedule outlining when the various echelons
of command should be notified of the plans. Each army commander was informed only of his particular role. Assault divisions were to be brought into the attack areas on the last day.
Daylight movement of troops was forbidden. No scouts were
allowed to make reconnaissance of the land over which the
attack was to be made. All artillery and antiaircraft positions
were surveyed by the highest commanders, who were not allowed to tell their subordinates of the plans. Combat planes
were to be held deep in Germany until the day of the attack.
All armies involved were required to retain their existing command posts. Fake radio messages were given out; a dummy
army group was established north of Cologne to confuse the
Allies further. Troops were told that the new *Volksgrenadier*
divisions were being assembled to relieve battleworn divisions
then in the line. As the troops moved into their assembly areas
immediately prior to the attack, motor vehicles were prohib-
ited nearer than five miles from the front lines, and airplanes
flew up and down the lines at night to drown out any possible
vehicle noises. Traffic was severely limited; telephone and tele-
graph lines were not to be used for messages concerning the

attack. Only officer couriers were allowed to carry the orders, and they were not allowed to fly. "Unreliable" elements, including Alsatians, Luxembourgers, Poles, and Russians, were weeded out of the attack divisions and sent to schools. Artillery pieces being moved up were halted during the daytime, and placed in woods near roads. Bridging equipment, a dead giveaway for offensive action, was carefully hidden. And high officers spread false rumors of their mission. Manteuffel, for instance, gleefully accounted to me how he announced in a stage whisper, while sitting at a cafe, that he was getting ready to attack the Saar. And other rumors and false clues, carefully planted, further misled us.

But the basic element of the secrecy plan was perhaps the most effective because it dovetailed so well with the Allied state of mind. It was the idea stressed by the code name *Wacht Am Rhein* which implied a defensive attack to prevent our reaching the Rhine River. This was emphasized throughout, and was formalized on November 5th when Field Marshal Keitel issued his camouflage order, which said:

> Large scale attack to be expected against line Cologne-Bonn. To attack this from flanks, two counterattack forces to be formed, one northwest of Cologne, the other in the Eifel. Latter to be concealed as far as possible, former to be made to appear more important. This is to be given as the reason for deployment of *Luftwaffe*.

By this device a clever plan was made diabolic. It was a clever plan because the German High Command knew that the Allies would be sure to spot some attack preparations, as they did, but it was diabolic because the Germans sensed the Allied frame of mind—exhilarated at the tremendous victories in France, overconfident, anxious to end the war with a final blow, intent on this end almost to the exclusion of other possibilities. Overwhelming proof of the success of this maneuver is the astounding fact that the only American intelligence officer who, in a printed report, mentioned the possibility of a large-scale German attack, predicted exactly what the Germans wanted him to predict—a defensive counterattack (see Chapter III for further discussion).

No one can deny that the secrecy plans were a great success. True, there were some slips, and some anxious moments in the German camp. The *Sixth Panzer Army* was spotted, as it was planned, in the Cologne plain in November, and many a cold night was spent around the Allied fireplaces speculating about when it would be used, but not once was the suggestion advanced that it would attack in the Ardennes forests. Two artillerymen from the *Sixth Panzer Army* were reported lost about four days before the attack began, but one had been killed before capture, and the second eventually returned. One deserter was lost from *Seventh Army*. Reports drifted through the lines mentioning concentrations of German troops in various villages behind the lines. Despite careful precautions, heavy vehicular movements were heard. All of these clues might have been important slips were it not for the Allied frame of mind and the cunning German cover-plan of *Wacht Am Rhein* which threw us completely off guard. The Germans scored their first major prerequisite for a successful attack—complete, utter surprise.

THE GENERALS

Gerd von Rundstedt, General Field Marshal, Commander in Chief of the German forces in the west, typified the German military aristocracy who, while finding much fault with the Nazi regime, were not inclined to fight an institution which glorified the military might of Germany. Rundstedt played a peculiar role in the Battle of the Bulge. Seventy years of age, he had once retired after a long, and in German military terms, distinguished career spanning nearly half a century. His had been an important role in the development of the German army, and especially the infantry, in the period between the two wars. But when war finally came, he stepped out of his retirement, and was in the forefront, brilliantly commanding an Army Group in the attacks in Poland and France and the subsequent campaign in Russia where he led the conquest of the Ukraine. Rundstedt was transferred to the west in 1942, and there he remained right through the Allied invasion, replaced for a time, but soon back in the saddle. Although we have no definite information that Rundstedt was implicated in the attempted *Putsch* of July 20, 1944, there are indications that Hitler was not prone to trust him or perhaps any of the other German Generals, following the abortive attempt on his life. However, others who looked for leadership from Rundstedt in the attempt to overthrow Hitler were also sadly disappointed, perhaps, as military commentators such as Liddel Hart have implied, because his ambitions had burned out his moral courage.

Rundstedt was a brilliant military leader, quick to grasp the significance of any particular operation, to analyze the obstacles, and then in turn successfully and oftentimes brilliantly to overcome these barriers. As General Jodl described him, "Rundstedt always enjoyed complete authority and had an excellent head for operations. He had studied in the old school." Whatever the reasons, whether because of his age, his fundamental doubts about the efficacy of an attack in the Ardennes, or his belief that Germany was defeated, Rundstedt divorced himself almost completely from the planning for the Ardennes offensive. Ironically enough, the "Rundstedt Offensive," as our press usually called it, was not directed by Rundstedt, who devoted himself almost exclusively to the supply phases of the attack. Perhaps he was purposely by-passed. Jodl hints at this when he reports: "On account of his (Rundstedt's) age, he was not so well-fitted to spur men on to superhuman efforts in an adverse situation."

Field Marshal Walter Model was a sharp contrast to the austere, haughty Rundstedt. Nothing better indicated this than the fact that Model was one of the few German generals to take his life at the war's end. This dramatic end to a spectacular military career indicates his fanaticism and devotion to the cause. Model was 54 and had been originally introduced to Hitler by Goebbels. From 1939 to 1941, he commanded a panzer division which made an enviable record as it slashed its way ruthlessly through the various opponents of Nazism. On the Russian front in July, 1944, at the time of the attempted *Putsch*, Model quickly proclaimed his loyalty to Hitler, and for this *Der Fuehrer* was eternally grateful. Being considered "reliable," Model was shifted to the politically more dangerous Western Front shortly after the abortive attempt to surrender to the English by von Kluge (see Chapter II). Here Model assumed command of *Army Group B* which led the rejuvenated German armies following the debacle in France. It was he, rather than Rundstedt, who masterfully planned the details of the German smash into the Ardennes.

Of the three army commanders, none matched Josef "Sepp" Dietrich for unashamed, rapid, fanatical Nazi political maneuvering. One glance at this short, squat Bavarian adds understanding to the bitter hatred for him evidenced almost unanimously by the German generals. His conceit is matched only by his apparently complete lack of the military wherewithal to make a good general. Dietrich's career mirrors the rise of the Nazi party in Germany. An enlisted man all through the first world war, Dietrich considered himself to be the greatest tank expert in the German army because of the few months he was a tank sergeant. After the war, he served in the army until 1928, when he went to Munich and joined the Nazi party. Trained as a butcher by profession, he resumed his civilian trade, only this time as head of the *SS Stubafu,* an infamous group which furnished bloody protection for party rallies. The return to butchery won for him a seat in the Reichstag in 1931 and the honored role as Hitler's personal bodyguard during the election campaign of 1932. From then on the name Dietrich is synonymous with everything violent in the Nazi career; first, he organized the *Liebstandarte Adolf Hitler,* a special unit for protection of *Der Fuehrer;* then it was the Roehm affair, when he was ordered to start the blood bath.

Later his *LAH* led the Germans across the Austrian border, marched into the Sudetenland, participated in the attack on Czechoslovakia, sustained heavy losses in the Polish campaign, fought in France, battled in Greece, joined in the attack on Russia, went as part of the relief army for Paulus at Stalingrad, fought in Normandy, and now head of the *Sixth Panzer Army,* the butcher had graduated to the head of his class—highest *SS* officer in Germany.

Dietrich had neither the training nor the mentality to become an army commander. Rundstedt admirably summed up his characteristics in one succinct sentence: "He is decent, but stupid." Goering said, "He had at most the ability to command a division." Why, then, did Hitler entrust this man with the cream of German armored might in his last great gamble?

The answer dates back to the shaky July 20 when Hitler so nearly met his death. The roots lie deep in Hilter's fundametal distrust of the military. Jodl suggested this when he said that there was certain political interference in the conduct of the war and that some things had been done which he would not have done on purely professional grounds. This is as near as Jodl would come to admitting the fact—Hitler had chosen his top-ranking *SS* General for this last attack, the man who has risen from captain to *Oberstgruppenfuehrer der Waffen SS* (Lieutenant General) in four years, to provide the fanatical base necessary to carry through with his daring plans. Not only did he provide Dietrich with the best equipment and men, but in addition, Hitler placed the main effort with the *Sixth Panzer Army.* Theirs was the shortest, but the hardest, route to the Meuse River, because this army skirted dangerously close to the huge Allied concentrations in the Aachen salient. Dietrich could be certain that his flank would be the first to be attacked.

But Dietrich was not wholly without assistance in the complicated task of maneuvering a panzer army. Although Rundstedt and Model had no say about the selection of Dietrich to lead the main effort, they did insist that Dietrich be given one of the most capable men on the General Staff, and to this end *Brigadefuehrer Der Waffen SS* Fritz Kraemer was assigned as chief of staff to Dietrich. Kraemer was the antithesis of Dietrich: regular army, trained by the General Staff, keen, witty, intelligent, and a gentleman, he had been shifted from the regular army to the *SS* during the course of the war. Not as fanatical as Dietrich, Kraemer was known and respected by the other army generals. His was the difficult task of pulling together Dietrich's army and plotting its strategy.

General der Panzer Truppen von Manteuffel, an alert *Wehrmacht* officer, was a master of armored tactics. Early in September of 1944, Manteuffel was given command of the *Fifth Panzer Army* which had been selected to launch the abortive attack against Patton's southern flank during the early days of September. Later, he was slipped into the line south of Metz, but in October Hitler shifted him to Aachen, where his army took over defense of that crucial city and the entire sector screening the Ruhr industrial area. Manteuffel remained in this sector until the second week in November, when he and his staff were withdrawn to prepare for the Ardennes attack.

Although the irascible Dietrich appears to have had little to do with the development of the tactical and strategic planning for the big attack, Manteuffel played a prominent role, even persuading Hitler to make certain basic changes in the attack hour and method. Being a brilliant tactician he commanded the respect of not only Hitler, but the General Staff and the field commander as well. Model leaned heavily on Manteuffel to carry out his plans. And here one of Hitler's basic inconsistencies caught up with him; after selecting Dietrich to lead the main effort, he practically ignored him in the planning phases. So obvious was the affront that Dietrich, like an apologetic schoolboy, told me how he knew nothing of the attack plans until December 12, four days before the start. I knew he was lying, and took great pains to point out chapter and verse to prove my point. But Dietrich stuck to his argument like the bully turned coward when cornered by bigger boys, and his bravado vanished when I asked him to explain how Manteuffel knew so much about the planning of the attack, and he, Dietrich, nothing. "Manteuffel had influence with Hitler," he innocently blurted out.

Steady Erich Brandenberger, *General der Artillerie,* unspectacular and little-known, was a soldier's soldier. Carefully trained in the various military schools, Brandenberger was well versed in the basic principles of attack and defense. Thus like Manteuffel, he was head and shoulders above fanatic Dietrich. When he first heard of the impending offensive, his army occupied the sector south of Manteuffel. His was the least spectacular of the three army missions: with six infantry divisions he was to pivot on the southern hinge of the attack, fan out to the south, and block any Allied attempts to hit the southern flank of the penetration. His hardest task, it was thought, would be to keep pace with the hard-riding panzers to his north.

These, then, were the major-domos of the attack. Except for Dietrich, all were steeped in German militarism. But there were others, perhaps not important in the over-all picture, but interesting as types, as personalities who appealed to Hitler. The first of these, Skorzeny, joined the Nazi party in 1932 at the age of 24. After the war began, he joined the *SS* and served at various times on the French, Balkan, and Russian fronts. Early in 1943 he was assigned to the German sabotage forces, having proved himself daring, courageous, and brilliant. He first won fame for his part in liberating Benito Mussolini in September, 1943. From that time forward this blonde, handsome, young giant became increasingly popular in palace circles. Active for a time in sabotage activities in the Balkans, where he was instrumental in counter-acting Allied agents' attempts to unite Tito and Mikhailovich, he was subsequently shifted to the west where, by June, 1944, he was charged with considerable sabotage activities. It was natural that when Hitler planned a massive deceptive "Trojan Horse" to accompany his Ardennes attack, he should choose this man for the job.

A second palace favorite was assigned a special role in the Ardennes offensive. Stolid, but loyal, Otto Remer has already come to our attention as "savior" of Berlin during the attempted *Putsch* on July 20, 1944. You will recall that it was Remer who went to Goebbels with news of the threat, and it was he to whom Hitler, temporarily only, entrusted the fate of Germany. Remer's "military genius" was immediately recognized by Hitler, and he rapidly rose from major to brigadier general. At first Remer's greatly expanded unit was deployed around Hitler's headquarters in the east at Rastenburg, ostensibly because *Der Fuehrer* had caught wind of rumors that the enemy was planning to capture him with a sensational parachute drop on his headquarters. But later, when Hitler left Rastenburg for Berlin, Remer was personally instructed by his idol to expand his unit to a brigade preparatory to participation in the big offensive.

Remer was also a big, rather handsome, young fanatic, but not so quick as Skorzeny. His was the third command given to one of the shrinking group of loyal Nazis. Remer's brigade in the Ardennes was the best equipped of the panzer units, even ranking on a par with the *SS* panzer units in Dietrich's army. Remer, like Dietrich, was a courageous fighter, but weak on the logistical side of warfare, and at a loss with the unit under him.

And so we have the Nazi leaders of all types and temperaments, some brilliant, some stupid. Americans who are sometimes quick to condemn their own methods of leadership will learn that one-man rule and absolute authority, backed by power of life and death, do not always solve the problem.

CRUCIAL OCTOBER

October was a crucial month for the Germans. Prerequisite for any successful attack by the battered troops still in the line was withdrawal. Hitler ordered top priority in relief to the four élite *SS* panzer divisions which were to form the new *Sixth Panzer Army*, led by "Sepp" Dietrich. This was not easy when, on October 3, 1944, heavy attacks began on the border city of Aachen. Because this was the first major German city to be attacked, Hitler ordered that the town be held at all costs. "No surrender, no matter what the odds," he decreed. By the middle of October, however, these four divisions had been relieved and had assembled in eastern Germany where they were given top priority for men and equipment. But other divisions were not as fortunate, and three of the chosen few were tied up in the fighting for Aachen. Then, in mid-October, the predominantly British push to relieve the port of Antwerp began. To ease the pressure of this attack and at the same time to test the possibility of a large-scale tank attack in middle Holland, Hitler committed two more of the panzer-type divisions which were allotted to the attack forces. This attack, which was only partially successful, was against the American 7th Armored Division, the first Allied armored division sent into the Battle of the Bulge on December 16.

In mid-October, Rundstedt, still unaware of the impending attack, reported to Hitler that he needed eight infantry and three panzer divisions to hold his 625-mile Western Front. His recapitulation showed effective strength of 47 infantry and 6½ panzer divisions against an estimated enemy strength of 42 infantry, 18 armored divisions, and 11 armored brigades. Between September 1 and October 15 Rundstedt received 150,000 men on the Western Front, mostly fortress troops not suitable for offensive fighting. He had lost 150,000 men; in additions, 80,000 men, mostly of the *Sixth Panzer Army,* had been withdrawn, he thought, for rest.

By the end of October, the initial painful steps had been taken. Dietrich's *Sixth Panzer Army* was being refitted and reorganized in eastern Germany. On October 27, Hitler decided to give Dietrich's units double their intended tank strength, and he ordered the entire supply for the Eastern Front diverted to Dietrich. He was ready and willing to risk all on this last great attempt to put out the enemy fire. Manteuffel had been withdrawn from a fighting sector on October 15, and was reorganizing the troops available to him, although most of his earmarked divisions had been thrown into the fighting either at Aachen or to the north against the American 7th Armored Division. Two days before the end of the month, Model's *Army Group B,* which had been holding down a wide sector, was given a small front so that Model might have more time to plan. Such was the situation in late October when Generals Westphal and Krebs, Chiefs of Staff to Rundstedt and Model, respectively, travelled to Hitler's headquarters to receive belated news that Hitler had decided upon an attack in the west.

COUNTERPROPOSALS

On October 24, Generals Westphal and Krebs were greeted by an exuberant *Fuehrer,* enthusiastic as a little boy with a new toy. Hitler, confidently predicting a complete change in the war in the west, outlined the general nature of the plan. Then for three days, the generals were briefed by Jodl and his staff. Both Westphal and Krebs were pleased with the prospect of an offensive on the Western Front, but were doubtful that they could be prepared by November 25, the tentative date selected for initiation of the attack. Both rather hesitantly hinted that possibly the final objective was outside the reach of the forces which would be available to them. However, they were sent on their way with a sketch of the operation plan and the unalterable directives ordered by Hitler. They were to study these plans, and then Model, through Rundstedt, was to submit to the High Command his views and intentions. Thus, a month after Hitler made his momentous decision to attack in the west, the field commanders were finally notified of the attack in which they were to play the leading role.

From the beginning, von Rundstedt opposed the plan as promulgated by Hitler and his staff. Perhaps this is why he divorced himself from the operation. Model, who also disagreed in principle, was a loyal enough follower of *Der Fuehrer* so that he would make the supreme attempt despite military misgivings. Rundstedt may have been too old for this, or possibly he was already convinced of the hopelessness of the German position. Whatever the reasons, it was Model who carried the brunt of the work, who ordered and executed Hitler's final grandiose dream.

On November 3, Rundstedt, through Model, issued his reply to Hitler based on study by himself, Model, and their chief assistants. The field commanders were in basic agreement that an offensive was needed to restore the balance in the west. But they submitted a counterproposal: instead of the gallop to Antwerp, the available forces should be concentrated for a gigantic crushing pincers on the packed Allied salient which jutted forth around the city of Aachen. This huge salient contained portions of the British Second Army, all of the American Ninth Army, and a large part of the American First Army. Although heavily loaded with troops and supplies, it was a bare 30 miles across the rear of this salient. Rundstedt and Model proposed to launch one drive from the north against the exposed flank of the Anglo-American forces, at the Anglo-American junction point, always a soft spot in any Allied lineup. They would accompany this by a projected attack through the weakly held front in the Ardennes forest, which would turn northward before it reached the Meuse River, and join with the northern attack. The two attacking forces would then combine to destroy the densely packed troops in the salient. Then, if successful, they could consider moving across the Meuse River toward Antwerp. Rundstedt and

Model further proposed that such an attack be dependent on an Allied offensive and suggested that if the Allies launched an attack before the Germans were ready to move, the German attack should be postponed. Then, as an antidote to the rejection they undoubtedly sensed, they proposed that if this proposal were turned down, any contemplated *Fifteenth Army* attack from the north of the Aachen salient should be abandoned entirely, and the troops tentatively allotted for this possibility thrown into the pool to be used in the lone dash through the dense forests of the Ardennes.

Hitler pitted his faith and clairvoyance against the military judgment of his field commanders. The former corporal reasoned that Germany's forces were not sufficient to kill off the mass of troops in the Aachen salient by chewing; that if after a successful break-through he were to turn on this mass, it would be as though he had attacked frontally. Either way the Allies would be able to defend or counterattack with no necessity for large troop movements. Hitler, backed by Jodl and Keitel, rejected the so-called "small solution" proposed by Rundstedt and Model and decreed that the only way to destroy the huge forces in the Aachen salient was by a rapid thrust which would destroy their lifeline of supplies—to kill by strangulation.

Hitler further rejected the suggestion that the attack be postponed if the Allies struck first. While he admitted that attrition would result, he angrily shouted that Allied attrition would be greater because of tenuous supply lines and difficulties of waging an offensive battle. He further felt that an Anglo-American attack would tie up many Allied reserves and make it more difficult for them to take countermeasures against the surprise German attack. Left open was the decision on the subsidiary attack from the north. Model accepted Hitler's insistence on the November 25 starting date with tongue in cheek; he doubted that supplies and men could be assembled that fast.

So Hitler arrayed himself against his generals in the field. That his objective was great no one will deny. That the Germans could mount an offensive at all in the light of the merciless pounding they had taken, both from the air and on the ground, is no small miracle. Whether Model's counterproposal, to bite off the huge Allied forces in the Aachen salient, would have succeeded, only a Monday-morning quarterback can answer. But now we begin to see more clearly why Rundstedt divorced himself from the details of the offensive;

why the frenzied Model and the fanatic Dietrich were given
the key positions in the attack. Only a loyal Nazi, ready to
do or die for his *Fuehrer,* could carry through such a doubtful plan. But Model, Johl, and Dietrich went ahead with no
heavy hearts; theirs was the faith sublime.

To Hitler the issue was clear: "Destroy the enemy north
of the Antwerp-Brussels-Luxembourg line; do not argue, but
destroy them." And then? Hitler had thought of that, too
(although one may wonder if he didn't have doubts deep within him). Jodl glibly echoed his *Fuehrer:* "We should have taken
further reserves from the whole front . . . and started con-
centric attacks on Aachen from Monschau, Maastricht, and
Central Holland, and crushed your forces in the Aachen
pocket, their supply lines having been cut. . . . It is difficult
to say whether we could have destroyed the forces in the
pocket or whether you could have supplied them by air, by
using your entire air force. But at all events, it would have
made a terrific impression on political, military, and public
opinion. But even with captured fuel and supplies, I doubt
if we could have reconquered France. . . . All the same it
would have been a big setback for you, and you would have
required many months to recover from it. You had many
divisions in the United States not yet ready."

"OPERATION CONFUSION"—THE SPECIAL BRIGADES

Once having decided on the grandiose scheme, the do-or-
die attack, it behooved Hitler and his intimates to meet two
problems which loomed high on their list, failure of which
could wreck the whole scheme before the attack was fairly
under way. The first was seizure of the Meuse River bridges
so the panzer formations could gallop across without breaking their stride, and the second was protection of the north
flank of Dietrich's panzer hordes to prevent the flood of reinforcements which might otherwise burst out of the heavily
loaded Aachen salient.

Goering was no longer the fair-haired boy of the regime
that he had been when the *Luftwaffe* was the terror of the
western skies. The *Luftwaffe* had inexplicably lost its staying
power, and with it went Hermann's prestige. Therefore, it
was natural that when Keitel said, *"Mein Fuehrer,* we must
have parachute drops to seize the bridges of the Maas," Hitler flew into a rage as he denounced Goering. All agreed that
the bridges must not be destroyed. Suddenly, in a flash of

inspiration, the idea was born: a gigantic hoax, a modern Trojan Horse, would be employed. And who better to carry this out than *SS* Lieutenant Colonel Skorzeny, rescuer of Mussolini, apple of *Der Fuehrer's* eye? And so it came to pass that on October 22 Skorzeny smartly saluted his god at Rastenburg to receive his newest orders. First, he was to select and train men drawn from all services who spoke English. He was to give them refresher courses in American slang and training in the use of American weapons. Then he was to form two groups, the first to split into small units of four to five men to operate behind the lines and create confusion wherever possible, the second to follow the leading panzer elements and in the confusion of the terrific break-through, act as one of the American columns fleeing the enemy, move to the Meuse River, and there seize and hold the bridges until the following day when the panzers would arrive. Three bridges, all in the sector of Dietrich's *Sixth Panzer Army,* were to be the targets. Skorzeny left Hitler that October day fired with enthusiasm for this daring plan.

Orders were shot out to the various services to provide their best English-speaking men for Skorzeny, and along with the men, all captured matériel. Gradually, the most desirable men were segregated, and the training steadily moved forward. Skorzeny picked from his men two groups, the first called *Kommandos,* who were to perform demolition work, reconnaissance, and disturb enemy leadership, and the *150 Panzer Brigade,* composed of two tank battalions and one infantry battalion, all with American or British uniforms and equipment, to make the peaceful road march to the Meuse River bridges.

Foremost among Skorzeny's worries was the danger that Allied intelligence might get wind of these plans. Actually, American and British intelligence officers were aware of the formation of Skorzeny's group and of the collection of captured equipment. Again our frame of mind was used to advantage, and Skorzeny spread the word that his group was to create confusion behind Allied lines, in conjunction with the big German counterattack which was to pinch off the Allied attack to the Rhine River.

Out of Skorzeny's mission grew one of the greatest hoaxes of the war. It all began with his imaginative men, who, unaware of their true mission, soon invented spectacular rumors of their pending deeds: they were to free German troops still holding out at Dunkirk or, singlehanded, drive to capture

Antwerp or push to Paris. These, and many other stories, began to seep out of the training camp.

One dark, windy fall night, Skorzeny summoned his two top henchmen to discuss their progress in training men for this 1944 version of the Trojan Horse. All agreed that the "OK Butch" lessons were a great success, but Skorzeny was alarmed by the rumors circulating about the brigade's intended mission. After some discussion, however, the three plotters decided to encourage the rumors as long as they didn't border on the facts. And so the stories spread. One young man with an extremely fertile imagination concocted a story centering about the capture and killing of Eisenhower. This story took several versions, one of which predicted a paratroop drop to surround and wipe out the headquarters. The most imaginative version visualized a dramatic rendezvous by Skorzeny with former cronies, now underground henchmen, at the famed Cafe de la Paix in Paris, and from there, a sudden swoop into Allied headquarters, where they would quietly and efficiently proceed with the business at hand.

This story traveled like wildfire among the men and on the first day of the attack seeped across the lines, possibly as deliberately planned by Skorzeny, where it rapidly spread from one Allied command to another, and finally to Eisenhower himself. Hundreds and thousands of guards were posted to seize Skorzeny, who was safely behind the German lines the entire time.

During the Ardennes offensive, the last actual German parachute operation took place. Far behind the pace of drops which had thrown terror into Allied hearts, such as the seizure of Fort Eben Emal near Liége, Belgium, in 1940, this last drop fell far short of the previous standard. Hastily organized by von der Heydte, a German lieutenant colonel and one-time Rockefeller fellow in New York, the drop consisted of a battalion of about 1,000 men. Their mission was to cut the key road leading south into the Bulge from the Aachen salient, and had they been successful, von der Heydte and his battalion could have materially hampered Allied reinforcements going into the Bulge. Van der Heydte and his men were assembled only ten days before the start of the offensive, when Hitler and his generals became concerned about their vulnerable north flank. As a result, the men were hastily briefed and organized, only to be dropped a day late. The plane crews were inexperienced in night drops, and the 1,000 men were scattered over three countries. Actually, about 300 got together at the assembly point, but they were too weak to stop the two divisions which rolled right through them oblivious of their presence. But like the Skorzeny mission, the psychological effect of von der Heydte's mission proved far more valuable than its operational effect. For days after the drop Allied soldiers everywhere were seeing visions of German parachutists who really were not there.

NOVEMBER TAKES ITS COURSE

The final, definite "no" which Hitler gave to Model's plea for the "small solution" ended once and for all any indecisiveness regarding the direction of the attack. However, all was not so simple in the designation of a date for the push. Hitler had tentatively set the attack for the last week in November. Called upon once again were his personal air force meteorologists who had played such an important and decisive role in the selection of previous attack dates, most conspicuously in the Lowlands in 1940. Lieutenant Colonel Schuster, head of the service, voted for November, when flying weather in Europe was notoriously the worst. He further stipulated the last week in November, when the new moon would be rising. This would tend to cut down night raids on troop reinforcements moving to the front. But Germany in 1944 was not the Germany of old; there was a considerable gap between hope and reality. Despite the superhuman efforts which had been made, the German war machine was not the vigorous youth it had been in 1940. Jodl plaintively bleated later: "This offensive could not be executed as speedily as those of the past. We were short on many things that had been overabundant in 1940." Actually, Hitler had laid plans for a 1940 attack in 1944; he refused to admit that Germany had gone downhill.

It is not at all strange, therefore, that on November 23, when Rundstedt, Model, Westphal, Krebs, Manteuffel, and Dietrich assembled in conference with Hitler and his planners, the first item on the agenda was the unpreparedness of the various commands. Unanimous agreement was reached that the attack plans were not sufficiently advanced to allow for an immediate thrust. Hitler reluctantly agreed to hold up his project; he then tentatively picked December 10.

Meanwhile, during November, other changes had vitally affected the course of the war in the west. On November 16 the expected Allied attack toward the Rhine River from the Aachen salient had begun. The German defensive positions were excellent, and despite hard fighting, the Allies were unable to make much headway. However, the threat was great; Dietrich's army began moving west on November 6 and had closed into the area in front of the Ruhr industrial section by mid-November. This served a dual purpose: first, if the American attacks became sufficiently grave, Dietrich's men could be thrown in as a last resort to stem the tide; second, the movement of the *Sixth Panzer Army* to the west at that time was the crowning stroke of genius to the German cover plan *Wacht Am Rhein*. It provided perfect meaning to the movement and gave the Allied intelligence officers the final kick in the wrong direction. But, actually, the American attacks had raised a more serious question. Four infantry and nine panzer or panzer grenadier divisions, which had been counted on for the great offensive, were tied up in the fighting east of Aachen and could not, according to Rundstedt, be relieved until the fighting had died down. In addition, the front of *Army Group G* to the south had all but collapsed, and *Panzer Lehr Division*, originally part of the *Sixth Panzer Army* and one of the crack German armored divisions, had been sent south in an attempt to stem the tide. So serious was the southern situation that on November 23 consideration was given to the suggestion that the entire Ardennes attack be dropped and that German efforts be concentrated in restoring the front in Alsace-Lorraine, where *Army Group G* had collapsed. Such attack, some argued would rewin coal and electrical supplies and destroy most of the élite units of the reconstituted French army.

Hitler vetoed all such suggestions. Citing the weakened condition of the Allies as a result of their attacks, the fact that they had placed all their reserves near the front, increasing supply difficulties, and continued light occupation of the Ardennes sector, he resolutely announced that the German attack would continue as planned. "Now is the time to attack," Hitler said, "when the enemy is most exhausted."

He was further encouraged by the excellent Roer River defenses, which the American forces were fast approaching. Hitler and his generals knew, and the Americans did not discover until too late, that the Roer River (not to be confused with the Ruhr), although small and narrow was actually a mighty defense barrier, because the dams at its headwaters could be so regulated that the river would be flooded for several weeks. The wide river valley was a perfect barrier which no sane military commander would attempt to cross, especially with a fresh, new panzer army waiting for him on the other side. In this, Hitler proved himself a prophet, because by December 1 the American troops were along the Roer River for most of its distance, and there the fall offensive in the north halted.

At the November 23 meeting final plans were laid for the movement of the various armies to the attack front. Dietrich was to remain north of Cologne until three days before the attack, when, in a series of night moves, he was suddenly to shift south into the attack position. Manteuffel's units were to assemble in secret in the dense woods of the Ardennes Forests, to move up to the attack line only at the last minute. Most of Brandenberger's units were already in the line. Reserves would be so distributed that in an extreme emergency they could be used in threatened areas, but were to be so arranged that the Allies would not be able to guess the German plan. The attack was divided into two waves and a third wave of troops who would act as a reserve. Transportation plans were worked out so that the last groups would just be coming west as the attack began. Actually, by the end of November, air raids notwithstanding, 100 trains a day were moving toward the Western Front.

Although supplies were being moved forward more slowly than hoped for, by scraping the bottom of various barrels the High Command was providing considerable material. In building up their supplies, however, the Germans were caught in their own web, not only because of the threat of the Allied November attacks, but also because the supply chieftains still believed that the preparations were for a defensive attack. As a result, many of the supplies were left on the east bank of the Rhine River. Later, many of these goods were never transported to the attacking troops because of Allied air attacks after the offensive was under way. For instance, Manteuffel was promised five refills of gasoline, good for 162 miles, for his tanks, but he actually received only one and a half refills. Dietrich was in a similar situation, and while on paper the High Command could report to Hitler that the gasoline and ammunition supply were sufficient for the entire attack, this was not apparent to the men in the field. But on the credit side of the ledger, the panzer divisions of the *Sixth Panzer Army* at least had been completely refitted, and those of Manteuffel's *Fifth Panzer Army* partially re-equipped.

By the end of November, plans were well along. On November 25, Model issued his field order outlining the attack, and the code name for the operation was changed to *Herbstnebel* (Autumn Smoke).

A SLIGHT DOUBLE CROSS

We have seen the picture as it appeared across the conference table at Rastenburg. Underneath the table, a polite double cross was probably being applied by the commanders in the field. Rundstedt, we know, was openly opposed to Hitler's "large solution" and so told his *Fuehrer* several times. He was an important enough man to be able to fade into the background. While Model was apparently against the "large solution" in principle, his zealous espousal of the Nazi cause carried him through this period despite his disagreement. Manteuffel, however, possibly in conjunction with Model, made enthusiastic preparations only for a "small solution," and although he made conscience-satisfying, but feeble, plans for crossing the Meuse River, he concentrated on the fighting east of the Meuse. Manteuffel, personification of the regular army field commander, believed that the forces were not sufficient for the ambitious objectives, but he was glad enough to tag along with the tide for the honor of old Germany. His personal cover-plan with the High Command was to say, "later objectives and direction of advance depend to a decisive degree on the measures of the enemy." Thus any planning for actions on the far side of the Meuse River was left in abeyance pending the "measures of the enemy."

Dietrich, on the other hand, engaged in some sabotage of a different sort. Friend that he was of Hitler, he took it upon himself to make some changes in the immutable plans of *Der Fuehrer*. Even Dietrich had favored the "small solution," the attack to pinch off the Aachen salient from north and south. Possibly he was influenced by Kraemer, his Chief of Staff, because Kraemer was a firm supporter of the regular army clique against Hitler, Jodl, and Keitel. Kraemer added to the other points in favor of the Aachen pincers, the psychological argument that German troops would fight more effectively when retaking a portion of their homeland.

Dietrich and Kraemer laid plans for the crossing of the Meuse River, which were in direct violation of Hitler's orders. Hitler continually stressed in all meetings the importance of staying south of Liége, the great industrial city on the confluence of the Meuse, the Ourthe, and the Vesdre Rivers. Dietrich ventured to argue this point with his tin god in the November 23 meeting in Berlin. Hitler was violently opposed to going near Liége for three reasons: in the first place it had a series of forts surrounding it, and, although they were not ideal for defense against mechanized forces, these forts could cause an attacking force considerable trouble; in the second place, going to Liége meant that the field commanders were still contemplating the "small solution," which would be possible if they successfully captured Liége and were to turn north; and in the third place, the bitter, costly lesson of Stalingrad had taught Hitler, to his satisfaction, that it was not possible to cross large rivers near strongly defended cities. Furthermore, Hitler believed that at least a division of armor, and possibly more, could easily be swallowed up in the street fighting which would result if Liége were stormed. In addition, the city itself was in a valley where the rivers joined, and could be dominated, if necessary, from the surrounding heights.

Notwithstand all this, Kraemer pored over the maps of the Liége area, spent wearying nights studying routes for his panzer columns, and he became convinced that the place for at least a part of the *Sixth Panzer Army* to cross the Meuse River was to the north of Liége. Kraemer had found what he considered to be the ideal crossing site: flat banks which would allow rapid access to the river, a large forest where he could hide much of his equipment and troops preparing to cross the river, and good roads leading to the crossing site. Kraemer agreed that no frontal attack should be made on Liége; he was simply going to surround it, and then announce the *fait accompli* to Hitler. Hitler and Jodl suspected that some thoughts of this kind were flitting through Dietrich's mind, and Hitler took great pains to instruct him time and again that he was to stay away from Liége. However, Kraemer blithely went ahead with his plan. Jodl later said in a fit of anger, "If mobile forces of 'Sepp' Dietrich were aimed at Liége, then Dietrich should be shot for disobeying orders." Dietrich only grunted and acted as vague as his mind probably was on the entire subject. Kraemer, however, when I told him of Jodl's statement, merely laughed heartily and said, "If I had successfully crossed the Meuse north of Liége I would have been decorated rather than shot."

A FINAL CONFERENCE

Numerous phases of the attack having not yet been ironed out, Field Marshal Model telephoned Hitler in the waning days of November, and urgently requested a final conference in Berlin where the last details could be settled. The request was granted, and on December 2, Model, Jodl, Keitel, Manteuffel, Dietrich, and Westphal, the latter representing Rundstedt, assembled. Hitler was astounded that Rundstedt lacked the interest to attend this important last meeting and was especially amazed when Westphal seemed very poorly briefed on details of the attack. The haughty aristocrat Rundstedt at seventy was unperturbed.

As the conference opened, Model quickly got to his feet to make the last, moving plea for the "small solution," pinching off the troop-packed Aachen salient. Model cited fact after fact to express his anxiety about reserves, difficulties with supplies and transportation, training of divisions. But again, in a burst of indignation, Hitler proclaimed irrevocably that the "large solution" would be followed to the letter. Model and the army commanders paid only lip service to this dictum; there was no arguing, but Manteuffel at least, as stubborn in his way as Hitler, had set his goal—the Meuse River.

Manteuffel, the shrewd tactician, presented two additional proposals which were accepted after long and bitter debate. First was the recommendation that the attack begin before dawn instead of broad daylight as originally planned. Manteuffel reasoned that the daylight attack would be subjected to devastating Allied artillery fire and might conceivably be subject to air attacks, even though the meteorologists promised dismal weather. Manteuffel took as his thesis the principle that the Allied ability to react to the attack should be the determining factor in setting the time. Despite the confusions of a night attack, he considered them to be outweighed by the advantages of catching the Americans when they could not readily react—the break would thus be achieved before air and artillery could swing into play. And he later added, "Everyone knows that the American outpost guards sleep in the early hours of the morning." His concurrent proposal revolved around the use of a preparatory artillery concentration. Hitler, the World War I soldier, had insisted on a huge preparatory concentration along the entire front line. Manteuffel argued convincingly that this would only alert the sleepy Americans. He favored a short concentration on selected points immediately prior to the jumpoff. Manteuffel's recommendations were accepted again after heated debate, although Dietrich ignored them when D-Day arrived.

At this last planning session, each army commander outlined the condition of his troops. Dietrich, the chronic complainer, was loudest in his protestations that he was unready for the attack, but his cries went unheeded by Hitler. However, to add strength for Dietrich's vulnerable north flank, Hitler provided a battalion of special *Jagdtigers*, with twenty-one huge Tiger tanks mounting 12.8 cm guns, total weight of each being 72 tons, with special armor said to be thick enough to stop any known shell. These tanks were to lumber up the roads leading into the penetration area from the north, and in conjunction with von der Heydte's parachutists prevent reinforcement of the Allied forces from this direction. The sad tale of this battalion we leave for a later section.

Following the lengthy and heated discussion of December 2, the field commanders again returned to their headquarters to make final arrangements for the great attack. Further aerial photographs of the Meuse River were furnished the army commanders on December 10. At the eleventh hour Hitler authorized postponement of the attack until the 15th, as weather conditions were to be best on that date. At this time Rundstedt received final orders from Jodl; scrawled unmistakably in Hitler's hand across the face of the orders were the words, "not to be altered." Final arrangements were made for the necessary reinforcements and reserves. Remer's *Fuehrer Escort Brigade* and the *Fuehrer Grenadier Brigade*, both élite guard outfits, were started toward the west; two mountain divisions from Norway were hurried toward the Ardennes (but neither arrived in time); and the units relieved from the fighting around the Roer River were hurriedly refitted and told to take a quick breather before running back into the greatest battle of all.

HITLER IS READY

From plans to attack, the German war machine rapidly began moving. *Sixth Panzer Army*, with its butcher boy "Sepp" Dietrich in the lead, began its sudden shift from the Ruhr industrial area where it had been standing guard, and by a series of night moves felt its way toward the weakly held front of VIII Corps. Meanwhile, to the south both the *Fifth Panzer Army*, sparked by crafty Manteuffel, and the *Seventh Army*, with stolid Brandenberger, had successfully completed their secret assembly in the heavily wooded areas of the Ardennes Forests. Manteuffel, like Dietrich, began moving his troops forward, first to the initial assembly areas, and then on the night before the attack, to the final assembly areas from which his troops would move out the next day. Brandenberger carefully shunted his attack divisions into their proper positions, always attempting to prevent detection of unusual movement. Our forces along the front heard these movements—even the Germans can't move seventeen divisions to within a few miles of the front lines complétely undetected—but interpreted them as a relief of front line divisions. As one intelligence officer later commented: "Hell, I thought they were moving troops either to the north or south to meet our attacks from these directions. I knew it couldn't be us they were after as this was the quiet sector where everyone got a rest."

When the cards were on the table, not all of Hitler's grandiose promises had been met. Although he had promised to have 2,000 planes in support of the attack, Hitler would not consent to move the fighter planes from the German cities, where they had been desperately clawing away at the Allied air birds, until the last minute. He didn't want to leave the cities unprotected, nor did he wish to give away his attack plans by the sudden shift of a large group of planes to the west. But Hitler also wanted bad weather to keep the *Jaboes*, American and British fighter-bombers, away from his attacking troops. He got his bad weather, but it was so bad that he couldn't move his own planes forward—the web had been spun too tight. And for the first seven days of the attack, the flying weather was non-operational most of the time. Not until the end of the month was *Der Fuehrer* able to assemble his aerial striking force, which was finally built up from 325 planes to between 850 and 900 planes by the first of January. But by then, it was too late.

Equally worrisome to the German field commanders was the failure of several trainloads of vital gasoline to arrive. From their carefully hoarded supplies of fuel reserves, built up during the calm period from September to December, the German High Command allotted 20,000 tons of fuel: 8,000 tons to carry the attack to the Meuse, an additional 8,000 tons from there to Antwerp, and a final 4,000 tons for a reserve. But again the Germans were caught in their own web, and because the supply officers had initially been instructed that the German attack was a defensive thrust—*Wacht Am Rhein*—much of the fuel was stored east of the Rhine River. Only a small portion of this hoard was available to panzers, sufficient for an average of two tank loads, rather than the five demanded. And in the rugged terrain of the Ardennes a tank load would only carry the slow-moving giants half the distance they could achieve once they burst into the level plains west of the Meuse River. With only sixty miles worth of fuel, the harassed commanders were forced to issue emergency orders to their troops to seize whatever gasoline they could find along the way. And equally serious, many of the artillery units and supply echelons were stranded while the fuel was diverted to the hungry tanks.

But in other ways the Germans were ready. Rundstedt's supply officer announced that the four SS panzer divisions in Dietrich's Army were 100 per cent supplied with tanks, while the three panzer divisions in Manteuffel's first wave were from 60 to 80 per cent equipped. One hundred transport planes were tuning up at the airfields deep in Germany, waiting to drop the parachutists on Dietrich's north flank. The last patrols of the "static" divisions, already on the front, were reporting on their final reconnaissance patrols, which ranged as far as seven miles behind the American lines, observing troop movements and installations. German intelligence officers issued their final estimates of our strength. Searchlights were brought up toward the front lines to light the way and guide Manteuffel's tanks in the early morning hours of December 16 (this was a trick the Germans and the Americans had learned from the British, first in Italy, and later in northern Europe). Directives were issued governing the conduct of troops in the occupied enemy territories: "The principle is to follow the behavior of the local populace." Former occupation governors were brought out of retirement: Dr. Seyss-Inquart for Holland, Grohe for Belgium, and Gauleiter Simon for Luxembourg, and the notorious Rexist Leon DeGrelle, the Belgian traitor, rode along far to the rear, sneaking through the back door into the country he so desperately wanted to control. And with true German thoroughness, Field Marshal Model issued a directive which must have caused ripples of laughter to crease even the dour, leathery Prussian face of von Rundstedt:

> The following is ordered: Use must be made of every opportunity for rest and sleep. All activity not necessary for the operation will be omitted. . . . The unit commander should consider: How can I tactically provide the best opportunities of sleep for my men? The soldier will then himself find the best technique of sleeping.

And so the final details were set. The last approach march
began on December 15. After the men were lined up for
the march, they were at last given the glad tidings: To the
attack! Forward over the Maas! Revenge for the bitter defeat
of the summer! Death to the Anglo-American invaders!
Scrawled in the flowery hand of one German officer, on a diary
lifted from his frozen hand, were these words: "There is a general feeling of elation; everybody is cheerful."

HITLER'S LAST CHANCE

On December 11, Hitler and his personal entourage boarded
the train from Berlin, bound for the Western Front. Headquarters were established in Ziegenberg near Giessen, west of
the Rhine River for the first time since the Allied invasion of
Normandy. Assembled before Hitler on December 12 were
his commanders; interspersed among them were scores of Gestapo agents. Imagine yourself for a minute, a member of a
proud, haughty Prussian army group, or even a division commander. After a hard day's ride, unaccompanied by any other
officer, according to orders, you arrive at a huge, towering
castle in the normally sleepy town of Ziegenberg, near the
Rhine River. After eating and talking with fellow-officers, you
are ordered to leave pistol and brief case in the cloakroom.
You are then herded out the door and into a bus, which rides
you around for about half an hour in the pouring rain. You
think you pass the same point several times, and on the way
back, later in the evening, you make the same trip in three
minutes. The bus grinds to a halt in front of a huge bunker,
and you, the pride of German military tradition, walk into the
bunker between two rows of grim-faced SS men who carefully
watch you at every step. Inside the bunker, lined with stern-
faced Gestapo men, you are seated in chairs carefully spaced
three feet apart, before a rectangular table, also flanked by the
pride of the Hitler gang.

Here is the way that one of those present described it: "Then
in filed the *Fuehrer* and his party. They sat at the table: Hitler, Keitel, Jodl, and two others. Hitler looked old and broken. He put on a pair of glasses. His hands, as he picked up
a manuscript, shook visibly. He read his entire harangue. It
began with a full hour's history of the party and of his own
gifts to Germany, which everybody had heard before, but during which they dared not even fidget or pull out a handkerchief
because the SS glowered at the slightest movement. Hitler then

launched, in the second hour, into the plan for the Ardennes offensive. He said he had scraped together everything available for this effort; if it did not succeed, the war was lost. The political consequences would be that Canada would withdraw from the war; the United States would not stand for the loss of a whole army group and would be so discouraged as to be a negligible factor thereafter. There was no need to worry about Allied fighters as 3,000 German fighters would 'clear the air for the *Wehrmacht.*' He said: 'There is no turning back; if things go wrong, we shall be in for hard times. For months our entire industry has been working solely for this at the cost of the Eastern Front. Our V-1 activities only represent harassing fire. We must attack and start a war of movement once more.' "

Der Fuehrer continued for hours in an almost unintelligible harangue on the glory of German might, from the days of the Treaty of Westphalia in 1648 to the present, touching on his struggle against the world and finishing with a stirring appeal for the absolute necessity of a successful attack. At the end of the speech each commander filed by. Dietrich related to me how he tried to tell Hitler, in the one minute allotted to him, of the need for additional time to prepare his plans. Hitler shrugged his shoulders, said the plans were set, and waved Dietrich on.

The die was cast: nineteen divisions prepared to move out with the three attacking armies; eight more in immediate reserve; an additional five waiting further to the rear. "Forward to and over the Maas!" shouted Hitler. Eager Field Marshal Model barked enthusiastically: "We will not disappoint the *Fuehrer* and the Fatherland, who created the sword of retribution. Forward, in the spirit of Leuthen! Our motto is especially now: no soldier in the world must be better than we soldiers of the Eifel and of Aachen." A more sober Rundstedt exhorted: "We gamble everything now. We cannot fail." Last minute shifts in troop assignments were made; in an eleventh-hour reprieve, Hitler postponed the attack to December 16 and decreed that it was then or never. Brandenberger complained he lacked bridging equipment. Dietrich still maintained that he needed time to prepare—the former butcher was still sharpening his knife. But at five-thirty on the morning of December 16, gray-clad troops sprang out of their hiding places to launch the last great attack of the Germans on any front.

An elated and ecstatically happy Hitler phoned General of the Armored Forces Balk, commander of *Army G* to the south, on that day. To win and retain forces for this offensive, Hitler said, he had imposed great burdens on other fronts and theaters of operations, "Yes, even discounted crises, and reconciled myself to loss of important terrain in the forefield of the West Wall, even of fortresses in the West Wall itself. But from this day on, no further foot of ground is to be given up. You are to hold the forefield of the West Wall between Voelkingen and Bitsch at all costs. No further bunker of the West Wall is to be lost."

Word was broadcast to an elated German people, "Our troops are again on the march; we shall present the *Fuehrer* with Antwerp by Christmas." And the German people felt happy once again.

CHAPTER II

Eisenhower's Great Decision

THE ALLIED DILEMMA

WHILE HITLER AND HIS GENERALS PLOTTED THE DIABOLI-cally clever attack into the Ardennes, Eisenhower was faced with the problem of beating the German armies in the field. Once having forced his foot into the supposedly iron door called *Festung Europa*, Eisenhower had to press onward and outward. After a tortuous month and a half on the beach-head, he broke loose, suddenly, dramatically, and set the Allied armies loose on a wild chase after fleeing Germans. So sudden, and in many ways so unexpected, was the breakout that it far outstripped our wildest hopes, and instead of being behind in our schedule, we were weeks ahead—so far ahead that the supplies couldn't keep pace.

As he approached Germany's border, Eisenhower found himself faced with a great decision: whether to attempt a final *coup de grâce* with a thin, rapier-like thrust to the heart of Germany or whether to push forward all along the front, maintaining a continuous line. Both Bradley and Montgomery pleaded for the wherewithal to make the thrust, each in his own sector. But supplies were short, and the Germans not as far gone as we hoped, and Eisenhower preferred to take it the sounder way.

THE CHASE

The Wehrmacht had failed in France. They had failed to contain the beachhead, as Hitler had so confidently announced they would do. They had failed to pinch off the sweeping armored spearheads, once the hole had been made. Now Hitler faced a blitz in reverse. Our air force raised havoc with his troop movements; his supply lines were long and tenuous with no air force to defend them; and he was still worried about our potential landing in the Pas de Calais. Coupled with this was a brilliant, bold strategy which turned the American armor loose.

Once we had broken into the open a myriad of possibilities became apparent. Hodges and Patton quickly closed two gigantic hooks into the rear of the German formations still fighting the British and Canadians around Caen and, in conjunction with a Montgomery drive to the south, created the so-called Falaise gap, which at one time contained 100,000 Germans. The gap was not completely closed, and some Germans made their escape. The boundary between the British and American forces ran through the mouth of this gap, which was a tactical error, but the dividing line was essential to prevent the fast-rushing British and American troops from colliding head-on in a second Bunker Hill. The Americans went faster than expected, but once the boundary was set by Montgomery, he had to stick with it, for to change in the middle of the battle would have created chaos. And although some American writers have contended that our forces could have completely closed the gap if they had not been ordered back across the line by Monty, the leading tank commanders of that attacking force say the Germans threw them out of Falaise, key to the gap; they weren't ordered out. Nevertheless, thousands of Germans were captured, and those who escaped were not in fighting trim. The German army in France was licked.

From mid-August until mid-September all hell broke loose in France. It was the happy period for the Anglo-American forces. Battle-weary soldiers often remarked during the bitter slugging in late fall that they wished all war was like those earlier days. It was a game of cat chasing mouse, of divisions racing toward the German border with German formations going the same way on the next road north. Many times the Germans were unmolested. LeMans, Chartres, Paris, Rheims, Verdun, all fell almost without a struggle. Patton raced and beat the Germans to many of the Seine River crossings. To the north, Hodges' First Army and Montgomery both rapidly swung forward, Hodges heading for Belgium and Luxembourg, and the British hugging the coast, pushing toward Holland. The advances were miraculously rapid, too fast for headquarters even to mark their maps, and unbelievable were the stories of chance encounters: part of the still untouched German *Fifteenth Army* was trapped by the American 1st Division which slaughtered thousands of unsuspecting Germans before they could fight; hundreds of historic towns were captured as Germans were caught in bed, often not alone—Brussels on September 3, Antwerp the next day, Liége, Lille, Dieppe—a bitter revenge for the Canadians—Le Havre, Luxembourg City. On September 5, a new army, the American Ninth, went into operation in the Brittany peninsula, took over the job left by Patton's VIII Corps, and in a costly, two-week campaign captured the port of Brest.

During June and July the Anglo-American armies were nourishing themselves, pouring in the lifeblood of men, food, and supplies across the flat beaches of Normandy, aided, once the extensive German demolitions were repaired, by a trickle of supplies from the small port of Cherbourg. It wasn't bad in those days when you could tour the entire battle front in a few hours and when from almost any point you could see the flash of artillery fire at night. But once the breakthrough came, the problems of keeping up with these armies multiplied. General Eisenhower reported to General Marshall:

> Losses of ordnance equipment have been extremely high. For instance, we must have as replacement items each month 36,000 small arms, 700 mortars, 500 tanks, 2,400 vehicles, 100 field pieces. Consumption of artillery and mortar ammunition in northwestern Europe averages 8,000,000 rounds a month. Our combat troops use up an average of 66,400 miles of one type of field wire each month.

With nearly 700 tons of supplies needed by each fighting division every day, it is no wonder that "Ike" early began to worry about his supply lines. Shortly after the hole was punched at St. Lo, Eisenhower wrote to General Marshall telling him to expect a break in the operations when the Allied forces would pause to catch their breath, regroup, resupply, re-equip, and then move on. Eisenhower originally thought the Germans would make a stand along the natural barriers of northern France, probably based on the Seine River line, but their defeat had been too decisive, the rout too complete, to allow them the time to prepare such a line. He, therefore, hastily revised his estimates and hoped that the Allied forces might be able to drive to the Rhine River before halting to regroup and refit.

Superhuman efforts were made to keep the supplies moving to the fast-charging troops at the front. Airborne lifts carried thousands of tons of supplies; the shattered railroad system of France was hastily rebuilt. But the railroad system was so badly smashed, and the rolling stock so depleted that we had to rely on trucks. We had an army on wheels, and trucks kept us going. From a modest beginning, the Normandy beaches to Chartres, the Red Ball grew and grew, like Topsy, until it stretched over 700 well-marked miles, thoroughly equipped with fast wreckage and servicing stations manned 24 hours a day. The Red Ball began operations on August 25 with 5,400 vehicles, hauled an average of about 5,000 tons of supplies for the eighty-one days of its operation. On its peak day of operation, over 12,000 tons of supplies were hauled to the front, more than enough for twelve fighting divisions. Operating on a circle route, it was a vast, one-way traffic circle, along which raced the life blood of the advancing troops. The driving was hard, the roads merciless on the vehicles, the turnover of equipment staggering, but the supplies were pushed through. By the end of the year, 9,500 vehicles were in operation hauling supplies.

Despite the gigantic efforts of the Red Ball Express and the supply forces in general, Eisenhower soon realized that the supplies which were being moved forward would not be sufficient to sustain all of his hungry armies at the same time. By August 25 when Paris was liberated, the forward elements were already over 150 miles from the beaches, and the German border was still a lengthy and tortuous 200 miles ahead. To a travel-wise, automobile-conscious American public, 350 miles seems no more than a fair day's drive. But just try moving a few hundred thousand men with all their equipment, supplies, and vehicles from Chicago to Detroit some day, and you'll get the idea. Then go out and destroy most of the bridges, use back country roads instead of our fine concrete highways, add some mud and a few planes dropping bombs, and you will soon decide that 350 miles isn't such a short distance after all.

There you have the problem in brief: a disorganized German army running for its homeland; an extended Anglo-

American army chasing them, getting farther and farther from its inadequate base of supply. Up to the middle of September, almost the entire supply of Allied material, which had to travel 3,000 miles before it even reached the English dumps, was coming across open beaches in Normandy, where the only port facilities were those which our own ingenuity had fashioned. You now have before you the background for the great decision.

THE DECISION

By late August, Eisenhower's great decision was full upon him. There were some who earnestly believed that if we could keep going we would completely demoralize the Germans and force their surrender. These people argued that we should concentrate all our supplies, equipment, transportation on one effort to rip through the German border defenses, plunge on to the Rhine River, possibly effect a crossing, and then just go right on to Berlin. General Bradley and his staff prepared elaborate plans which envisaged a drive right through Metz, the West Wall, and on to the Rhine. Bradley possibly believed that one army could again make the hole behind which all of the others could follow, as we had done at St. Lo, that such an army could destroy the usefulness of both the West Wall and the Rhine as military obstacles and might, with luck, take Berlin. Montgomery came up with the same idea. He wanted to rush around the German West Wall in Holland and take the short route to Berlin, across the northern German plains. And he, too, appealed to Eisenhower, with all the eloquence that was his, to divert the entire force to the north so that Montgomery could effect this great push to end the war.

Here was the great decision. Political and personal as well as military decisions were involved. The Allied High Command had faced the same decision in the invasion of Europe, deciding between invasion of the soft underbelly, as Churchill so often and so eloquently preached, or the direct approach through France. Once France was agreed upon, the argument centered on the short route through the Pas de Calais area, north of the Seine River, as opposed to the more southerly route through Normandy. Many of the British strategists favored the direct approach: hit the enemy at his strongpoint; crack him once and for all; drive through on the shortest route. The so-called American point of view had triumphed in the invasion, and we had struck the longer way through Normandy. It had been successful; how successful, we were just beginning to realize. Bradley and his staff reasoned that the indirect approach was again the best: through the Frankfurt gap where they could strike in any one of three directions. Harder? Yes, but trickier; more possibilities. Against this, Montgomery held out the opportunity of a short, direct sprint to Berlin by the northern circle route. History had proved, said Montgomery, that the short, direct route across the plains, where armor could be employed, represented the only way to win.

Eisenhower, with headquarters still in London, studied the myriad supply figures available to him and reached a different solution from either Montgomery or Bradley. His plan was to close up along the Rhine with Bradley's army group, joining Devers coming up from the south, to get a bridgehead across the Rhine in the north with Montgomery, and then to clean up the supply situation preparatory to the final push. Once the supplies had caught up with the troops, the armies would again push forward, Eisenhower said, and, as he had long proclaimed, they would meet and defeat the German armies west of the Rhine River. He rejected the finger-like approach, recommended by Montgomery and Bradley, as impractical in view of the acute supply situation. How, he said, could we push through to Berlin with a narrow salient, perhaps twenty miles wide, in which we would have possibly three good roads and, if we were lucky, one railroad? How would we get the 700 tons of supplies needed for each division into that narrow finger, and how would we ever beat off the German pressure on the sides of that finger?

Eisenhower has much history to back up his decision. An American finger pushing through the forests of the Ardennes early in September was nearly chopped off and was pushed back through the West Wall. Another finger at Metz was horribly mangled, when we discovered that the Germans were not through fighting. And finally, the finger poked across the Neder Rijn at Arnhem was hacked off, and the troops lost. Had we lost an entire army in a dangerous gamble, it would have been a grave disaster to our still small field force.

The immediate result of Eisenhower's decision is ancient history. The air-borne drop to secure the lower Rhine bridgehead failed; even this modest attack was projected too far beyond the following ground troops, and the reinforcements could not reach the most advanced paratroopers, the British, until too late. The bridgehead across the Neder Rijn was lost, but the British lines were pulled forward sixty miles. Even the limited offensive had been a gamble, based on 100 per cent luck. The drop had landed in the midst of German panzer forces, and the British paratroopers were overwhelmed—only 2,000 of the total 7,000 escaped to the far shore of the river. Meanwhile, farther south, Hodges pulled up along the West Wall, but fierce German attacks forced him to withdraw his thin penetration through the West Wall in the Ardennes region.

Still farther to the south, Patton's troops ran smack into a hornet's nest at Metz, the traditional fortified city which had never been taken by direct assault, and he too received a bloody nose. Despite the supply shortages, blustering Patton laid plans to strike through the Frankfurt corridor into the heart of Germany, and if a shoestring was all that they would give him, then he intended to do it on a shoestring. In any event on September 6, one of Patton's corps was ordered to, "Attack and seize the area east of the Moselle River, capture Metz and Thionville, and continue east to secure bridges over the Saar River, thence east to secure bridges over the Rhine River vicinity Maintz, and prepare to continue the advance to seize Frankfurt." For six long days the lead 7th Armored Division lay at Verdun waiting for gasoline. When the gas arrived, the tankers fueled up, and started to execute the corps order. The division ran into a murderous defense at Metz, which cost thousands of casualties, and it was unable to advance into or around the city. Historians who have spent months studying this campaign report that if our forces had received the gasoline and had reached Metz six days earlier, they would still have taken a beating—the troops defending Metz were largely young officer candidates and their teachers, and they had been there all the time. The town was never abandoned, contrary to persistent stories still being repeated.

The critical link in the contention that Eisenhower made the greatest mistake of the war, when he failed to follow through after the chase across France, is the suggestion that the German armies in the west had ceased to be an effective force by late August. German records do not confirm this belief. There are many indications that the German withdrawal from France, although disorganized and costly, was not the complete rout that it has so often been pictured. "It was never in our minds to retreat as far as the Rhine at that time," Goering later reported. "Instead, in September, 1944, we wanted to make use of the West Wall and even before that, of the Vosges Mountains, the Albert Canal (in Belgium) and the Maginot Line. Anybody who would have suggested retreating to the Rhine would have been considered mad."

The facts, when carefully evaluated, indicate a planned German withdrawal. They avoided any major pitched battles as they streaked across France, and although thousands of German prisoners were captured, among them many combat troops, the majority of those captured were service and rear echelon troops left behind in the precipitous retreat. In many cases, the fighting cores of divisions and armies were maintained. A series of covering actions in a progressive leapfrogging withdrawal took the German armies back into the West Wall: the *Fifteenth Army* on the north; *Seventh Army* covering the Aachen Gap, *Fifth Panzer Army* further to the south, linking with the *First* and *Nineteenth Armies,* hastily pulling within the shelter of the West Wall from the south. We moved too fast for the Germans to establish a Scheldt-Albert canal line, but failure of the Arnhem drop gave the Germans the lion's share of Holland. And already, Hitler was talking of counterattack. Even he would not dare think of attack were his armies gone.

THE CALM

Late September and October were weeks of preparation: most of the combat troops were engaged in badly needed organization and consolidation. Thousands of tons of supplies flowed from the beaches and, finally, the ports to dumps near the German border. Casualties were replaced, and the new men worked into their fighting units. Railroad lines were slowly put in running condition; hundreds of blown bridges were replaced, and roads were repaired. The new American Ninth Army was brought into the line after completing the reduction of Brest. Placed at first in the center, between the First and Third Armies, in the quiet Ardennes sector, Ninth Army was shifted north of First Army on October 23, two days after capture of the first major German city—Aachen— by First Army. At last the stranded divisions of the Ninth Army, temporarily converted into trucking regiments, were brought to the West Wall and given their battle indoctrination. Only Montgomery to the north, and Hodges at Aachen were engaged in heavy fighting.

Montgomery's 21st Army Group was conducting an attack

from the corridor, formed as a result of the air-borne drop, to enlarge the corridor and drive the Germans from the Scheldt peninsula and Walcheren Islands, which dominated the water approaches to Antwerp. Finally on November 3, the Scheldt peninsula and the islands were cleared, and minesweeping operations were begun to open the port of Antwerp. In addition, reconstruction work at Le Havre and Boulogne advanced rapidly, and by the first of November supplies were finally moving in quantity from these ports. However, Antwerp itself was not in operation until November 27.

During this quiet period, Supreme Headquarters planned the next offensive against the Germans. In late October, the preliminary build-up sufficiently advanced, General Bradley issued a letter of instruction to his three armies—Ninth, First and Third—calling for an advance to the Rhine River. At the same time, Montgomery issued orders for his army group to swing east and attack across the Meuse River in conjunction with the general attack as soon as Antwerp's approaches were cleared. The Third Army was to concentrate on Metz, then move rapidly east, but the main effort was to be with the First Army which was to strike for Cologne. Ninth Army on Bradley's north was to protect the flank of First Army and to link up with British forces attacking southward after crossing the Meuse. Target date for the main attack was November 10 or as soon thereafter as weather permitted the extensive aerial bombardment which was to precede the jump-off. Supplies were constantly brought up, replacements readied to take their places, attack plans perfected, and finally after six days of bad weather, the attack jumped off on November 16.

NOVEMBER OFFENSIVE

Once again in November Allied soldiers began the advance all along the seething front. Steady pressure in the south began on November 8, brought about the capture of Metz by the Third Army on November 22, following which the Germans began a withdrawal to the southerly West Wall positions. Seventh Army and the First French Army, attacking on November 13, had pushed and groaned their way up from southern France and were holding down fourteen German divisions as they closed in to the Palatinate border. By November 27, Strasbourg had been liberated by the Seventh Army, and the first Allied troops were on the Rhine River near its headwaters. Only around Colmar near the Swiss border had the

Germans been able to maintain a substantial bridgehead across the upper Rhine. Third Army had driven east from Metz, had generally closed along the Saar River, and had already established three bridgeheads across the Saar. On the far north, by December 4 the British had cleared the Meuse River of Germans, but a direct drive across the Meuse to the Rhine was considered impracticable, and extensive regroupings and shortening of Montgomery's line would have been necessary before he could possibly begin to strike southeast from Nijmegen along the watershed between the Meuse and the Rhine. This attack was, therefore, held up. But the main effort of the First and Ninth Armies was still batting its head against an iron wall as it attempted once more to break out into the open to the Rhine River.

"I anticipate one hell of a fight," General Simpson, commander of the American Ninth Army, had told his staff prior to D-Day for the November offensive. The Germans fighting on their home soil, shielded by the massive fortifications of the West Wall, reorganized and at least partially re-equipped following the retreat from France, fought hard and well. The weather was miserable, and the mud was an enemy, but there was more to it than that. To the north, the Ninth Army was fighting across the gently rolling plains leading to a small river, the Roer. Defensive positions were a dime a dozen, maneuvering area for the tanks small; it was a straight line plunge, and the Germans knew that and were ready for it. Further south, the First Army had similar terrain due east of Aachen, but more serious, their right flank was fighting through the Hurtgen forest, a densely wooded area which had to be penetrated before the Roer River could be reached. Again, lack of room to maneuver made necessary this line plunge through the dense forests. We had rejected as impractical the possibility of going south and turning the flank of the Germans by attacking through the Ardennes forests. The fighting in the Hurtgen forests was the bloodiest and most costly Allied experience on the Western Front. Parts of three entire divisions were cut to pieces. Two of these were later sent to the static front along the Our River, in the Ardennes forests, to rest and recuperate.

After two weeks of the most bitter fighting, the Ninth Army and the northern wing of the First Army had advanced ten miles and were along the Roer River for a distance of about twenty miles. First Army's exhausted remaining attacking forces were just poking their heads through the east end of the Hurtgen forest when a new obstacle arose. The headwaters of the Roer River, in the northernmost hills of the Ardennes forests, east of the town of Eupen, were bottled up by a series of huge earthen dams built by the Nazis for purposes of flood control, but with military defense in mind. Although we knew about these dams, we failed to realize the apparent invulnerability of their defenses to a straight attack from the west. The plan was to capture the dams by the push through the Hurtgen forest, but the German resistance was too stubborn. Key to the dams was a little town called Schmidt, which had been captured in the early push to the German border, but recaptured by the Germans. Suddenly we realized that we could not cross the Roer River until the dams were taken or destroyed. If the troops crossed the river, puny though it was, the Germans could loose a torrent of flood waters, which would cover the mile-wide river valley, and make it very difficult, if not impossible, to supply and reinforce the attacking troops. And sitting on the opposite side of the Roer River were not only the infantry divisions defending in this area, but further to the rear "Sepp" Dietrich's *Sixth Panzer Army*, which had already been brought back to the west and whose mission was unknown. And so began a period of frantic bombing to knock out the Roer River dams. But the planes could not turn the trick. Direct hits were scored on the huge earthen dams, it is true, but day after day at the briefings at the First and Ninth Armies, the air officer would report, "No results." It got to be something of a standing joke when they would announce that the planes were going out for the dams. Finally, the air attacks were called off, and General Hodges hastily organized a ground attack which was to capture the Roer River dams by hitting at them from the south, just north of the Ardennes. This was on December 13.

THE DAM ATTACK

Hodges' First Army on December 13 was composed of three corps containing a total of three armored divisions, eleven infantry divisions, and three cavalry groups, arrayed as follows: the southern flank of the Army stretched north for eighty miles from the southern boundary of the army at the junction of the Moselle and Sure Rivers, just east of Luxembourg City. This was the Ardennes sector, some eighty miles covered by four divisions and a cavalry group of Major General Troy Middleton's VIII Corps; North of Middleton was V Corps commanded by Major General Leonard T. Gerow,

Chief of the War Plans Division at the time of Pearl Harbor. This Corps of four infantry divisions, with parts of two armored divisions, and a cavalry group, was assigned the mission of capturing the Roer River dams; on the extreme north flank of First Army, Major General J. Lawton Collins' VII Corps was generally along the Roer River with four infantry divisions, an armored division, and part of a second, and a cavalry group. North of First Army, Ninth Army with two corps and six divisions was sitting along the Roer River waiting for capture of the dams to launch an attack across the River toward the Rhine.

While Gerow's V Crops prepared to attack the Roer River dams, Collins' VII Corps and the two corps of Ninth Army rested and licked their wounds from the war of attrition they had fought with the German forces defending the approaches to the Rhine River. While small infantry forces held the Roer River line, the bulk of these forces north of Gerow were resting in reserve. These included all four of the armored divisions and two infantry divisions none of which were engaged with the enemy. Several days later this fact was to assume paramount importance in meeting the German attack. South of Gerow's V Corps, the four divisions of Middleton's Corps, stretched thinly along the forests of the Ardennes, continued their inactive role.

While the remainder of First and Ninth Armies marked time, except for local adjustments in the line, three infantry divisions of Gerow's V Corps started on December 13 to push across the hills and through the woods of the northern highlands of the Ardennes mountains, generally in the vicinity of a small town called Monschau in Germany, to capture the Roer River dams. One command of Middleton's 9th Armored Division was loaned to Gerow, and it lay in readiness, waiting to strike for the dams as soon as the attack was out of the woods. In three days of attack Gerow's troops made slow but steady progress when, on December 16, the German blow fell, mostly in the Ardennes forests further south, partly on this very attack. Not until December 17 was the attack of V Corps halted and the divisions thrown on the defensive. For one day, both sides were attacking.

South of First Army, Patton was once more girding his forces for a gigantic smash. Having successfully breached the stubborn German defenses around Metz and driven to the Saar River, Patton was generally along the line of the German West Wall. That his threat was taken seriously by the Germans is attested by the fact that one of "Sepp" Dietrich's panzer divisions, the crack *Panzer Lehr*, which had valiantly fought in France, was dispatched in mid-November to the Saar to meet Patton's threat, was relieved only on December 1, and given two weeks to prepare for the new attack. Patton's plan was to launch a massive attack on December 19 with three Corps to smash the Siegfried Line and drive to the Rhine River. Preliminary preparations had been completed; they included the largest aerial bombardment ever to be attempted during the war: 3,000 planes were to blast a huge hole in the West Wall, through which Patton was prepared to pour three of his four armored divisions and his infantry. Patton was racing against time because Eisenhower had set a time limit on his attack, after which part of his army, regardless of the attack results, was to be transferred to the north.

THE DIE IS CAST

The great decision had been made. The chance for a speedy end to the war was lost as supply lines creaked and groaned those last weeks in August. The war of movement was ended. It became, in those grimmer days of October and November, a battle of supply, a war of attrition. Both German and Allied forces were being steadily used up. American divisions were terribly under strength; replacements could not keep pace with the rapid casualty rate. Divisions were fighting with service personnel, rapidly converted to fighting troops; a massive training program was about to be launched to prune out the seemingly top-heavy headquarters and service staffs. Urgent pleas were made by Eisenhower for troops, and General Marshall, in Europe during October on a personal inspection tour, went home to order the immediate shipment of nine infantry regiments ahead of their divisions to relieve this critical situation. And in early December, Marshall announced that 65,000 troops, air force and service personnel, would be transferred to the ground forces for training.

The Germans, too, suffered heavy casualties. Our best estimates indicated that the equivalent of three-fourths of a German division was being destroyed a day—actually this meant about 10,000 casualties a day scattered along the 625 mile front. Our Intelligence indicated that this attrition was going on at a faster rate than the Germans could expect to replace men. But we underestimated the Germans' ability to recover and overestimated the damage we were inflicting. The Germans were able to hold our main effort toward the Ruhr with the troops they had in the line at the time; they held out their trump cards, the *Sixth Panzer Army* and the *Fifth Panzer Army*. They were partly able to achieve this seemingly impossible task because of the West Wall, partly because they had flooded great areas of central Holland and were able to withdraw troops from there and use them farther to the south, and also because their homeland was being invaded. Nazi and non-Nazi could now be exhorted to the final great effort. "We stand again alone on the front against our enemies," Hitler cried; "we will throw them back." The *Volkssturm*, composed of all men between 16 and 60 who were able to carry arms, was formed to defend the homeland; more soldiers were drafted; Germans everywhere in the threatened areas dug and dug and dug. Daily our aerial reconnaissance showed more and more antitank ditches, more fire trenches, more road blocks. All of Germany was aroused for the last great effort; Hitler was playing his last trump card. He was fighting for his very life this time. And behind this screen, he plotted and planned for the last great gamble—the Ardennes offensive.

CHAPTER III

All Quiet

SETTLING DOWN

IT WAS A GHOST FRONT. EVER SINCE THE FIRST TANKS OF THE 5th Armored Division had poked their noses through the Ardennes forests and into the West Wall, this had been the "phony" sector.

We have already seen how the leading tankers charged across the German border on September 11, first to march on the sacred soil of our mortal enemy. Finding no opposition in the bunkers of the West Wall, the tankers and infantrymen hastily streaked through the fortifications and into the open, the German plains beyond. For one week these forces moved around well within the German border, but they were far ahead of their supporting troops and supplies. Shortly, the Germans, who were supposed to be on their last legs, recovered, counterattacked in substantial force, and drove the Americans back through the West Wall across the Our River. Our offensive action in the Ardennes had ended. The troops sat down to wait impatiently for the supplies and reinforcements to catch up with them.

General Hodges, the First Army Commander, was then faced with a dilemma. His last static front had been less than fifty miles long, which he could cover with the limited number of divisions available to him. But St. Lo was now far behind, and he was drawn up along the German border on a sector stretching nearly one hundred and fifty miles. Allied forces were still gravely limited in numbers and operating on a shoestring. With determination to carry the war to the enemy wherever and whenever possible, it was necessary to hold portions of the long front lightly, if sufficient troops were to be made available for the attacks elsewhere. Natural barriers behind which small forces could hold with little likelihood of an enemy attack were sought out: the "calculated risk" began. In those days of unbridled optimism, almost every sector seemed immune from a German attack, but because of the hills, the forests, the paucity of good roads, the lack of apparent strategic objectives behind the front, and the scarcity of Germans in this area, the Ardennes sector was selected for the "calculated risk." The ghost front was born.

While the larger part of Hodges' First Army was attracted toward Aachen and further north, where heavy fighting was taking place, the Ardennes sector of eighty miles was loosely held by three divisions of General Middleton's VIII Corps. Middleton's Corps was brought into the Ardennes from Brittany where it had been dispatched soon after the breakout at St. Lo to contain the German forces in the channel ports of Brest, St. Lazaire, and Lorient. Middleton's three divisions— on the north the 4th (Ivy), in the center the 8th (Pathfinder), and on the south the 83rd (Thunderbolt)—were confronted with a serious situation from the start. Each division was ordered to hold a front of about twenty-six miles compared to the average four- to five-mile front usually recommended by military manuals. But it was not a new situation for Middleton, who once had a forty-five mile front with one division in Sicily, and nearly as large a front at one time in Italy. The Corps mission was to defend in place.

Eisenhower's decision to push ahead in late August and September, despite the acute shortage of supplies and transportation, was a bold one. Few people stop to think that the Americans had only thirty-three divisions in Europe by the end of September, augmented by approximately fifteen additional British and Allied divisions—just under fifty in all. The Germans, despite their stunning defeat in France, had more than this number and were fighting for their homeland from fixed, fortified positions. It was absolutely essential to concentrate the relatively small Allied forces at the most vulnerable German spots in order to achieve maximum effectiveness. In early September Eisenhower extended the First Army's front northward to permit Montgomery to mobilize his forces for the Arnhem landings, and again Hodges had to stretch himself somewhere. He did it in the Ardennes. Again, early in October, during the drive to open the port of Antwerp, additional American units were lent to the British to bolster their forces. Only in mid-October was Eisenhower able to provide Hodges with a reserve for this long, vulnerable front. At that time the 9th Armored Division, fresh off the beaches of Normandy, was assigned to the VIII Corps, and its three combat commands were scattered along the front to provide the mobile reserve considered sufficient to restore positions lost in any attack in this sector. But already Hitler had spotted the weak point.

Opposite the Americans, the Germans were busy withdrawing their élite troops for refitting and for a long time used the Ardennes sector for resting battered divisions and instructing new ones. Patrols from both sides moved back and forth through the thin lines with ease, and each brought back reports that the enemy was weak. Middleton, faced with a choice of fortifying his entire line in depth by keeping the men digging or maintaining an offensive attitude, chose the latter and was supported by his boss, Hodges. The German inactivity influenced his decision. Trucks and a few trains, which could have brought up mines and other defensive weapons to strengthen the front, were busily engaged in hauling ammunition and gasoline for the attacking troops in other sectors, since offensive needs were deemed most urgent. American soldiers—unused to defense, and poorly trained in it—grew restless and, in some cases, careless as day after day passed with no apparent German action in the Ardennes sector.

Shifts were made in the Allied lineup in the Middleton sector. On September 30, the 2d (Indianhead) Division replaced the 4th (Ivy) Division at the northern end of Middleton's line as the 4th was moved north to take a shot at the Roer River dams. In the middle of November the 28th Division, labeled the Bloody Buckets by the Germans because of its red insignia and vicious fighting tactics, traded places with the 8th (Pathfinder) Division and returned to the center of Middleton's line to recuperate from the horrible fighting for the Roer River dams. Unable to get through the dense Hurtgen forest, the only gateway to the dams, the division had been pulled back, badly mauled, after having been attacked by the *116 Panzer Division*. Less than thirty day later the same *116 Panzer* hit them again, only this time together with twenty-eight other divisions. And on December 6 the 4th Division returned again to the Middleton sector after having lived through one of the worst periods of fighting in the entire war. Working in the area in which the 28th had been mauled, the 4th Division suffered 7,000 casualties in its attempt to drive through to the Roer River dams. Still short 1,500 infantrymen and exhausted from the bloody tree-to-tree fighting in the Hurtgen forest, it replaced the 83rd (Thunderbolt) Division at the southern end of Middleton's line. The 83rd went north to join the 8th Division in the continuing Hurtgen fighting. On December 10, the Golden Lion Division, the 106th, took over the sector of the 2nd Division in the Schnee Eifel to free the 2nd Division for participation in the new V Corps attack toward the Roer River dams. The Golden Lions left the States in November, spent a few pleasant weeks in England, were brought across the channel to France in the first week of December, and in a series of moves in freezing weather were shuttled to the VIII Corps sector, where they were to get their battle indoctrination. This was the last major shift, but one other movement is important to our story. In the first week of December Middleton staged, on orders from higher headquarters, what is known as a "rubber duck" operation. Middleton's "rubber duck" involved the fake movement of a new division into the VIII Corps sector. Its purpose, as understood by Middleton, was to draw German divisions away from the vital Aachen sector, where we were preparing our attack to the Roer River dams. And all this time German forces in the Ardennes appeared to be light.

Middleton's defense line lay deep in the heart of the rolling wooded hills of eastern Belgium and Luxembourg, commonly called the Ardennes forests. Long known for its quaint charm, this famed vacation area, with alternate gorges and ridges interspersed by areas of gently rolling hills, is covered with large forests and criss-crossed by a sparse network of roads generally following the valleys. Bordered on the east by the Our River and on the west by the majestic Meuse River, the Ardennes region has been visited by thousands upon thousands of pleasure-seeking vacationists. Its famed chateaux have played host to many an international gathering. Twice before, the region had been trampled by boots of conquest-bound German troops headed for the richer lands of France and Belgium. Over half of Middleton's defense line was based on a series of river lines, principal of which was the narrow, but deeply etched, Our River, separating first Luxembourg and then Belgium from Germany. However, on the extreme north of his line, the 4th (Ivy) Division had penetrated a portion of the West Wall due east of the road center, called St. Vith, and was perched in German territory on a large ridge, called the Schnee Eifel. The northern positions, strategically important because we possessed this segment of the West Wall, were nevertheless difficult to hold because of their exposed nature. Several times General Middleton requested permission to withdraw from this penetration of the German defensive positions to straighten out his line along more tenable positions some ten miles to the west. Permission was not granted because of the tactical importance of the penetration of the West Wall. So exposed were two of the battalions, however, that they could be supplied only at night. Finally Middleton, in desperation, withdrew these two battalions without authority from higher headquarters and blew up some twenty-five pillboxes which had been occupied in that area. But still Middleton was alarmed about the possibility of an attack around the Schnee Eifel from both exposed flanks, and to counteract this possibility, he concentrated ten of the Corps' thirteen artillery battalions in this northern sector to give added support to his revised positions.

Middleton's defensive positions were nothing more than a series of widely separated strongpoints, each with barbed wire, minefields, probably a machine gun, and covered shelters. These strongpoints were scattered along the front, but between them the ground, usually including the roads, was wide open. It is no wonder that large parties of Germans were able to filter through the lines at night, almost at will, and some of them wandered about for days on end. Driving along the roads immediately behind the front lines, one had something of an uncomfortable feeling, wondering just how many "Krauts" might be staring from behind bushes.

The Germans knew we were weak in the Ardennes. Field Marshal Model reported about the Ardennes front to his troops: "The enemy does not have a continuous main line of resistance. He carries on defensive battle from strongpoints about four to five kilometers in depth. In the most forward line, relatively strong security elements are placed in well-developed positions. These security elements yield systematically in the case of strong attacks and retreat to strongpoints behind them. The strongpoints are organized chessboard-fashion, with flanking effect, well adapted to terrain sectors, localities, woodpatches and crossroads. At the strongpoints, which are defended even when surrounded, well-camouflaged and dug-in tanks, tank destroyers and heavy weapons, especially antitank and mortars, form the backbone. Stronger reserves are in position several kilometers behind the zone of strongpoints at centrally located points, such as villages or forest patches near main highways. They are fully motorized and are committed in combat groups of two to three infantry companies with eight to ten tanks. They go into action about six hours after the attack starts."

Model's analysis of our defensive positions was quite accurate. But, as important as the physical aspects of the defense was the environment as etched by a frame of mind. One day spent there, and you, too, would have called it the ghost front. For one beautiful Indian-summer week I shared a room with some officers from the 8th Infantry Division in a charming little town called Wiltz, nestled in the side of one of the many rugged hills in the Ardennes forests of Luxembourg. I remember well how we joked privately about the owner of that house who, we were certain, constantly carried a swastika with him. Although friendly and sympathetic to us, this Luxembourger was afraid, afraid of a Nazi threat that they would return to Wiltz. We laughed at the absurdity of this fear; it was the laugh of a victorious army waiting to move forward again, flushed with confidence engendered by one of the most decisive encounters in modern warware—the defeat of the German armies in France. None of us, even in our wildest dreams, ever imagined that Hitler was at that very time plotting and planning an attack, which two months later would strike through our thinly held lines some eight miles east of Wiltz, to capture this beautiful little town in a bloody battle.

From Wiltz, we moved out toward what people had dubbed "the sieve." Imagine, if you will, a ridge road running along a high plateau, just west of the Our River. As I rode along this European sky-line drive one day late in October, I asked my guide where the Germans were located and what they were doing. All was peaceful; farmers in the fields along the road were plowing their fields for the winter fallow, and some were taking in the last of the summer harvest; cattle were grazing lazily. I was green, and my guide knew it, so he said suddenly, with a dramatic flourish of his hand, "See that ridge line over there just across the valley?"

I nodded.

"That's it."

"What?" I naively inquired.

"The German line," he replied.

We were riding along the top of a huge ridge, silhouetted in plain view of an enemy no more than eight hundred yards away, guns of the West Wall supposedly bristling behind every bush, and nothing happened. "Have to be careful at night," my talkative guide continued, "Krauts like to sneak over patrols, just to make a social call. Ambushed a jeep in daylight the other day, and got a new battalion commander. Hell, he didn't even get a chance to report in. But the only shelling we get is when a Jerry goes to the latrine; seems like they have a machine gun and a mortar there, and each one fires a burst—hope they don't get diarrhea."

We left the ridge road and wound our way into the valley along a narrow secondary road which twisted and turned its way through the thickly wooded hills until it came to a beautiful resort town called Clerf. There, eight miles behind the so-called front line, the 8th Division had a rest center, where the men frolicked, drank beer, flirted with the pretty Luxembourg girls, seduced them when they could, and relaxed from the worries of war. Just such a group was frolicking in Clerf on December 16, less than two months later, when the Germans suddenly burst into the town.

After lunch I motored further north to see a friend of mine in one of the companies holding the line. Everyone assured me it was safe to go up there; nothing ever happened in this sector, they said. That was the day General Jodl was giving preliminary orders for the attack which was to engulf that very road.

"Hughes isn't here," his company commander said, "you'll find him on the rifle range."

"What?" I asked in astonishment, "Where did you say he was?"

"On the rifle range," the Captain said, deadpan. "I'll take you there."

Our jeeps wound around the side of a hill into the Our River valley, and finally we found Hughes. He *was* on a rifle range, but it was no ordinary range; the backstop was the Our

River, and the ridge on the opposite side was German-occu-
pied. The Germans were shelling the road on our ridge. The
shells were passing directly overhead, but my friend was saying, "Ready on the right. Ready on the left. Ready on the
firing line. Commence firing!" And the men were practicing
under the shadow of the West Wall. "Nearly had some
trouble," my friend quietly drawled; "it was just before you
came. Goddamned Jerries must be using poor-grade ammunition. Anyway they had a short, and it dropped right behind
the targets. The boys out there were in the pits, and none of
them were hurt, so I said 'mark those targets,' There were
nine jagged, shelf-fragment holes in the bull's-eye; pretty
damned good shooting for a Kraut." That was the phony front.

Back in Wiltz that night we stayed in a modern apartment
house, had a dance with the Red Cross girls across the hall,
and wandered around the beautiful little town talking with the
lucky soldiers who were holding this dormant front.

IT CAN'T HAPPEN HERE

Meanwhile, the Germans continued with their plans for the
attack. In early November, the *Sixth Panzer Army* was
brought west of the Rhine, where it sat in front of Cologne in
plain sight of all. And there it waited, apparently for the day
when we would cross the Roer River. The movement of other
divisions to the Western Front began late in October and continued steadily to Christmas day. Twenty-three of the divisions
moved at least a part of their journey by rail, and this involved
a grand total of 1,050 trains or an average of twenty-one trains
per day during the fifty-day period, exclusive of supply trains
which probably averaged another twelve trains per day. Rundstedt's supply officer reports that for the pending offensive and
the troops already in position, a combined total of one hundred
trains a day were being shunted to the Western Front in early
December. Naturally, a number of these troop movements
were sighted by our air force, which, during this same period,
attacked sixty-three marshalling yards in Western Germany in
a total of 133 raids. The Director of Intelligence of the United
States Strategic Air Force concluded that the German troop
movements were not seriously affected by this concentrated
bombing because of the facility with which repairs were made
and because of the complex network of railroads in Western
Germany, which offered infinite possibilities for alternate rout-
ing. However, the detraining points, some sixty-seven of which

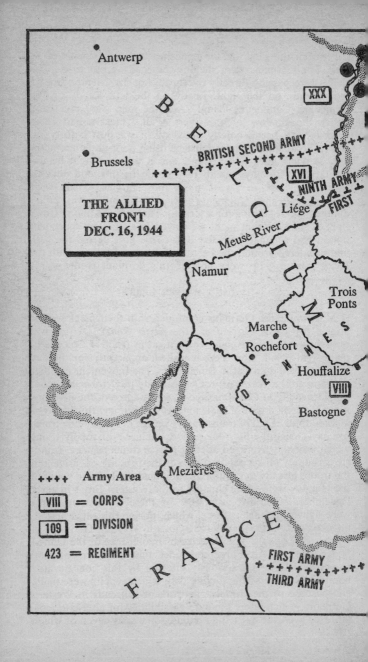

Antwerp

BELGIUM

XXX

Brussels

BRITISH SECOND ARMY

XVI

NINTH ARMY

THE ALLIED FRONT DEC. 16, 1944

Liége

FIRST

Meuse River

Namur

Trois Ponts

Marche

Rochefort

Houffalize

VIII

ARDENNES

Bastogne

Mezières

FRANCE

++++ Army Area

VIII = CORPS

109 = DIVISION

423 = REGIMENT

FIRST ARMY

THIRD ARMY

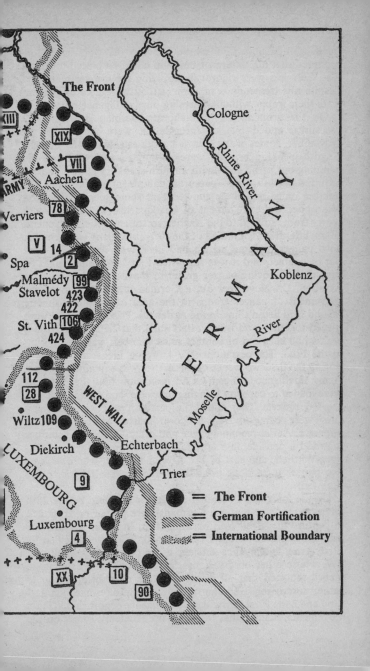

have been identified in subsequent reports, were so widely scattered that no pattern of build-up could be pieced together. The Germans were rigorously applying their cover plan, and despite this tremendous movement they were able to concentrate their troops without alarming our intelligence officers.

On the ground, despite elaborate German precautionary measures, added bits of information were picked up. In November, copies of the German order establishing Skorzeny's English-speaking brigade were captured which directed the combing-out of all men with English-speaking ability and re-required release of all captured equipment available to the fighting units, and these showed that some special operation was under way. Movement of headquarters of the *Fifteenth Army* from Holland to the Aachen sector and relief of General Manteuffel from command of the *Fifteenth Army* were known. Two panzer divisions which had been with Manteuffel were out of contact, and it was suggested that Manteuffel might be organizing a roving panzer group to move to danger spots as required. On November 30, a German prisoner reported the movement of panzer troops in the area of Wittlich, directly behind Middleton's line in the Ardennes. Prisoner reports were pieced together, and it was established that *2 Panzer Division*, which had been out of contact since October, was the division in the Eifel. The cessation of V-1 fire on Liége and Antwerp during the first two weeks of December was explained by First Army intelligence officers as an indication that the railroads were loaded to capacity bringing up troops and could not carry the V-1 rockets. They added the possibility that the launching sites were being moved to co-ordinated with a potential offensive. Aerial reconnaissance and other unidentified sources reported a considerable German build-up in the area of Bit-burg-Wittlich, due east of the Ardennes front, where at least two panzer formations in addition to *2 Panzer Division* were reported.

On the fourth of December a prisoner captured by the 28th Division reported that the Germans were preparing an attack to capture the West Wall positions then in Allied hands. One prisoner captured before December 10, who was classified by First Army intelligence officers as "an extremely intelligent PW, whose other observations check exactly with established facts," reported that all possible means were being taken to gather forces for a coming all-out counteroffensive. On December 12 the First Army daily intelligence report said, "Train movements indicate that the build-up of enemy forces on the

western slope of the Moselle Valley continues. *Grossdeutschland Division,* crack infantry division of the German army,
has again been reported to be in the area by PW's [actually
this was Remer's brigade]. A conservative estimate would place
at least two *Volksgrenadier* and one *Panzer Grenadier* division
in the enemy's rear area opposite VIII US Corps." The next
day, prisoners of *3 Parachute Division* reported that they were
to be relieved in the northern portion of the Ardennes sector
by the *12 SS Panzer Division.*

Other reports made on that same day indicated a southward
movement of *116 Panzer Division* from its rest area east of
Aachen. And on that same day a German woman came
through the lines of VIII Corps and told of her observations
during the three days beginning December 10. Her statements
were considered as reliable by intelligence officers of VIII
Corps. They included observation of many horsedrawn vehicles,
pontoons, small boats, and other river-crossing equipment
coming from the direction of Bitburg; and moving west, many
panzer troops in Bitburg and many artillery pieces. First Army
intelligence officers also reported: "Build-up of troops has been
confirmed by Tac/R [aerial reconnaissance] and PW statements. Presence of large numbers of engineers with bridging
equipment suggests preparation for offensive rather than defensive action."

The next day in the First Army intelligence summary,
Colonel Dickson reported "Reinforcements for the West Wall
between Dueren and Trier [a broad limit of the Ardennes
sector], continue to arrive. The identification of at least three
or four newly reformed divisions along the army front must
be reckoned with during the next few days."

Many prisoners began to speak of the coming attack between
December 17 and 25, while others related promises of the
recapture of Aachen as a Christmas present for Hitler. About
the same time, VIII Corps announced an abrupt change of
routine in the enemy personnel opposite it. On that same day,
considerable vehicular traffic was noted on the southern flank
of the Schnee Eifel salient. Perhaps most startling was the capture of two prisoners on December 14 who reported that
members of the divisions in the line opposite Middleton's
VIII Corps were ordered back to their divisions from rest areas
on December 11 and that the Germans were preparing to attack. So novel was this suggestion that when the report was re-
printed, it read that the German prisoners said they were ex-
pecting us to attack. "We must have made an error in translat-

ing their statement," said Intelligence, "it's obvious they couldn't be preparing an attack." Another prisoner captured on December 15 reported that the Germans were preparing to attack, but this report was not sent on to higher head-quarters. Most startling of all, we knew that the Germans had imposed a radio blackout on December 12, that new troop movements had begun, and we could estimate the general direction of these columns. This information, gathered at high levels, may not have been transmitted to lower headquarters. I found no record of it down below, and, at any rate, we can examine the record of our behavior in the face of all of those indications to discover how they were read or misread.

SIX AND SIX ARE THIRTEEN

No person of stature among the American leaders claims we knew at the time that the Germans were going to launch such a huge attack in the Ardennes. Eisenhower, Bradley, and Hodges all told me they were surprised. Two operational moves made by our forces, prior to the German attack, indicate with-out doubt the surprise with which we were taken. First, was the very presence of the 106th Division, the Golden Lions, in this quiet section where Hodges wanted them to get their battle indoctrination; and, second was the "rubber duck" operation conducted in conjunction with the First Army attack to the Roer River dams. This operation was initially conceived as an exercise to contain German units then on the front, but as it passed through various headquarters, was changed in concept and became an operation to lure German divisions from the Aachen sector to the Ardennes. Wags have facetiously and perhaps unfairly suggested that this was the greatest deception in the history of organized warfare—29 German divisions brought down on Middleton's neck to meet one American division which wasn't there. Actually, although this deception was of no assistance to First Army's December attack, the fault revolved around a matter of timing and changing objec-tive rather than any fundamental weakness of the idea of de-ception. But even more complete than these operational moves are the written reports of the various intelligence officers in the weeks before the attack. They are both pertinent and revealing.

On December 9, one week before the Germans sprang out of the protecting forests of the Ardennes, Colonel Reeves, Middleton's intelligence officer, issued an estimate of the situation, which was a summary of the known facts concerning the enemy along his front. Reeves, representing the considered judgment of Middleton's intelligence staff, concluded that, "the enemy can continue the active defense of his present positions with forces now on his front . . . it is believed that the enemy will continue this line of action until VIII Corps goes on the offensive. The enemy's present practice of bringing new divisions to this sector to receive front-line experience, and then relieving them out for commitment elsewhere, indicates his desire to have this sector of the front remain quiet and inactive." And in a discussion of the terrain in his sector, Reeves pointed out in this same report that the terrain favors the defense, and added that there would be little opportunity for the use of armor. And on December 9, Reeves reported that an estimated 24,000 German troops representing four infantry divisions, three of which were *Volksgrenadier* Divisions, the new streamlined, 1944 version of the German infantry, with horsedrawn artillery, fewer troops, and less training, were defending the VIII Corps sector against Middleton's 40,000 men. Reeves did not know of the attack, and he has said as much, nor did any of the intelligence officers in any of the divisions in VIII Corps.

What about the higher echelons of command? Although normally most intelligence information begins at the lowest level and is then disseminated upward, oftentimes the lower echelons do not have sufficient information to interpret correctly the material they have gathered, and, therefore, all intelligence information is passed up the chain of command regardless of its seemingly inconsequential nature.

Skipping the First Army intelligence officer for a moment, we will examine the prognostications of General Bradley's intelligence officer, General Sibert. Four days before the German attack, Sibert issued his weekly summary of the enemy situation. He was in an exuberant mood, and his enthusiasm bubbled over in his first sentence: "It is now certain that attrition is steadily sapping the strength of German forces on the Western Front and that the crust of defenses is thinner, more brittle, and more vulnerable than it appears on our G-2 maps, or to the troops in the lines." Although Sibert recognized the capabilities of the *Sixth Panzer Army*, which everyone knew was lurking west of the Rhine River, his optimism stemmed in part at least from the reports of Eisenhower's intelligence officer, General Strong, who had recently announced that the Germans were losing the equivalent of twenty divisions a

month and that the maximum new personnel available to them
were fifteen divisions a month. Mathematically it was simple:
every month the equivalent of five less German divisions on
the Western Front; every month new American divisions (the
British were already down to the bottom of their barrel).
Net result: the Germans undoubtedly would be forced to
commit their reserves into the line to replace the losses caused
by the war of attrition. Sibert recognized, in passing, the possibility of a German offensive, but only as a counterattack
against our crossing of the Roer River. And this happy man
concluded his report with a statement which was to warm the
cockles of many a homesick soldier's heart: "With continued
Allied pressure in the south and in the north, the breaking
point may develop suddenly and without warning." This was
Sibert's last written word before the great attack, but in all
fairness to him, it must be reported that in his weekly summary
two weeks previous to this he discussed in some detail the possibility that the Germans would use "Sepp" Dietrich's *Sixth
Panzer Army* in a counterattacking role. However, because
of the serious situation to the south and the Allied concentration east of Aachen, he concluded: "While it is likely Rundstedt would employ a part or all of the *Sixth Panzer Army* in a
counterattack against any bridgeheads east of the Roer, in conjunction with flooding the river, in order to protect the Cologne
corridor, it seems unlikely that he would bring them westward
across the Roer to commit them in a major counteroffensive.
This counteroffensive use of the *Sixth Panzer Army* is a capability that appears less probable now than it did a week ago."

General Strong, Eisenhower's intelligence officer, reported
on November 26 in his "Weekly Intelligence Summary": "The
intentions of the enemy in the Aachen sector, therefore, become quite clear. He (the enemy) is fighting the main battle
with his infantry formations and army panzer divisions, and
with these, he hopes to blunt our offensive. Meanwhile, *Sixth
SS Panzer Army* waits behind the River Roer, either to continue the defensive action, and prevent bridgeheads from being
established, or, if Rundstedt gauges that we are becoming
exhausted, to counterattack and regain lost ground." But the
next week Strong's report presaged the wave of optimism which
was to sweep down from Eisenhower's headquarters through
the entire army in the field when he reported: "The problems
still facing the enemy are naked enough. The longest term
problem is to find enough men and equipment to stand up to
the present rate of attrition . . . . So far this rate has been met,

partly by replacements *but to a large extent by feeding the fat from the Ardennes and from Holland to the battle sectors"* (italics mine).

Strong was aware that German panzer divisions began to disappear from the line about December 1 and that there seemed to be more *Volksgrenadier* divisions in the Eifel than warranted by a static front, but he did not guess the Germans' true intent nor did he visualize the potential striking force and determination of the German attackers. On December 14 General Strong's war maps still showed only four German divisions opposite Middleton, with two panzer divisions lurking far to the rear of this area, apparently moving north.

At First Army, Hodges' intelligence officer, Colonel Dickson, had been considering the possibility of a German attack since early November, when he indicated that the Germans seemed to want to mount an offensive, probably in the area Aachen-Venlo (in Holland). He concluded that there was high probability of an attack against the British and the Ninth Army, but low probability of an attack against First Army. Later, on November 20, shortly after the First and Ninth Armies began their attack toward the Roer River, Dickson lost his cautious touch, and predicted that the possibility of a German spoiling attack in any sector had been lost with the beginning of the American attacks. The remaining German capabilities, Dickson concluded, were continued defense or surrender—attack was impossible. But again about the first of December, when the American attacks were dying down, the additional clues, already noted, indicated the renewed possibility of a German attack.

Throughout the first week of December, many additional indications of a German build-up came through, as the railroads were working overtime pouring the German troops and supplies into the Western Front. On December 10, Dickson issued his last estimate of the enemy situation before the attack, which has led some to credit him with the prediction of the German attack. After citing numerous indications of a German build-up, Dickson concluded: "It is plain that his (the enemy's) strategy in defense of the Reich is based on the exhaustion of our offensive, to be followed by an all-out counterattack with armor, between the Roer and the Erft (which is between the Roer and the Rhine Rivers), supported by every weapon he can bring to bear. It is apparent that von Rundstedt, who obviously is conducting military operations without the benefit of intuition, has skillfully defended and husbanded his forces, and is preparing for his part in the all-out application of every weapon at the focal point, and the correct time to achieve defense of the Reich west of the Rhine by inflicting as great a defeat on the Allies as possible. Indications to date point to the location of this focal point as being between Roermond and Schleiden" (the area due east of Aachen, and north of the Ardennes sector).

Did we have, then, foresight of the German intentions by First Army headquarters? No, we did not. Dickson came closest to outlining the possibilities of a German attack, but his prediction was mentioned only on this day and then was dropped. From then on, the clues which had led to these conclusions seemed to die down. In summing up the enemy capabilities in the same report, Dickson concluded that the concentrated counterattack "is to be expected when our major ground forces have crossed the Roer River."

And tucked in the heart of Dickson's summary was the death blow to his divining ability: "During the past month there has been a definite pattern for the seasoning of newly formed divisions in the comparatively quiet sector opposite VIII US Corps prior to their dispatch to more active fronts." And on December 15, Dickson said: *"Although the enemy is resorting to his attack propaganda to bolster morale of the troops, it is possible that a limited scale offensive will be launched for the purpose of achieving a Christmas morale 'victory' for civilian consumption"* (italics mine).

In addition the following items were variously noted: (1) when prisoners of *3 Parachute Division* reported they were to be relieved by *12 SS Panzer Division*, First Army reported it unlikely that the *SS* division would be used then, because it was being saved for the big attack; (2) when VIII Corps reported the abrupt change of routine opposite it, First Army said, "Very likely a recently arrived *Volksgrenadier* Division came in to relieve *212 Volksgrenadier Division.*"

Certain definite conclusions may be drawn from this array of statements and facts. Most important, no serious consideration was given by any echelon in the entire command in the west to the possibility of a strong German attack through the weak "calculated risk" in the Ardennes. The nature of the divisions occupying the front, the written statements of intelligence officers, unconcern for secondary defensive positions in the Ardennes, loan of part of Middleton's only armored division to V Corps, all combined to confirm the candid statement of Middleton's intelligence officer, "It surprised me," and to deny that in their wildest dreams or predictions anyone gave consideration to this location for the German attack.

However, we should recognize that the various intelligence officers had seriously considered the possibility of a German attack, and that Hodges' intelligence officer, for one day at least, had gloomily forecast a rather heavy German attack which would risk the entire German future. But all of these predictions were based on the presumption that the Germans would attack our concentration in the Aachen sector and that attacks would occur only after we had battered our way across the Roer River and were lunging for the fattened industrial area of the Ruhr, barely twenty miles east of the Roer River on the opposite shore of the Rhine.

During the war no armchair strategist's theories so infuriated American GI's as the statements in which several of our leading civilian "military experts" insinuated we knew all about the Battle of the Bulge in advance. Several even hinted that it was merely a trap to get the Germans into the open. Today certain columnists, military analysts, and commanders are still suggesting that they knew the Ardennes attack was coming all the time. If they did, they concealed their knowledge as well as the Germans did their troop movements. The German cover or camouflage plan, *Wacht Am Rhein,* had exceeded its fondest expectations. We were completely, utterly fooled.

For just one minute let us cast our eyes back to the German plan, to review how its strategy had succeeded so well. First, *Sixth Panzer Army* was brought west of the Rhine, where it sat in front of Cologne, in plain sight where we could not fail to see it. Was it not logical to suppose that it would be used to defend the approaches to the Ruhr? Had not the Germans always reacted bitterly to any attempts to push east of Aachen? Secondly, new *Volksgrenadier* Divisions were moved into the deep forests of the Ardennes. Was it not probable, said the Germans, that some of them will get in there without being detected at all? And cannot we presume that the Americans will assume that the divisions they may spot are simply relieving other divisions which have been there for some time, a practice we have been following for the three months this front has been static? We figured just that way. And then, said the Germans, just before the attack we will suddenly shift these panzer divisions south in a series of night moves, hide them in the woods during the daytime, and hope that our weather forecaster was right when he said there would be no flying weather those days. We will be ready for the attack which the Americans will not expect. And we will attack before dawn, before that quiet dawn, when we know the few American sentries will be sleeping. And while Eisenhower tries to figure out our intentions and then argues with Roosevelt and Churchill, we will drive forward and cross the Meuse River before he can turn on us. And thus would *Wacht Am Rhein* emerge as *Herbstnebel* (Autumn Smoke), and in that cloud of smoke, they would suffocate the entire northern group of Allied armies. German deception at its best had outfoxed us. The guards were napping, and we were shocked and rocked on our heels, but there the reasoning broke down.

THE OPTIMISTS CLUB

Despite the crushing, grinding, fighting of October and November, optimism, which reached its height during the chase across France, continued to pervade all ranks of the Anglo-American armies, sometimes to the blinding of reason. Ralph Ingersoll, one of Bradley's staff officers, now says that he was gloomy when Eisenhower missed "The Great Decision" in September, but he seems to have been alone. Certainly Bradley's intelligence officer did not show any gloom in his glowing intelligence reports. The intelligence officers of all commands seemed to enter into a deliberate contest in those fateful days to see who could make most fun of the critical German situation. Wisecracks and serious reports alike, led to only one conclusion: the Germans were on their last legs even if they did not act that way. I well remember the day we received our copy of the 12th Army Group intelligence report which said: "the crust of defenses is thinner, more brittle, and more vulnerable than it appears on our G-2 maps or to the troops in the line." I was in the G-2 office of the 7th Armored Division at the time. We were comfortably sitting astride the little river which separates Holland and Germany, in reserve, waiting and planning for the big push across the Roer River. We did not have much to do in those days, and we sat around discussing this report. I was ready to pack my bags and prepare to go home, but some of the more sober individuals rather hesitatingly pointed out that it seemed as though the *Sixth Panzer Army* was waiting across the river, licking its chops in anticipation of our crossing. It did not happen that way, but less than a week later, the 7th Armored Division was fighting portions of both Dietrich's *Sixth Panzer Army* and Manteuffel's *Fifth Panzer Army,* and nobody was joking then.

A symptom of the times was the talk in higher headquarters of issuing a joint Churchill-Roosevelt statement which might break the will of the Germans to resist. However, Eisenhower recommended against this. Nevertheless, his aide, Captain Butcher, writes that on November 11 he ordered a mobile radio transmitter ready by December 15, ironically enough the eve of the German attack, so that it would be ready in time for the fall of Berlin; and on December 13, Eisenhower sent a letter to Montgomery describing the irreparable damage done to the Germans by the then current offensive. On December 16, General Eisenhower's chauffeur and orderly, Micky, was married to a WAC in a military ceremony attended by the Supreme Commander.

The lack of concern with any secondary defensive line for VIII Corps was another indication of this optimism. No matter what the "calculated risk," sound defensive tactics would seem to call for the establishment of alternate positions in any defense, even if it be for one night. But Middleton's VIII Corps had been in the Ardennes sector for nearly three months.

The underestimation of the German ability to recover was the most flagrant example of this overoptimism. We thought that all German divisions were down one-third to one-half strength, but much to our surprise, we discovered that the panzer units of "Sepp" Dietrich's *Sixth Panzer Army* carried their full strength and more. And most of the *Volksgrenadier* divisions were in the same condition. We thought the Germans did not have enough tanks, guns, ammunition, and fuel, but they turned up with vast quantities of all of these in the Ardennes forests in December.

Germans captured before their December wave of high morale, fed this optimism of ours. From general to private they confided that they were licked and knew it. Some asked that we take letters to their wives in Berlin because they knew we would be there in a few weeks (this was during the chase across France). Others "admitted" that the German war machine was through; some confided that great unrest was stirring Germany, and, of course, the attempt on Hitler's life added fuel to this type of thinking. In addition, our newspaper reports, as you will remember, glowed with satisfaction and overoptimism—it couldn't be long, they said.

Those were certainly days of smug satisfaction, when people felt that the glorious day of victory could not be far off. And with this optimism was another factor, the general strategic conception of our fight. Eisenhower's goal at all times was to apply continuing pressure to the Germans, to deny them the breathing space which would allow them to rebuild their armies further. Time and time again he reiterated his belief that the Allied armies must attack, attack, attack throughout the winter. Butcher summed it up when he said, "Ike's problem is to continue his attacks as long as the results are so much in our favor, but, at the same time, to prepare a full-out and heavy offensive when weather conditions become favorable, *assuming the enemy still holds out*"* (italics mine).

It was this strategy which had prompted the November offensives and the V Corps attack toward the Roer River dams in December, for the weather was foul and the fighting conditions miserable. The Allied strength in Western Europe was actually small; just before the offensive there were all told sixty-three Allied divisions in Europe, of which forty-one were American. In order to conduct two or three major offensives against an identified seventy German divisions, weak as they may have been, or as we suspected them of being, along a six-hundred-mile front stretching from the Swiss border to the North Sea, it was impossible not to hold some sectors thinly. The theory of the "calculated risk" has been thoroughly hashed over; it is certainly true that the Ardennes sector was rugged, had a generally poor road net, did seem to be remote from any strategic objectives. These were the very reasons that Eisenhower had thinned out this sector, and that was the reason the Germans attacked there.

Let us for a moment suppose that the Allied High Command had intercepted messages or orders definitely proving that the Germans were going to attack as they did. If Eisenhower had decided to meet this attack, it would have been necessary for him to divert troops being readied either to the north or south of the Ardennes to attack and shift them to meet this German threat. The Germans would have achieved one of their objectives without a fight, because they would have weakened our offensive strength in the crucial sectors either around Aachen or in the south. Of course, if we had obtained any inkling of the magnitude of the German attack, we would have been better able to plan our defense, to prepare to bite immediately into the German flanks, and possibly to trap a goodly portion of the German fighting force, with far fewer casualties to ourselves. Actually such a plan was proposed on November 30, whereby a vast pincers with 12th Army Group on the southern flank, driving northeast through the Ardennes to the Rhine,

---

* *My Three Years with Eisenhower*, p. 714.

and Montgomery's 21st Army Grou, driving south between the Meuse and the Rhine Rivers, would trap the known German concentration of twenty-one divisions between the Roer and the Rhine Rivers. This plan was abandoned because of the difficult terrain in the Eifel or northern Ardennes region and because the British were not yet ready to attack from the north.

Intertwined with the optimism and the strategic situation was the belief on the part of our commanders that the Germans would under no circumstances dissipate their forces on an attack in so difficult a terrain as that in the Ardennes. Several weeks before the German attack, Eisenhower and Bradley, at one of their periodic conferences in Bradley's headquarters, discussed the situation in the Ardennes. Both of them noted that there were no strategic objectives in the Ardennes sector, and they agreed that an attack in winter through this rugged territory would be very difficult. Furthermore, they noted with satisfaction our large concentrations both north and south of the Ardennes, and then agreed that even should the Germans attempt an attack, these large formations would rapidly be turned around to hit the German flank. But neither Eisenhower nor Bradley guessed the extent of the German power nor the fanaticism of the German leadership.)

WHAT WENT WRONG

Why, in the light of the considerable array of information available to us, did we not predict more accurately not only the time, but the nature of the German offensive? Numerous apologies, excuses, or rationalizations have been offered, suggested, or ordered to explain this situation. They seem to consolidate into five general categories: (1) our optimism; (2) the situation; (3) the cleverness of the German plan; (4) poor interpretation of intelligence; and (5) lack of aerial reconnaissance.

The first three reasons have been thoroughly discussed in previous sections. Just a brief glance at the last two:

Poor Evaluation of Collected Intelligence—Although they came in driblets rather than bucketfuls, isolated clues to the German intentions dripped through the Allied lines for nearly a month before the attack. Admittedly, some of the intelligence media were not producing at full strength. Combat patrolling by the divisions occupying Middleton's sector was at a minimum. The Golden Lions of the 106th Division had only closed into their positions four days before the German attack, and when they arrived, they were cold and wet and disheartened after a miserable truck ride from Normandy. The weather had been rainy all the time, and the division commander ordered his regimental commanders to get the men rehabilitated before doing anything else. The shelters were full of water, and many of the men already had trench foot because of their continuously wet feet from the ride, wet shelters, and lack of dry socks. Similarly in the other two infantry divisions, rehabilitation was taking place, and extensive patrolling was not undertaken despite corps orders to send out strong feelers behind the enemy lines. Then, too, the Germans began to react violently to American patrol activity, but this should have been an indication that something unusual was in the air. In addition, misfortune befell some of the line crossers sent into the German-held portion of the Eifel; five were sent through the lines in early December, and none of them returned.

Despite these rather awkward limitations in intelligence material gathered during the crucial period, the opinion of this author, backed by other serious students of the intelligence picture, is that intelligence officers were not fully alert. Several factors helped build this intelligence blind spot. First was the general overconfidence of the times, already discussed in detail. Second was the smugness of the intelligence officers, who are supposed to be pessimists by training, if not by nature. And third was a more fundamental weakness in our intelligence organization. The function of an intelligence officer is first to collect, then to evaluate, and finally to disseminate to other levels of command, information of the enemy. Through a process of over-specialization, intelligence officers seemed to operate in a vacuum, charged with describing enemy intentions without reference to our plans. Because our actions directly affect theirs, it is very difficult to say what the Germans may do if we do not first say what we intend to do, but this is exactly what our intelligence officers were doing. For example, to discuss German intentions in the Ardennes without analyzing the weakness of our positions there, our present and pending attacks elsewhere, is to overlook the true situation. An intelligence man who only considers the German potentialities without assessing our own aims and desires, soon is no longer an "intelligent" man. This we have learned the hard way. The more aggressive intelligence officers conquered this weakness; the others did not, and we suffered accordingly.

Lack of Aerial Reconnaissance—It is perfectly true that the weather in the weeks immediately preceding the German attack precluded much of the aerial reconnaissance, on which our intelligence officers relied so heavily. Between December 5 and 16, five reconnaissance missions were flown for VIII Corps, and all but one of these fought bad weather over the target. Either at the bases, or over the front itself, cloud formations prevented flying or photographing. Such tactical reconnaissance has always been a keystone of our intelligence, and the lack of it seriously hampered our efforts. Of the missions flown only one was a photographic mission, and it reported heavy rail activity at Trier, directly behind the German lines in the Ardennes, but this sampling was not sufficient to warrant any conclusions. The other missions were for observation, and weather prevented successful observation. The week before December 8 was also bad for flying, and there were similar negative results.

In the end, it seems we did poorly by the forgotten front in the rugged, foresty hills of the Ardennes. There can be no argument that we did not know of the attack plans. We did suspect some sort of attack, but not in the Ardennes and not in strength. We had numerous bits of information which might have been pieced together to outline the picture of the German attack—it seems easy now—but our frame of mind was such that the possibility just didn't seem to exist. We were derelict in our interpretation of the information gathered. We should have given more thought to the possibility of a German attack in the Ardennes.

Maybe we can blame it on Hitler, and say that the army would not have sprung the attack if they had been in control. But we had been fighting an irrational Hitler for three years ourselves, and we had been watching our friends fight him for two years before that. We had followed the pattern of conquest and surprise through Poland, France, Russia, to Stalingrad, Norway, the Balkans, Italy, and yet we had not learned that we were dealing with a desperate genius. It should not have been new to us, because we had been subjected to the mastermind's intuition before, first at Mortain when he attempted to rally his forces to bite off Patton's fast moving armored tentacles, and later by a series of three sudden, unexpected, and unheralded attacks at various points along our West Wall line. In each of these cases, he struck hard and cunningly from a surprise build-up of forces. So astonishing were these attacks, that they prompted the alert intelligence officer of XIX Corps to report these attacks in November and conclude, "The German's selection of the swamps west of the Meuse as a spot to employ two of his best mobile divisions (against the 7th Armored Division in southern Holland, where the Germans massed two divisions without our knowledge), alerts us to the fact that the enemy cannot be trusted always to attack according to the book. He remains a clever, aggressive foe." This officer then cautioned his readers to combat this by alert observation posts, listening posts, air observation, aggressive patrolling, and defensive preparation for a variety of eventualities. "Rapid and complete dissemination of each bit of information," he continued, "to the next higher echelon can frequently produce the picture of lurking dangers and avoid disaster . . ."

We failed to heed the message from this one intelligence officer, a lesson that was available to anyone who cared to examine the record. We were lured to sleep by the lilting music of Hitler's muses, as we had been before at Pearl Harbor, and once again we were saved, this time not only by our own resilience and ability to bound back from a shock, but also by the real weakness of the German arms. But we should have learned from these lessons. As it was, it might have been the spring of 1940 all over again.

CHAPTER IV

The Penetration

NOT A CREATURE WAS STIRRING

AMERICAN SOLDIERS BEDDED DOWN IN THE HILLY FORESTS OF the Ardennes on the night of December 15, peacefully oblivious that late into the night the German commanders labored over plans for the morrow. Although Dietrich begged unpreparedness, while one of his commanders complained that his route was for bicycles, not tanks, and Brandenberger cried for more bridging material, Hitler would brook no further delays: "It is now or never," he said. "Quick exploitation of the success of the first day of the attack is decisive," remarked Model. "The first objective is to achieve liberty of movement

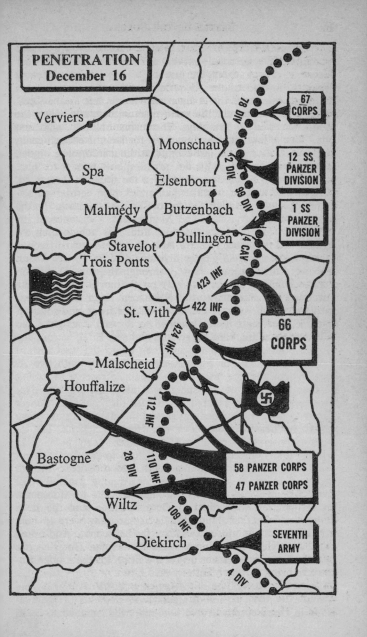

PENETRATION
December 16

Verviers

Monschau

Spa

Elsenborn

Malmédy

Butzenbach

Stavelot
Trois Ponts

Bullingen

St. Vith

Malscheid

Houffalize

Bastogne

Wiltz

Diekirch

67 CORPS

12 SS PANZER DIVISION

1 SS PANZER DIVISION

66 CORPS

58 PANZER CORPS
47 PANZER CORPS

SEVENTH ARMY

78 DIV

12 DIV

99 DIV

14 CAV

423 INF

422 INF

424 INF

112 INF

110 INF

28 DIV

109 INF

4 DIV

for the mobile forces." Last minute decisions were made: Luxembourg was ruled out as an objective for Branden-berger's *Seventh Army* because he had only four infantry divisions, instead of the six promised him. The attack from the north to cut off the Aachen salient was left in abeyance, to be launched should the main push successfully reach the Meuse River in the first days. The formations were split into three waves, separated by two days, for lack of enough roads and routes. And at the last minute, without informing Model, Hitler moved in two of his pet brigades, both named for him, which were to be used as reserves as the situation warranted.

As finally ordered, the German attack plan earmarked ele-ments of seventeen divisions for the first day's attack. To the north between Monschau and Manderfeld, a distance of fif-teen miles, four infantry divisions and a parachute division, all attached to Dietrich's *Sixth Panzer Army,* attacked to open a hole for the two *SS* panzer divisions of *1 SS Panzer Corps,* who were then to move rapidly through the gap. The *12 SS Panzer Division* (*Hitler Jugend*) on the north was to strike out over the absolutely vital Elsenborn ridge, situated im-mediately to the rear of Gerow's V Corps front, and south of this *1 SS Panzer Division* planned to thrust through the gap between the Elsenborn ridge and Schnee Eifel, across the Ambleve River at Stavelot, and then on to the west toward the Meuse River. For *2 SS Panzer Corps,* also with two *SS* panzer divisions, the task was to remain in reserve to exploit further the gains of the spearheads after the Meuse River crossings had been secured or to pass through *1 SS Panzer Corps* to maintain momentum should the attackers slow down or receive heavy counterblows from the north flank. The in-fantry divisions attached to *Sixth Panzer Army* planned to wheel rapidly through the hole and turn to the north to cut the three main roads running south into the break-through area and to establish a defensive line running generally east from a point south of Liége through Verviers to Monschau. In conjunction with the parachute battalion and the huge *Jadgtigers* with their impenetrable armor, they were to hold off any Allied attempts to reinforce the battle area. And riding with Dietrich's lead columns were the Trojan Horse troops of Otto Skorzeny's panzer brigade, waiting for the proper mo-ment to break for the Meuse River.

South of *Sixth Panzer Army,* the *Fifth Panzer Army* planned to make its initial attack with elements of six divi-sions in three corps. Unlike Dietrich, who planned to leash the tanks of his *Sixth Panzer Army* until he could charge through like the cavalry attacks of old, Manteuffel, wiser and sounder military tactician, grouped his forces so that his tanks would be in the fray for the first assaults. Manteuffel planned to light the way with the huge searchlights which had been so laboriously moved to the front, and unlike Dietrich, he scheduled only a light artillery preparation prior to the actual attack. Immediately to the south of *Sixth Panzer Army*, Manteuffel's *66 Corps*, led by General Lucht, was allotted two infantry divisions to envelop the Schnee Eifel and the two regiments of the green 106th Division, who were perched atop this small segment of the West Wall. These two German divisions planned to meet behind the Schnee Eifel, and then drive rapidly on and capture St. Vith, vital road and rail center in the northern portion of the Ardennes. The two attack corps—*58*, led by General Kruger, and *47*, led by the bombastic General von Luttwitz—with two divisions each in the initial attack wave, were to burst through the 28th Division on to the west and then isolate Bastogne with panzer thrusts, leaving capture of the town to infantry divisions while the panzers moved on to the Meuse.

The *Seventh Army*, with four divisions of two corps in the initial assault, was ordered to push back the 4th Division; then wheel rapidly to the south to establish a defensive line from Echternach west to Givet on the Meuse River. Its one mobile division, *5 Parachute,* was somehow expected to keep pace with the panzers and tie in with their southern flank as they reached the Meuse. The army would thereafter stem any attempts to reinforce the battle area from the south.

Although the High Command, headed by Keitel, had itself perfected many of the details, the initial objectives were left to the attacking divisions themselves. However, three objectives were stressed by Keitel and Jodl in their final orders: to the north, the vital Elsenborn Ridge; in the north-center, the Schnee Eifel; and to the south, the confluence of the Sauer and Our Rivers, a key hinge upon which they hoped to swing their southern pivot.

"Hold the reins loose, and let the armies race." Thus General Kraemer, Chief of Staff to Dietrich, later described the plan of attack to me. He further stated, "The main point was to reach the Meuse, irrespective of flanks; this was the same principle we employed in the French campaign of 1940. I never worry about my flank. As Clausewitz said, 'The point must form the fist.'" A mailed fist struck in the early morning hours of December 16, 1944, a haymaker which sent the world reeling.

THOSE FIRST TWO DAYS

Roaring cannons along an eighty-mile front served as the alarm clock for thousands of sleeping American troops that murky morning. It electrified men who felt safe in the assurance that theirs was a rest area. Commanders and their staffs tumbled out of bed to eye with wonder the flashes of the distant artillery and listen, amazed, to reports from their outposts. They didn't wait long: shortly after six o'clock, the first reports were hastily relayed back to the command posts that through the early morning dark could be seen German infantry, moving forward slowly. Behind them snorted the tanks, ready to roar through the gaps cleared by the infantry. In at least one instance, the infantry were driving a herd of cattle before them to detonate any mines which might have been planted in the earth by defending troops.

"I told the *Fuehrer* on the first day of the attack that the surprise had been completely achieved," a still smug Jodl announced after the war. "The best indication was that no reinforcements were made in your sector before the attack." So complete was the surprise that not until the next morning did even Middleton, VIII Corps commander, realize the extent of the attacks. "Just a local diversion," one intelligence officer remarked that first day. The Germans had played their cards well, had further confused their intentions by organizing on the spur of the moment a two-battalion attack on the vulnerable north flank of the Ninth Army. You ask, how could we mistake an attack of seventeen divisions, representing probably a total of 200,000 men, for anything but a major attack? One must always remember that at any given time no more than a handful of the total troops of any unit are actually fighting. In the confused situation in the sparsely held Middleton line, where communications rapidly broke down, it was not easy to grasp immediately that this was the great German attack of the Western front. Small groups of Germans, perhaps thirty to forty, were moving forward, feeling their way through the weak points, eliminating the few strong-points we had manned in the Ardennes forests.

On the far north of the German attack line, the infantrymen of the five attacking divisions ran into the stiffest opposition of the day. They collided head-on with General Gerow's V Corps, which was reaching for the Roer River dams, key to the next great Allied push. Through the rain and fog the German infantrymen drove, only to be met by the stubborn resistance of infantrymen from the 2d and the 99th Divisions. Initially surprised at the strength of the resistance, the Germans recoiled and searched out weak points in the divisions' line. The Germans were cognizant of our attack towards the Roer River dams, but they banked on meeting only the 99th Division and expected the 2d Division to be further to the rear in reserve. Because of the peculiar nature of the American attack front, with the 2d Division attacking along a corridor running through the 99th Division's lines, the German attack rapidly disrupted the two American divisions, which became inextricably intermingled, but managed to hold their own. Enraged at the failure of his infantrymen to break through this combined defense, Dietrich ordered his northern panzer division, *12 SS*, to attack at midmorning instead of noon as originally intended. But it, too, was held up by a stubborn defense and a dynamited bridge, a vital one which took hours to repair. The roads were so muddy that travel was difficult and the fields too soggy to risk tank movement. The *12 SS Panzer Division* with its infantry help nearly succeeded in battering its way onto the Elsenborn Ridge, but the badly shaken defenders of 2d and 99th Divisions held, not only on the first day of the attack, but the second as well. With the 99th Division badly disorganized, in this its first major engagement, General Gerow placed the intermingled forces under General Robertson, commander of the veteran 2d Division, and turned over the protection of the vital Elsenborn Ridge to him. Gerow requested permission on the afternoon of December 16 to discontinue his attack toward the Roer River dams, this attack having been in progress all during the day, theeoretically at least. But First Army's Commander, General Hodges, still unaware of the critical nature of the German attack, refused him permission to withdraw to the protection of the heights of Elsenborn Ridge. Next day, however, the situation had sufficiently cleared, and Hodges gave Gerow a free hand to act as he saw fit. Early on December 19 these badly depleted divisions drew back several thousand yards to the heights of Elsenborn, where they withstood all German onslaughts during the remainder of the offensive. A solid anchor had thus been welded on which a new First Army line would be built in the days to come.

Just to the south of the 2–99 Division section, in the gap between Elsenborn and the Schnee Eifel, lay the 14th Cavalry Group, which was attached to the 106th Division. The cavalry group, ordinarily a reconnaissance rather than a defensive force, garrisoned a series of six small hamlets along the boundary of Gerow's V Corps and Middleton's VIII Corps. It was here that Dietrich concentrated the southern half of his striking force, consisting of two infantry divisions and the élite *Liebstandarte*—the *1 SS Panzer Division*. Again the infantry led the way. Slightly before noon the panzers of *1 SS Panzer Division* were turned loose on the cavalry group which vainly tried to stem the fanatics as they advanced. Rapidly overwhelmed, the group commander withdrew his troops without orders from the 106th Division, for which he was subsequently relieved, and *Kampfgruppe Peiper,* lead command of the *Liebstandarte Adolph Hitler,* passed through this gap. Many men of the cavalry group successfully kept ahead of the charging panzers. They were eventually stopped by new divisions rushing into the breach, and then the group was reorganized for a further fight. Peiper rapidly moved west toward Stavelot, Trois Ponts, Werbomont, and Huy, first major objective on the Meuse River. With him went a large portion of Skorzeny's *150 Panzer Brigade,* the Trojan Horse which was to sprint through the confused Allied defenses on the night of December 17, to seize and hold Meuse River bridges pending the arrival of Peiper and his companion *Kampfgruppe* from *12 SS Panzer Division* to the north.

During the late afternoon and evening, units of the *1 SS Panzer Division* continued to pour through the gap left by the 14th Cavalry Group. Fearful for his flank, General Robertson of the 2d Division, ordered the southern flank of the 99th Division to fall back and face south to prevent, if possible, the panzers from turning north behind the forward troops and thus gaining Elsenborn Ridge for the Germans. Actually, the strength of the American forces facing south was so small, and the men so shaken, that the Germans could have broken through to the north almost at will, thus isolating the two divisions holding on by the skin of their teeth. In Butgenbach, the key town on this route to Elsenborn ridge from the south, only a handful of men with several guns stood between the Ridge and the Germans. But the Germans, always mindful of their orders to reach the Meuse River as rapidly as possible, were not interested in isolating a mere two divisions. So *Kampfgruppe Peiper* of *1 SS Panzer Division* continued on west, and Elsenborn Ridge was saved by default from a flanking thrust.

Peiper also had his eyes on another goal to the west; he knew there was gasoline in the small town of Bullingen, dead ahead of him, and he wanted that gas badly. Already he suspected that his supply facilities would not be able to keep up with his lightning swift advance.

While the Germans pounded at the defenders of the Elsenborn Ridge from the east and *1 SS Panzer Division* continued almost unmolested toward the west through the gap it had found, additional steps were taken on December 17 to protect the southern approaches to the Ridge. Seaching for infantry reserves to plug this vital gap, Hodges of the First Army turned again to the wheelhorse of the army, the 1st Division, veteran of nearly every campaign from Africa through Sicily to Italy, and then D-Day in Normandy. The Big Red One, insignia of the division, was only too well known to the Germans who had come to respect the fighting ability of this Division. The 1st Division had been in a rest area following heavy fighting in the November offensive, and its men were scattered as far distant as Paris. A hasty call summoned all men to return by early morning, December 17, and by that night the first regiment of the division was attached to Gerow's V Corps and speeding on its way to bolster the new southern flank of the 2–99 Division protecting that approach to Elsenborn Ridge. By late night, the first regiment was in contact with the Germans, who sent only light patrols toward their north flank for sounding out purposes, rather than attack.

Too late the Germans realized they could not crack the 2–99 Division line by a frontal assault from the east. First, they tried to slip *12 SS Panzer Division* around to the south behind *1 SS Panzer Division* to turn north, as they could have done late on December 16. But the roads were poor, and when the division attempted to strike cross country, most of the tanks mired in the mud, some of them up to their turrets. Then part of the High Command reserve was thrown against this new American southern flank protecting the Ridge, but again the Germans were too late. The Germans experienced their first great setback. Dietrich blamed it on bad roads; Rundstedt said it was caused by superfluous heaping up of strong attack units in difficult terrain and the tactical incompetence of butcher boy Dietrich.

While all this transpired to the north, the Germans were meeting with better luck further south. The second great objective from north to south was the Schnee Eifel, captured portion of the West Wall, on which sat two of the green regiments of the 106th Division. In a vast pincers movement, infantry and supporting tanks of the German *66 Corps* rapidly closed around the ridge mass and by early morning of December 17 had snapped the pincers on the town of Schonberg at the western base of the Schnee Eifel, shoving the southern regiment of the 106th Division, at the base of the ridge, to the south as they brushed by. Both Middleton, the corps commander, and General Jones, the division commander, divined the threat of this German attack. Middleton promptly regained control of the northern combat command of the 9th Armored Division, which had been in reverse in V Corps to the north, and ordered it to St. Vith, 106th Division headquarters, to meet this threat. He further recommended to Jones that he withdraw his exposed troops from the Schnee Eifel before they were cut off. And then late in the evening of December 16, Middleton obtained the release of the 7th Armored Division from Ninth Army reserve for immediate movement to St. Vith to assist Jones in his already grave situation. When Jones was informed by Middleton that the 7th Armored Division was on its way and scheduled to arrive by early morning of December 17, he immediately shifted CCB of the 9th Armored Division south to assist the southern regiment, the 424th Infantry, in restoring the southern flank of the 106th Division sector. CCB attacked and was making progress on December 17, when suddenly orders came to cease the attack and withdraw just west of the Our River, which it had crossed, pending stabilization of the situation on the Schnee Eifel. The 424th Infantry had already begun a rather disorganized withdrawal after being buffeted on both sides by onrushing Germans.

Meanwhile, further to the north in the 106th Division sector, all was not well. Middleton, not yet realizing the gravity of the situation, expected the 7th Armored Division to make a rapid sixty mile night road march from its Ninth Army assembly area to arrive in St. Vith in ample time to launch an attack on the morning of December 17. Actually, the division, its route lit by German reconnaissance planes dropping flares, made a hectic journey south into the unknown, where its staff was told, "an attack of three or four German divisions is underway." Moving on two routes, the division was exasperatingly delayed by many retreating units, and actually CCR on the most eastern route, came within a half hour of colliding with the spearhead of "Sepp" Dietrich's *1 SS Panzer Division* bursting toward Malmedy. Only luck or fate let CCR through Malmedy, and caught Battery B of the 285th Field Artillery

Observation Battalion, which had wormed its way between the march columns of the 7th Armored Division; this latter group was trapped and then liquidated by order of an ardent *SS* Lieutenant leading a tank column in the infamous "Malmedy massacre," which aroused the entire Allied world. The 7th Armored Division artillery columns, following CCR, were forced to backtrack and join the remainder of the division on a road further to the west. As a result, the artillery was not in firing position until December 18. Whereas Middleton had estimated that the first combat command of the 7th Armored would arrive at seven-thirty in the morning of December 17, advance reconnaissance elements did not get to St. Vith until about three in the afternoon. It was too late; the Schnee Eifel was already cut off, and advance elements of the German *66 Corps* were advancing on St. Vith itself. St. Vith was a scene of wildest confusion, befuddled by conflicting rumors, aided by few concrete facts about the enemy's intentions or whereabouts. The Germans had completely achieved their first objective—isolation of the Schnee Eifel.

In the center of VIII Corps, the Germans were equally successful in those first two hectic days. Immediately south of the Schnee Eifel, one panzer corps, the *58th,* steam-rollered through the southern portion of the 424th Infantry, which had also been squeezed on the north by the pincers around the Schnee Eifel. The 424th Infantry pulled back in disorder toward the Our River in the vicinity of Winterspelt, just south of CCB of the 9th Armored Division which had been attacking in this region until recalled by Jones, 106th Division Commander. Simultaneously, the main effort of *47 Corps,* with an infantry and two panzer divisions, was directed at the eleven-mile front of the 110th Infantry in the center of the 28th Division sector. Hit on the first day by the *2 Panzer Division* and the *26 Volks-grenadier Division,* the regiment reeled back, only to be hit again on the next, by a second panzer division, the *Panzer Lehr.* This aggregation of armor and infantry bridged the Our River, cut the ridge road along which I had so peacefully ridden several months before, completely overwhelmed the regiment, and rapidly moved toward the beautiful town of Clerf, the rest center eight miles west. A second combat command of the 9th Armored Division, behind the 28th Division, was alerted on December 16 by Middleton. It shipped tank destroyers and then a few tanks to the front; but they, too, were overwhelmed, and the rest of the command began to pull back to the west, confused by the turn of events. Just north of the ill-fated 110th Infantry, its sister regiment, the 112th Infantry, fought in a pocket around which the Germans flowed. It was cut off from the division by the fierce attack through the 110th Infantry and was finally withdrawn by Middleton, the corps commander, in the absence of any orders from its divisional commander. This splintered regiment eventually found its way northwest and crossed the Our River on the night of December 17 to join with the defenders of St. Vith far to the north of its starting point.

In the south, the German *Seventh Army* hit the southern regiment of the 28th Division, the third command of the 9th Armored Division, which occupied a small sector south of the 28th Division, and the 4th Division. With no armor, and lacking adequate bridging equipment, Brandenberger's *Seventh Army* was less aggressive than its northern mates, and these three American units were able to slip to the south across the Sauer River, where they successfully formed a southern hinge on which a new line, facing north, was eventually formed, bit by bit. Heavy fighting took place along this front, but the combination of the rugged terrain and the smaller striking force of *Seventh Army* saved the situation for these southern forces despite a bitter nip and tuck fight. Here, too, help was forthcoming on December 17 when a major portion of the 10th Armored Division was rushed north from the Third Army and put in to bolster the 4th Division and supporting troops.

Surprise, complete and devastating, had indeed been achieved. Caught unawares, overwhelmed by the weight of the German attack, uncertain about German intentions and objectives, front line divisions could only give out a welter of confused reports. So suddenly did the tide turn that the returning flow of information from corps, giving the bigger picture, was vague and uncertain. During these first critical hours, each division or group shifted for itself, finding salvation as best it could.

Thus, by the evening of December 17 the Germans had knocked two distinct gaps in the American lines, both in the VIII Corps zone. The northern gap, roughly in the nine-mile sector of the 14th Cavalry Group, was between the forming southern flank of the 2–99 Division and the Schnee Eifel on which the two cut-off regiments of the 106th Division still held. Through this hole the *1 SS Panzer Division* was pouring its armor, its leading formations already riding far to the west. The southern gap, ten to twelve miles in width, had been forced through the 28th Division sector, and pouring through it were the troops of both *58* and *47 Corps* with a combined total of three armored and two infantry divisions. *58 Corps* on the north was heading generally for the second "Ridge Road," running from Bastogne to Houffalize, the first objective, from where it was to hinge along the east bank of the Ourthe River. *47 Corps* on the south was directed toward Wiltz and then Bastogne, which the Germans hoped to catch in a quick surprise thrust, and then to the Meuse River at Namur. Manteuffel's third corps, *66,* had swept around both sides of the Schnee Eifel and was heading for St. Vith with two infantry divisions, whose final objective in the first phase of the attack was St. Vith. Only in the extreme north, where the infantry and panzers were stalled in front of the Elsenborn Ridge, and the south, where Brandenberger's *Seventh Army* was more slowly plodding southward, had the Germans failed to break completely into the open. No wonder that despite these two setbacks, the initial reports to Hitler at Zeigenberg, where he awaited word of his destiny, were optimistic. No wonder that smiles again wreathed the faces of German civilians. Once again Germany's invincible armies were on the march. No wonder that veteran French liaison officers with American divisions were wringing their hands in trepidation; to them it was once again 1940, and they remembered only too well the denouement of the break-through at Sedan four years before.

WHAT'S GOING ON HERE?

Our forces reacted slowly, and only slowly did the news of the forceful German attacks trickle up the chain of command to Paris. Hitler, confident that Eisenhower was only a puppet in the hands of the "democratic demagogues," Roosevelt and Churchill, was basing his high hopes for quickly reaching the Meuse River on the theory that before Eisenhower could abandon his planned offensives, he would first have to assess the true German intentions, and then speak to his masters. While Eisenhower was making such duty consultation, Hitler further prognosticated, the Germans would roll through the hills and forests of the Ardennes, cross the Meuse River, and be well on their way toward Brussels and Antwerp.

But Hitler was wrong. General Bradley was closeted with Eisenhower when first word of the German attack came through, discussing the serious replacement problem facing his armies. Although claims have been made that Eisenhower

instantly gauged the seriousness of the situation, the truth is
that none of the Allied commanders, from Eisenhower down,
realized the true extent of the German attack on that first day.
Eisenhower *did* suggest to Bradley that he send an armored
division to each side of the apparent attack area. So the 7th
and 10th Armored Divisions, from Ninth and Third Armies
respectively, were ordered to move during the night of December 16-17 into the Ardennes. Always aware of bombastic
Patton, Eisenhower told Bradley that if "Blood and Guts"
objected to losing a division, Bradley was to inform him that:
"Ike said he is running this damned war." But not until the
17th, when the German paratroopers were discovered, and
the Skorzeny "Greifer" told all, did even Middleton, the corps
commander, realize the extent of the German plan. Ample
evidence of this is offered by Hodges' insistence that Gerow's
V Corps continue its attack toward the Roer River dam on
December 16.

"Fold with the attack," Major General Kean, Hodges' Chief
of Staff, told Middleton early in the attack. Middleton wasn't
just sure what that meant, but did what he could to stop the
penetrations. Both General Bradley and General Hodges
agreed that the attitude of all forces should be strongly offensive, that the armies should check the enemy with local counterattacks and then hit him from both sides with a co-ordinated
attack on the flanks. This was in the first days of the attack,
before its full force had been felt. General Patton went even
further and said, "Fine, we should open up, and let them get
all the way to Paris. Then we'll bite off the rear of their
attack." But more sober heads ruled at SHAEF (Supreme
Headquarters Allied Expeditionary Force).

By the morning of December 17, the local commanders were
finally aware that the Germans were planning something quite
out of the ordinary. It had already become painfully apparent that the Germans had an excellent opportunity to break out
in the clear if American troops were not bolstered. Strangely
enough, Supreme Headquarters had no reserve of its own.
Ordinarily, every echelon of a fighting organization, from the
platoon on up, has a reserve which can be used as a counterattacking force to be thrown in at a critical moment to break
the back of enemy resistance in just such a situation. However,
because of demands from various armies, always hungry for
more divisions, SHAEF had never been able to build up its
own reserve properly. After the Battle of the Bulge, SHAEF,
you can be sure, was never again without a reserve.

In a look for immediate help on the morning of December 17, the SHAEF staff found only two divisions available. These were the 82d and 102d Airborne Divisions, recuperating and re-equipping in training camps near Rheims, France, from their recent heavy fighting in the Arnhem drop. The two divisions were part of the First Allied Airborne Army and were being readied for a new mission—a drop on the east bank of the Rhine River. They, together with the 17th Airborne Division, still in training in England, formed the XVIII Airborne Corps, a new unit under command of General Ridgway. Late on December 17, the rest period for the two divisions was abruptly ended when they and the Corps were instructed to proceed with all possible haste to the town of Bastogne, Belgium. Bastogne had been selected because of its excellent road net. Moreover, its central location made it an ideal assembly point from which the divisions could move out as the situation required. At that time, nobody was thinking about defending Bastogne itself; it was simply a meeting point.

All during the nights of December 17-18, the paratroopers hastily reassembled their forces. Hurried trips were made to collect men and weapons scattered about during the training period. Many of the men were not completely equipped; many of their weapons were still being repaired. The staff of XVIII Airborne Corps was in England on a "dry-run" maneuver, and the commander of the 101st Airborne Division was in the States, but by morning of December 18 the 82d Airborne Division, packed into huge ten-ton truck trailers, began the chilling journey to Bastogne. It was followed in late afternoon by the 101st Airborne Division. By early morning of December 18, General Gavin, commander of the 82d Airborne Division, arrived at First Army headquarters to get his orders from Hodges. The perilous situation on the northern flank of the German break-through was to change the original mission of XVIII Airborne Corps. But for SHAEF, the first big step had been taken; it remained for the field armies to plot the use of the new reserves.

All through the 18th, scattered reports of new German advances poured into Supreme Headquarters at Versailles. As the day advanced, the Germans seemed to be making rapid strides forward, as well as one could surmise from spotty reports. By late afternoon, Eisenhower had made his decision, the one Hitler thought was not his to make. Patton's big attack to blast the West Wall, scheduled for the next day, was cancelled, despite "Blood and Guts' " plea to let him go ahead and "see who can get the farthest." Dever's 6th Army Group was to stretch its forces thin, abandon its offensives, and take over Patton's sector north along the Moselle River, giving up the three bridgeheads across the Saar River. Then Patton was to assemble a force of six divisions to strike the southern flank of the German's penetration by December 22; one of Patton's Corps was to remain in position along the Moselle with the 6th Army Group. Using both Patton and Hodges, General Bradley was to check the enemy advances and secure the line of communication from Namur to Liége to Aachen. Then he would relieve the 21st Army Group west of the Meuse River. There Montgomery was immediately to place protective forces. Finally, after the German attacks had been stopped, Bradley was to prepare a counterattack in the direction of Bonn-Cologne and meet with Montgomery's 21st Army Group which would at the same time launch an attack from the north along the Rhine River plain to meet with Bradley's attack coming from the west. In other words, we were simply to continue our original strategy.

Because of unbelievably poor communication with the field armies, there was only a slow flow of information trickling back to SHAEF at Versailles where the big plans were being shaped. However, throughout December 18-19 news began to come through indicating the true German strength, and the power with which the Germans were moving. With it was waged a German war of nerves. There is no doubt it affected the highest planners; everyone was worried. And so, on December 19 at the meeting, a revised plan was adopted: Patton's III Corps was to attack northeast from the area of Arlon —Patton issued ambitious orders to attack directly toward St. Vith, which he hoped to reach in several days (St. Vith was finally liberated on January 23). At the same time Patton's XII Corps would concentrate in the vicinity of Luxembourg to attack northwest in the direction of Bonn on Army order, but no date was set for this attack. Middleton's shattered VIII Corps, with the 101st Airborne Division and the 5th Division now added, was to continue to contain the western German penetration and go over to the offensive on Army order. The XVIII Airborne Corps was already moving to close the northern portion of the German penetration, and this fitted into the new plan. A new Corps, XVI, with two brand new divisions, would assemble in the area of Liége as an army group reserve.

Even this revised plan, which evolved from the first big

strategy meeting at Verdun on the morning of December 19 was unrealistic and failed to measure the power of the German offensive adequately. The VIII Corps, badly damaged, was nearly useless except for the 101st Airborne Division, which was just arriving in Bastogne. Gerow's V Corps was given a sector which was split through the middle by the northern German penetration of *1 SS Panzer Division*. The new XVIII Airborne Corps, just assembling in the Ardennes forests, was to seal off the German penetration with a parachute, an infantry, and an armored division. This corps was soon engaged with parts of four German corps. The inescapable conclusion can only be that the initial SHAEF plan was based on faulty information from subordinate units. Mute testimony to this is the letter of instruction from Hodges to his Corps on this same day: "The enemy continues his efforts to penetrate our lines in the southern portion of the V Corps zone and the northern and central portions of the VIII Corps zone. *Isolated parties have made deep penetrations, but the enemy have not penetrated our lines in force*" (italics mine). Said Hodges in a burst of optimism: "Our position is not critical. Reinforcements are constantly arriving. Our position improves each day."

LET NO MAN SPLIT ASUNDER

The optimism which sparked every section of the Supreme Allied headquarters at Versailles began to flag December 19 as the trickle of information from the tangled, confused battlefront swelled to a roaring stream. When Eisenhower returned from the morning meeting at Verdun with his commanders, this torrent of new facts burst upon him. What "Ike" heard, gave him cause for great alarm. Supreme Headquarters learned the true extent of the German penetrations, both along the V and VIII Corps boundary where *1 SS Panzer Division* was steadily bouncing forward, and farther to the south in the center of VIII Corps where Manteuffel's three corps were striking hard and fast for St. Vith, Houffalize, and Bastogne. News of the threat to Spa, the subsequent evacuation of this town by First Army headquarters, the loss of Wiltz, the German capture of Houffalize on the main north-south road from Arlon to Liége was relayed to the Supreme Commander. Only then did Eisenhower appreciate the magnitude and audacity of the German plan. Here was something far more serious than anything he had reckoned with. The die was cast. For to

Eisenhower, always fearful that Germany would crack the secret of the atom and turn it loose on his armies with a vengeance then unknown to man, speed was of utmost importance. The atomic bomb could cancel out his months of careful planning and fighting—*Der Tag* had arrived.

Four critical areas, to be held at all cost, had been outlined by the Supreme Commander's staff: the port of Antwerp through which supplies must flow during the winter months when the beaches in Normandy are wind-swept and storm-ridden; the British advance bases at Antwerp and Brussels; the city of Liége, signal, road, and rail center, stocked high with supplies; and the line of communications from Antwerp to Louvain to Liége. Without these, forces in the low countries could not be maintained. Access to Liége, the planners said, was essential to support forces in the Aachen salient. The rough sketch of the German plan had been pieced together by careful study of various captured orders and reports from interrogations of prisoners. Antwerp was definitely the final objective; the general trend of the German attack was to the northwest, and it appeared to the allied commanders that Liége was an intermediate target.* Every one of the four critical areas was in the line of this German attack: all of them were north of the area through which the Germans were driving their wedge. All this is background for Eisenhower's next move.

Back from Verdun, Eisenhower made a new decision— without consulting his staff. Only afterwards did he notify Bradley, Montgomery, Marshall, and Churchill. Aware that the brunt of the attack would be felt in the north where not only Hodges, but eventually Simpson and Montgomery, would be directly menaced, Eisenhower split the battlefield through the middle of the break-through area with a line running from Givet on the Meuse River east to Prum, in the West Wall. All forces north of the lines went to Montgomery's 21st Army Group, while the southern forces, including most of VIII Corps' remaining troops, were left with Bradley. This was no reflection on Bradley. To make that indisputably clear, Eisenhower urged Marshall to promote Bradley immediately; he denied that Bradley was to blame for the German break-through. The shift in command should not reflect on Bradley's

* Even after the war in his *"Story of the War"* Eisenhower erroneously assumes that Liége was a primary goal of the Germans. It was a logical assumption, and only after interviewing scores of German planners and fighters and analyzing their r are we able to say that Liége was specifically excluded from the German

excellent work, Eisenhower declared, and must be explained as such to the American public. He added that everyone had failed to predict the attack, and placed the chief blame on lack of aerial reconnaissance because of bad weather.

Startling though the decision was, and much as it shocked Bradley's staff, it was based on sound premises. Two factors motivated Eisenhower's decision: first, for both psychological and strategic reasons, it was imperative that Bradley maintain his headquarters in Luxembourg City. To move an entire Army Group headquarters at that time would not only have upset its work, but further shake morale in that area. Secondly, and even more important, in the entire northern area which was threatened by the German attack, there was only one corps in reserve, and this was the British XXX Corps, which was near Brussels on its way to join the next British attack to the east.

Each of these reasons unfolds into other subsidiary considerations. Related to the decision that Bradley should remain in Luxembourg City—on this there was unanimous agreement—was the problem of communication between Bradley at the southeastern end of the German bulge, and Hodges on the northern side of the enemy penetration. The vital communications network between Bradley and Hodges was threatened by the German penetration. The three principal means of communication were a buried cable, an open-wire circuit, and a radio-link system.

The buried cable was cut on December 23; the open circuit, on December 25; the radio link, on December 23. Only sporadically could the repeater station at Jemelle hear the noise of its operation because of the noise of battle, and even this channel was cut off altogether on December 26.

Once the momentous decision had been made to split the battlefield, the operation of the battle was conducted mainly at the two army group headquarters, Bradley's and Montgomery's. SHAEF immediately took a new armored division just arrived on the continent, the 11th Armored, and assembled it near Rheims for use in the center of the break-through area if needed. Also hurriedly assembled and flown to France from England, was the 17th Airborne Division, third of the three divisions in XVIII Airborne Corps. Additional infantry divisions were rushed from England ahead of schedule to provide a much needed reserve. Later, these divisions were to enter into the bitter slugging match which was to liquidate the German penetration. But for the time being the crucial action

centered on the fighting line, and there we may assess more
thoroughly the wisdom of Eisenhower's decision. But first
one vital, however intangible, factor in the fighting must be
considered—the psychology of the battlefield.

THE WAR OF NERVES

Before reviewing the crucial eight days which turned the
tide in the Battle of the Bulge, it is necessary to diverge
slightly to consider the most effective weapon in Hitler's great
attack—psychological warfare. You must understand the
frame of mind which temporarily gripped large segments of
the Allied command and troops to comprehend the events
which followed the first crash of shells early on the morning
of December 16.

In analyzing the phenomenal spread of despair in the Allied
armies and in assessing the success of the German war of
nerves, one must emphasize the motif of pessimism which
pervaded the Allied forces.

I doubt that Hitler in his wildest dreams foresaw the success which attended "Operation Confusion," as I label the
unorthodox German units which operated with the ground
troops in the big attack. Really to understand the phenomenal
success of this operation, you would have to see the terror
and doubt which races like wildfire through all the ranks in the
midst of a great enemy attack. The German attack had
shocked the complacency of the "Pearl Harbor" mind, typical
of the thinking of most Allied soldiers in the days following
the break-through and chase across France. When communications break down, when units appear to be swallowed up,
and men go down roads never to return, one can run the
gamut from extreme optimism to supreme pessimism in a
matter of minutes. Suddenly, Germans are seen at every corner
and in every bush. To all this panic, doubt, and uncertainty,
the Germans, quite purposefully and skillfully, added their
inimitable touch.

Topmost in the German bag of tricks was the now famous
Operation "Greif," which, with sad wisdom, we later called
"grief." Led by swashbuckling Otto Skorzeny, scourge of the
counterintelligence corps, foremost espionage agent on the
Western Front, Operation "Greif," you will recall, envisaged
two separate missions: first, seizure of the Meuse River
bridges by the Trojan Horse 150 Panzer Brigade, completely
outfitted with American and British tanks, guns, and equip-

ment; secondly, creation of confusion behind the lines by small *Kommando* groups, four men in a jeep, who would not only spot and report on vital installations, but would disrupt communications, change road signs, rearrange signs covering minefields, misdirect traffic, and generally upset an already groggy enemy. Skorzeny's men had been carefully chosen and almost as carefully trained. Each jeepload of the *Kommandos* had one man who spoke excellent English; the other three spoke it with varying degrees of skill.

When the attack opened up, Skorzeny's men began to filter through the lines. All told, he had one hundred fifty *Kommandos* scattered among the attack divisions of Dietrich's *Sixth Panzer Army*, from where they were to fan out at the proper moment. Because of the failure of some of Dietrich's units to break into the open, many of these men were unable to blaze their way to glory. When the German attack began to show signs of failing to meet optimistic hopes, as early as the third day, Skorzeny, already aware that some of his men had been captured, forbade the remaining groups to pass through the lines.

Altogether, forty-four of the *Kommandos* made their way into Allied territory. All but eight of these returned. Nor were their efforts unavailing. One jeepload drove through the important center of Malmedy, about which we will hear much later, on December 17, to discover with amazement that the town was practically deserted. A second jeep group reported on American troop movements south of Liége. A third group canvassed rear areas for airports. A fourth group located munitions dumps at Liége and Huy, both towns on the Meuse River. A fifth spotted a large gasoline dump and reported this to Dietrich's panzers. A sixth group ingeniously stationed one member at a road junction to act as an MP; he directed an entire American regiment down the wrong road as it was hurrying south to fight this huge German attack. At least two jeeploads were caught, one by the British as it attempted to cross the Meuse River, and a second, on the first day of the attack by First Army MP's near Liége.* It was this latter group which did us both a service and a disservice by revealing the mission of its men. One scared officer prisoner disclosed much of the truth about the mission. He also passed on some rumors which had been circulating among Skorzeny's men before the attack began. Among them, you can chalk up

---

* Other Germans, dressed in American uniforms, were later caught and shot. But they were part of the "orthodox" *150 Panzer Brigade*.

the famous rumor about the attempt on Eisenhower's life. Although Counterintelligence Corps men (such as John Schwartzwalder in his book, *We Caught Spies*) opine that Skorzeny really did intend to get Eisenhower, *they have only the statements of this one German prisoner to support this thesis.* In a previous section, I traced the origin of this story. After several sessions with Skorzeny and by piecing together his movements, I am thoroughly convinced that no such plot existed. We know from prisoner reports that during the entire offensive Skorzeny was behind German lines. Not only high commanders spoke with him, but soldiers of lower rank actually saw him at various points. Skorzeny himself directed the tactical operations of his *150 Panzer Brigade* when in its normal infantry role it attacked the town of Malmedy.

The second German scare-weapon was the paratroop mission which was dropped along the northern flank of the penetration to cut the roads leading south into the bulge. Originally scheduled for the early hours of December 16, the drop was postponed one night because of bad weather. But about midnight on December 16, about sixty Junkers transport planes roared over the battle lines, and 800 of Rockefeller scholar von der Heydte's men were dropped. The wind was so brisk and the drop so bad, only 300 of the men successfully found their way to the rendezvous point at the junction of two roads leading into Malmedy. Many of the other 500 men were hurriedly rounded up by units of both First and Ninth Armies. But again the war of nerves was a howling success. The shock of the sudden German attack, when coupled with word of the Skorzeny mission and the parachute jump, spread panic through the ranks. Almost immediately, one entire combat command of the 3d Armored Division was placed north of the jump area to guard against any possible attacks, and it remained there for nearly a week while the sister commands of the division were desperately attempting to stem the orthodox German advances.

Von der Heydte immediately judged his assembled men too weak to block the road successfully, and when the promised relief failed to arrive by December 18, he gave up hope of accomplishing his mission. He did, however, send scouting parties far and wide, which reconnoitered as far away as Stavelot, Malmedy, Verviers, and Werbomont, where one of his patrols witnessed the arrival of the 82d Airborne Division, about which we shall hear more later. But von der Heydte's radio had been smashed in the drop, and he had no communication with headquarters. (In vain he had pleaded with Dietrich for carrier pigeons, which he had observed the American paratroopers using in Normandy, but Dietrich scornfully asked him, "if he thought he was running a menagerie.") Von der Heydte sat along the roadside, while three American divisions rolled through his positions; first the 7th Armored, then the 1st, and finally the 30th. He was helpless to interfere. Finally, weary of the wait, he decided to contact the German forces who were supposed to be in Monschau on the first day. Von der Heydte walked into the town, only to find American troops still there in force. His career was suddenly ended.

Despite total failure of the parachute jump, its psychological effect was great. Not only did it tie up part of the 3d Armored Division, but all up and down the Front it further addled the nerves of already jittery staffs, who began to see paratroopers everywhere stalking through the countryside. When one leafs through the many official reports of units engaged in the fighting, he finds literally hundreds of messages reporting German paratroopers sighted en route to terra firma. These reports naturally increased the uneasiness. The Germans, doubtless well aware of the confusion their jumps had wrought, cleverly fostered this fear by dropping dummies on a number of occasions. But after the initial drop, we now know, no further parachutists were dropped into the battle zone. Yet reports still were made of other parachute drops. For example, Walter Millis in his recent book, *The Last Phase*, told how Patton fought his way north through the parachutists to reach the Ardennes. And General Eisenhower himself said in his own *Story of the War* ". . . parties of paratroops were dropped throughout the battle area . . . while small paratroop units and agents who had remained behind during our advance were active in attempting to sabotage key bridges and headquarters as far to the rear as Paris" (page 76).

Still another aspect of the Germans' thorough plans was the amazing scheme, somehow transmitted to Britain, for a break by all German prisoners of war. By all odds, the most Wellsian phase of the German war of nerves, it has still not been completely explained. We do know that German prisoners began organizing for a mass break; that they plotted to seize arsenals, obtain tanks, and actually prepare the way for German landings in England. The original date set for this break was December 16. All this we learned from agents among the German prisoners. Was it pure coincidence that the break plans coincided with those for the attack? I don't know. In any event, the break, as you already knew, did not come off.

Word of these German measures spread like wildfire through the Allied ranks. Hastily counter-measures were adopted; road blocks sprung up at every junction; guards were stationed on every bridge for miles north and south of the threatened area. At all of these blocks, American soldiers stopped all comers, regardless of rank, and questioned them on typically American customs, such as names of presidents, nicknames of ball teams, popular songs, football scores; and woe to the man who was not up on his folklore. Many of the humorous incidents arising from these questions have already appeared in print. My most vivid remembrance is of one brigadier general the day after the report was issued that one of Skorzeny's men was dressed as a brigadier general (actually Skorzeny's highest ranking "American" for a colonel). This particular general, hero of the dash across France with the 4th Armored Division, was almost unable to perform his duties because of the number of times he was hauled into headquarters to confirm his identity. GI's with relish welcomed the opportunity to talk back to the "brass."

Even General Montgomery, in despair, went to General Simpson, commanding the Ninth Army, to see if he could get an American identification card; he had been stopped so many times by skeptical GI's, unfamiliar with British cards, that he feared he was getting no work done. A hasty staff conference produced the card, despite strict rules to the contrary.

Those who could arrange it did not travel after dark, and those who could not escape the ordeal usually came home considerably aged by so many sudden demands to halt at unexpected points. Back in Paris, Eisenhower was virtually held prisoner in his own headquarters by overzealous counterintelligence men, who even sent a double through the streets of Paris in an attempt to smoke out the would-be killers. So serious was the situation deemed that an eight o'clock curfew was clamped on Paris; the order was to keep all soldiers off the streets after dark. And all this time Skorzeny was safely behind the German lines, innocent of the havoc he had wrought.

More serious was the inability to get reports on various units. The headquarters of First Army, originally at Spa (headquarters of the Kaiser in the last war), went to a small town called Chaudfontaine near Liége, and finally to Tongres,

west of the Meuse River, between Liége and Maastricht. Spa
seemed to be in the path of the onrushing German armor,
and forward elements of *1 SS Panzer Division* actually were
within several miles of the town on December 18. On the
seventeenth, the headquarters had been hastily evacuated;
those of us who were there later found many secret documents
left by various hastily departing staff divisions. Others found
new pistols and other types of equipment left behind in the
departure. At Malmedy, near panic gripped the town as the
Germans approached, and an evacuation hospital hastily
loaded up and left, as did the other units in the town. All
these people were scared, most of all because they did not
know what was going on. Nobody seemed to comprehend
what had happened. Communication with the forward divisions had in many cases been cut or greatly reduced, and
higher commanders were unable to obtain sufficient information to put together the pieces of the puzzle. Retreating troops
clogged the roads and blocked reinforcements on their way to
the front. At times complete panic gripped some of these
units as rumors of approaching Germans were heard. In one
instance, eight huge 240-mm. guns, in perfect working conditions, were abandoned in a ditch with no demolition because
the Germans were approaching. Much equipment was also
jettisoned in perfect working order, despite previous careful instructions on how to disable matériel if need be.

I was trying to find the 7th Armored Division, which apparently had been swallowed up in the center of the German
penetration. Officers at First Army were actually uncertain
exactly where the Division was located. On December 19, three
days after the start of the German attack, two privates from
the 7th Armored Division went to First Army headquarters at
Chaudfontaine, searching for a trailer full of Christmas pack-
ages which they had abandoned on their trip south. Suddenly
someone spotted their patch, and the dazed privates were
rushed from a captain to a major, to a colonel, finally to General Kean, Chief of Staff to General Hodges. General Kean
questioned the privates closely concerning the whereabouts of
their division, the roads they had used to get to Chaudfontaine,
the troops they had seen along the way. The privates knew
only the location of the division command post and nothing of
the fighting troops. Yet, as they left this unexpected grilling,
they heard the General remark to his aide: "This is the most
information I've had all day." Said one of the men: "This
shouldn't happen to a private."

Rumor dominates the battlefield at any time. The rumors which begin in time of stress, like the Battle of the Bulge, are beyond description. Those which sweep through the ranks may not ordinarily be damaging, but when the enemy is on the march, they can transform battle into a rout. Uncertain gossip of a more serious nature flooded the American intelligence officers, whether planted by German agents or merely because of lack of information, we do not know. In any event, a sudden tide of German divisions began to be identified by our intelligence officers, divisions which failed to appear in the fighting. For example, the *11 Panzer Division* appeared on most of intelligence maps for more than a week of the fighting, when actually it was south of the Bulge during all that time. Eisenhower's maps showed the Division in the center of the Bulge area. The two Hitler brigades caused endless confusion because of their identity with the *Grossdeutschland Division*, famed German formation, from which the brigades drew their replacements. This led to the legitimate assumption that the Division was on the Western Front. It was some time before the Russians confirmed our earlier understanding that the Division was on the Eastern Front.

On December 22, the intelligence officer of the First Army, Colonel Dickson, issued an estimate of the enemy situation in which he reported, without expressing doubt, that thirteen German divisions were reported to be in reserve in the battle area, that five and one half more were possibly in reserve, and four additional divisions were reported in reserve, but not confirmed. This was six days after the attack's beginning when twenty-four German divisions had already been identified. In addition, Colonel Dickson predicted that Germany proper could supply an additional four *Volksgrenadier* divisions within a week; the Italian front could yield up to four divisions; the Eastern Front possibly five, and Norway four to five more divisions.

Here was the intelligence officer at his gloomiest. So grave was this report that all copies were ordered destroyed after they had been distributed, and the divisions which had received them were ordered to send signed certificates indicating they had destroyed them. General Hodges was afraid of its effect on already low morale, should such a report be made public. Here you have a very dangerous and concrete example of the state of mind which grips an overconfident army suddenly jolted with a haymaking punch.

Do not jump to the conclusion that everyone in the Battle

of the Bulge was scared and panicky. Many of the most heroic deeds of the war were performed by small, isolated groups of soldiers, unaware of the situation, without adequate equipment or support, who stood and battled it out with the Germans until overwhelmed. Some of these deeds will be discussed later. But, although we like to think of our soldiers as always heroic, it's time the public began to view them as the human beings that they really are, with the weaknesses which one finds in any group or individuals in any working situation. This talk of fear and panic is not recited to deprecate the American soldier, but rather to bring into focus a vital consideration in the Battle of the Bulge. We were not used to defeat; that made it more difficult to take.

The over-all result of "Operation Confusion" was an over-cautious reaction to the German attack. Thinking that Liége was the goal of the Germans, not being blessed with the German plan which appears so simple when expounded later, First Army officials needlessly maintained an impregnable defense due south of Spa, long after the German main effort had passed far to the west. Here was another concrete example of the effects of the German war of nerves.

This war within a war affected the development of the fighting in the Ardennes forests. It is true that our reaction can never be completely assessed because of the hundreds of intangible manifestations which arise in an army in a state of near panic. But reports of parachutists behind every barn, overestimation of German strength, uncertainty regarding our own troop dispositions, the infuriating inability to get information, all are facets of the same problem. And caught in the middle of this indecision and doubt were the civilians, completely out of touch with the military developments, dazed by the sudden change of events, frightened beyond description by the imminent arrival of Germans. I shall never forget the looks on the faces of the Belgians in the little town of Chaudfontaine, nestled into a river valley just south of Liége, as headquarters of the First Army packed up and rolled away to the west. Stark fear gripped the faces of those dazed peasants as the last trucks vanished around the final gentle curve in the road. "Is there no one who can help us?" one of them asked me. I could only stammer helplessly and vanish into the distance myself. In Liége I had a young friend who suddenly disappeared. He had been a Belgian prisoner, released because of illness. His wife was from Detroit. They and most of the remaining young people in Liége had fled to the country to hide so the Germans would not find them and impound them once more. Liége became a seemingly empty town where one could rattle through deserted streets, completely shorn of all signs of life. It's no fun to be on the losing team, especially when a pale, wan, dazed civilian says, "And what is to become of us?"

CHAPTER V

The Crisis (December 18-26)

AMERICANS ARE AROUSED

DESPITE THE CRUSHING BLOW OF THE FIRST TWO DAYS AND the unrelenting war of nerves embodied in the German "Operation Confusion," the immediate effects began to wear off during the course of the first week's fighting in the Ardennes. It is impossible to tell the exact date when "Operation Confusion" waned; certainly the First Army intelligence officer's dire prediction of German strength of December 22 was a part of this. But, in general, after the first few days of shock, the dazed, uncomprehending feeling gave way to new determination and resolution born from the first jolting setback on the Western Front.

To the highly disciplined Germans, our normal unmilitary bearing, our apparent lack of discipline seemed completely contrary to their conception of a good soldier. The Germans felt that the American soldier was inexperienced, not completely interested in the war, and somewhat slipshod in his methods. Although there was considerable justification for their feeling so, in times of crises our citizen army invariably rallied quickly and effectively to the defense. At Kasserine Pass in Africa, Salerno in Italy, and Anzio beachhead, our troops were at their best; at those times the issue seemed clear, and the stakes the highest. And these same Germans were unable to comprehend the sudden stiffening of the backbone, the complete change of attitude which occurred each time our forces seemed trapped. Being a big and strong and undisciplined colossus of the New World, we often seemed casual in our interest and fighting ability. But when backed against a wall, our troops suddenly became fighting demons. The same inconsistency showed up in the Battle of the Bulge.

Those first two days on the Ardennes front were complete

chaos. Many Americans ran. Some stayed to fight. Others surrendered in large groups. The Germans wrung their hands with glee and said, "Did we not tell you that the Americans were cowards? Did we not say they would wilt if surprised and overwhelmed?" But once again they failed to understand the psychology of our young nation. As the initial shock wore off, and the terror and dismal uncertainty of those first hours diminished, a perceptible change swept through American ranks. Rudely shocked out of their complacency, the grim truth suddenly dawned on our dazed troops and leaders—the war was far from over.

Partly because of the humiliation at being caught asleep, partly because of the sobering realization that much hard fighting remained ahead, and partly because of the surprising German strength, the often careless, casual, and even uninterested Americans suddenly buckled down to the grim business of killing Germans in large numbers. Too often overzealous correspondents have described in sweeping, colorful terms, the sensational ripple of an idea through the ranks; hence the discerning reader has become skeptical of generalizations about morale of fighting men. But here was the great "shock treatment" of the war in the west; the German attack was the insulin injected under American skin. The sudden serious light in which the war was viewed was a subject for comment by all. Stung by the surprise punch of the Germans, we staggered and then rebounded. Our minds suddenly cleared.

As never before, since D-Day in Normandy, all of the troops and the commanders were aware of the dangers ahead. By mutual consent they banished the wisecracks about the Germans, forgot for the moment their desire to get home, and placed first things first. Those first things were Germans unendingly streaming through the shattered American line.

The job centered on the two German breakouts punched through Middleton's Ardennes front: one was to the north through the Losheim gap running between the Elsenborn Ridge and the Schnee Eifel, where *1 SS Panzer Division* was pouring westward toward the Meuse, and in the center of the line a large hole had been ripped through the 28th Division line, allowing Manteuffel's Corps to pour through toward Houffalize and Bastogne. The third immediate danger area, at St. Vith, was an unknown factor, with both forces struggling toward the town. All this we know now, but no such clear picture was available to Hodges at First Army headquarters or to Bradley, Eisenhower, and Montgomery. For the most part, the front, as seen on the war maps, seemed to be a confused series of German and American lines, representing only vaguely the locations of the various units.

What happened during the next few days, as the Allies attempted to plug these gaps, was never fully known to Allied or German commanders, high and low, and has only emerged now as a result of nearly two years' study of voluminous documents, interviews, and orders, supplemented by hundreds of personal conversations with officers and men who participated. The events of that hectic week of December 18 to 26 are most clear when we understand the principal actions encompassed by it. Beginning at the northern end of the line where the crisis first developed and where the Germans applied their main effort and moving our eyes southwards, the battlefield resolves into segments capable of some degree of isolation. Little consideration is given in this chapter to the shoulders or hinges of the Bulge, both north and south, where by tenacious defense the Americans were able to hold, although forced at both ends to swing back and face in toward the ever-expanding Bulge. Keeping these facts in mind, let us examine the fighting as it developed.

FORMATION OF THE AMBLEVE RIVER LINE

To trace the formation of the meager First Army defensive line, formed on an east-west axis to replace the shattered line through the Ardennes forests, we must look again at the attack plans of "Sepp" Dietrich's *Sixth Panzer Army*. You will recall that Dietrich had massed five divisions of infantry and two divisions of armor on a twenty-five mile front generally straddling the boundary of Gerow's V Corps and Middleton's VIII Corps. He intended to open a hole with his infantry, and then following through with the two panzer divisions, *12 SS*, on the north, bursting over the Elsenborn Ridge and then on the Malmedy, Spa, and Verviers, and *1 SS*, on the south, passing through the Losheim gap between the Elsenborn Ridge and the Schnee Eifel, south of Malmedy, across the Ambleve River at Stavelot and Trois Ponts, and then on to the west through Werbomont and, eventually, Huy on the Meuse River. Then the following infantry was to swing to the north, and assume a defensive position to block any attempted Allied reinforcements from moving into the battle area from the north. To aid him, Dietrich had the paratroops drop north of Malmedy and Skorzeny's "Trojan Horse" panzer brigade, which was to pene-

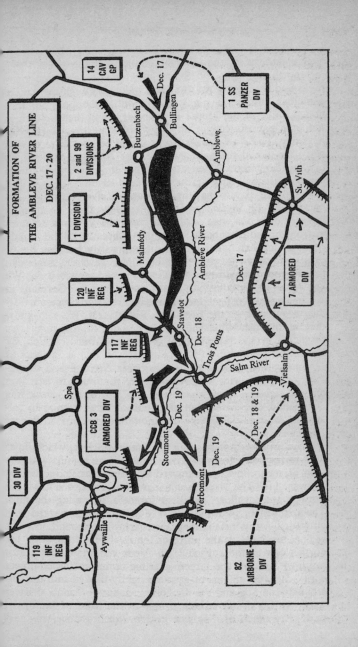

FORMATION OF
THE AMBLEVE RIVER LINE
DEC. 17-20

14 CAV GP

1 SS PANZER DIV

Dec. 17

Butzenbach

Bullingen

2 and 99 DIVISIONS

1 DIVISION

Ambleve.

St. Vith

Malmédy

Ambleve River

120 INF REG

Dec. 17

Stavelot

Dec. 18

7 ARMORED DIV

117 INF REG

Trois Ponts

Salm River

Spa

CCB 3 ARMORED DIV

Dec. 19

Vielsalm

Dec. 18 & 19

Dec. 19

30 DIV

Stoumont

Werbomont

Dec. 19

119 INF REG

Aywaille

82 AIRBORNE DIV

trate American defenses when *1 SS Panzer Division* reached a point abreast of the mountainous area of the Hohe Venn, just north of Malmedy. Skorzeny's brigade, with American tanks and equipment, was to move quietly through the American lines during the night to take without opposition, they hoped, three of the Meuse River bridges and then hold them until the panzers caught up, probably some time during the next day. The *2 SS Panzer Corps* would be kept in reserve to carry on should the momentum of the attack slacken off, to hit any dangerous Allied attack from the north flank or to run with the ball once across the Meuse River.

We already know that the Germans received their first setback when *12 SS Panzer Division*, and its three companion infantry divisions were unable to crack the V Corps defenses in front of the Elsenborn Ridge, partly because of the muddy roads which hampered movement and partly because the V Corps attackers, 2d and 99th Divisions, gave the American forces more strength than the Germans had reckoned on. We know that the 2d and 99th Divisions held off the Germans in a grim, uncertain fight for three days, until on December 19 they drew back to the Elsenborn Ridge itself. We also know that in the meantime the southern flank of the ridge was protected by the rapid arrival of the 1st Division which, by December 18, had filled in a new east-west line as far west as Malmedy. The attacks of *12 SS Panzer Division* and the infantry divisions with it were fruitlessly continued for six days of hard fighting, after which time this half of the attack was abandoned, and *12 SS Panzer Division* turned around to follow the route of *1 SS Panzer Division*. But what of *1 SS Panzer Division*?

From Malmedy west along the Ambleve River, which flows west to the small town of Trois Ponts where it joins with the Salm River to flow north toward the Meuse, existed a natural defense line. The rivers are narrow but swift, and they cut through steep valleys, excellent for defense among the hills. The area just north of the Ambleve River line was packed with vital First Army installations. First Army's command post was at Spa, ten miles to the north of the river line, located on the north slope of the rugged Hohe Venn mountain range. Just south of Spa was the largest gasoline dump on the continent with 2,500,000 gallons of gasoline tightly packed into the forests between Spa and the Ambleve. Along the Ambleve River were two important crossings: one at the town of Malmedy, itself very much of a service center with ordnance, engineer maintenance, medical and military police units, and an evacuation hospital, all in or about the town, and the second at Stavelot, which contained the First Army map depot with over 2,500,000 maps. These two crossing towns covered the approaches to the gasoline dumps, where most of the First Army reserve was stored, and controlled the roads leading north toward Spa and eventually Liége.

The town of Spa seemed remote from any battle area on the morning of December 16 as staff members of the First Army headquarters awoke from their billets in the very beautiful resort hotels which abounded in the town, to receive the first reports of a small German attack along the VIII Corps front. But in a few short hours, the lightning-like thrusts of *1 SS Panzer Division* had completely revised this picture, and by evening it was becoming clear that the panzers had broken through the Losheim gap into the open, that they were heading west toward Spa. During the first uncertain, nightmarish hours of the German attack, in the midst of the horrible confusion caused by the reports of the parachute landing north of Malmedy, steps were taken to provide a defense for this approach to Spa and Liége. First, engineer units were sent to Malmedy and Trois Ponts, and they were followed by First Army and 12th Army Group security forces, commonly called the Palace Guard, who went to Malmedy and Stavelot. Additional small units were rushed to the defense of the gas dumps and Spa itself on December 17 and 18 when the full significance of the German attack began to be felt. Finally, on December 18, the 30th Division was rushed into the breach from its reserve area in the Ninth Army some forty miles to the north, barely in time to meet the full weight of *1 SS Panzer Division* which already was arrayed in front of Stavelot by the evening of December 17. This split-second drama formed the frame for the picture of the defense of the Ambleve River line and the second great defeat of "Sepp" Dietrich's roughriding panzers.

For a moment we will follow the vagaries of *1 SS Panzer Division*. Leading the attack *Kampfgruppe* of *1 SS Panzer Division* was Colonel Peiper, arrogant Prussian officer. Peiper burst through the Losheim gap, captured a divisional gasoline dump at the town of Bullingen on the morning of December 17 and then headed for the Ambleve River, where he was to cross at Stavelot. About noon on December 17, his lead forces arrived at a road junction just to the south of Malmedy, at the time defended by a handful of engineer and security troops which had arrived during the day. Peiper did not turn north toward Malmedy, two miles away, because it was supposed to be in the sector of his running mate, *12 SS Panzer Division*, and Peiper did not yet know that *12 SS Panzer Division* was bogged down in the mud and defenses of the Elsenborn Ridge. At the crossroads, however, Peiper's lead tanks did bump into Battery B of the 285th Field Artillery Observation Battalion, which had sneaked into the march column of the 7th Armored Division, also using the Malmedy road on its way to St. Vith, an addition twelve miles to the south. As we noted, part of the 7th Armored Division was on the road just a few minutes ahead of Peiper. In a short struggle, the artillerymen were overwhelmed, captured and lined up in a field by the crossroad. Then at the command of one of Peiper's fanatic lieutenants, the men were mowed down as they stood there helplessly with their hands over their heads. Most of the seventy-odd men were killed outright; those still alive were shot by guards who kicked the bodies of victims to find out whether they still lived. All who were not dead were then shot with pistols. Some fifteen lived to tell the story by feigning death and then escaped several hours later. The perpetrators of the crimes have been convicted after a trial in Germany.

At this time the only troops in Malmedy belonged to the 291st Engineer Combat Battalion. They were weak and would have been unable to withstand the onslaught of the panzers, but Peiper turned south on his way to Stavelot and the Ambleve River. Early in the morning of December 18, Peiper attacked Stavelot, which was held by a company of armored infantry and a squad of the engineers from Malmedy. Peiper rode roughshod over these troops as he seized his vital Ambleve River crossing. Part of his outriders started north toward Spa and were only turned back by a torrent of 100,000 gallons of gasoline from the southern edge of the great gasoline dumps, which was poured into a steep cut in the narrow road, and then ignited. This fire forced Peiper back and turned him on his main route to the west. Peiper knew that if he could cross the Salm River at the town of Trois Ponts, some four miles to the west of Stavelot, he would be out in the open into the better road net, and free for a straight run to the Meuse. Success seemed within his grasp as he started confidently along the Ambleve River road which wound toward Trois Ponts. But he was halted. An engineer company of the 51st Engineer Combat Battalion, which had been operating sawmills in the Ardennes forests, had been ordered to Trois Ponts and had arrived there about midnight on December 17, the night Peiper arrived at Stavelot. Their orders were to blow the bridges at Trois Ponts if the enemy approached. When Peiper arrived, they were waiting—140 men, 8 bazookas, 10 machine guns, and an antitank gun which had been commandeered as its crew wandered through the town, looking for its organizations. This small group halted Peiper's lead tanks with the antitank gun, then retreated across the river and blew the bridges. "If we could have captured the bridge intact, it would have been a simple matter to drive through to the Meuse River early that day," Peiper lamented later. But as speed was of the essence, he again turned to the north, into the very steep valley of the Ambleve River as it turned north toward Liége. And this was his undoing.

Once again Peiper attempted to burst out into the open as he found a crossing of the Ambleve River north of Trois Ponts, and sent his main body along a new road toward Werbomont. Once again a squad of engineers, this time from the 291st Engineer Combat Battalion, blew a bridge in his face, this one only four miles from Werbomont; and again Peiper, without adequate bridging equipment, and with orders to avoid all resistance, turned north deeper into the valley of the Ambleve River. He bivouacked for the night near the town of Stoumont, less than twenty-five miles from Liége. That afternoon his columns had been heavily pounded for the first time since the start of the attack by four fighter-bombers, alerted to hunt for the panzer column, and finally directed to the column by a reconnaissance plane which had skidded under the cloud bank to spot the panzers as they moved west. The fighter-bombers inflicted telling damage on the panzers and slowed them down; and then for the first time the true location of the blitzing panzer units was reported to First Army.

Meanwhile, the 30th Division, veteran of many a hard fight in the European Theater and heroes of the battle of Mortain when Hitler had attempted to cut off General Patton's forces bursting out of Normandy, had been alerted late on December 17 for movement to the Ambleve River line. Here they were to meet the onrushing panzers and counterattack to close the twelve-mile gap between Malmedy and St. Vith, where the 7th Armored Division had been sent the previous day. The Division spent most of the day trying to keep abreast of the reports on the hard-driving *1 SS Panzer Division* so that its commanders could plan their deployment. By the morning of December 18, one regiment was spread along the Ambleve

River between Malmedy and Stavelot; the west battalion of the regiment recaptured Stavelot, which Peiper, in his utter confidence, had left only lightly defended while his main forces sped westward. Peiper later said that *3 Parachute Division*, part of Dietrich's infantry, was to take over the defense of Stavelot the following day, and he did not believe that any American reinforcements could reach the town before then. A second regiment was rushed around the tip of this huge German finger, poking into the American rear areas. One battalion wormed its way into the little town of Stoumont, literally under the noses of the bivouacking German guns, and a second sped all the way around to Werbomont, where they took over from the valiant engineer squad which had blown the bridge. Neither of these battalions arrived a moment too soon: the battalion near Werbomont caught and ambushed a German reconnaissance force which had finally found a bridge that would get them back on the road to Werbomont, and the battalion at Stoumont found itself locked in a vicious battle with Peiper's main spearhead of over sixty tanks on the morning of December 19th. The Germans gave up on the Werbomont tack, concentrated on the battalion at Stoumont and sent it reeling back, badly beaten. And then the Germans began inching their way up the steep river valley road, only to be frustrated once more by the rugged terrain and by a portion of the third battalion of this 30th Division Regiment (the 119th Infantry) and by a company of tanks hurriedly assembled from the First Army ordnance shops to the north, where they were undergoing major alterations. A see-saw battle raged throughout December 19 in the canyons of the Ambleve River, but the defenders were stubborn and the terrain friendly. Finally, the Germans, unable to find a way around the relatively small American force, drew back to Stoumont to await further developments. The second major blow had been dealt the German hopes.

In the meantime, happenings along other parts of the now-forming Ambleve River line further sealed the doom of *Kampfgruppe Peiper*. The 117th Infantry of the 30th Division, which recaptured part of Stavelot on the afternoon of December 18, beat off a continuous series of German counterattacks, as the desperate Germans, in fanatical charges, waded icy waters of the Ambleve River in an attempt to regain Stavelot, and reopen the route to their now stranded leading *Kampfgruppe*. The fighting at Stavelot ranks among the most bitter of the war, and German casualties were terrific. The defenders stood their ground, and Stavelot remained in American hands. To the west, General Hodges diverted a combat command of the 3d Armored Division which, as we shall see shortly, was on its way to prepare for the counterattack which Hodges and Bradley hoped to organize to help hold and clean out the trapped *Kampfgruppe Peiper*, which was caught in the Ambleve River valley. General Hodges, noting first that *1 SS Panzer Division* was steadily advancing into his rear area, hastily diverted the 82d Airborne Division, en route to its assembly area at Bastogne, to Werbomont to meet the sudden bombshell which had penetrated the American defenses. All during December 18, troops of the 82d Airborne Division closed into an assembly area at Werbomont, their assembly itself only made possible by the defenders of the bridges at Trois Ponts and just to the east of the Werbomont. Throughout December 19 and 20, the 82d Airborne Division cautiously felt its way forward, closed along the west bank of the Ambleve River, across from the German concentration at Stoumont, and sealed the sack into which Peiper had stuck his head. Other units of the division moved due east to the Salm River, where, to their amazement, they found far to their front the defenders of St. Vith still holding out despite overwhelming German concentration. The remainder of the German formation which had been ambushed as it attempted to get into Werbomont on the night of December 18 was found and driven back into the main German pocket at Stoumont. For the most part, the 82d Airborne moved forward cautiously, uncertain of the location of friend or foe, and anxious to maintain its balance to meet any new German attacks.

Back on the other side of the Ambleve River, the 30th Division, set off balance by its sudden and dramatic contact with the enemy, felt that it was in no position to attack south to join with the defenders of St. Vith. Worried about future German intentions, General Hodges piled unit upon unit behind the 30th Division to strengthen its defensive position preparatory to an attack he was sure would hit the division as the Germans drove north toward Liége. Here, the war of nerves caught up with Hodges, and the psychology of depression which gripped the American command diverted it from the primary German intention: that of getting to the Meuse River. It was during this period, on December 22, that the First Army intelligence officer, Colonel Dickson, issued his gloomy report of German capabilities, and at the top of his list of probable German actions was an attack through the 30th Division toward Spa and Liége. But the Germans were already preparing plans to attempt a new breakout far to the west of the 30th Division.

From December 20 to 23, pressure by the 30th and 82d Divisions and Combat Command B of the 3d Armored Division was unrelentingly applied against Peiper's *Kampfgruppe* trapped in the sack which was hastily thrown around it. Finally, when he realized he would be unable to break through to Peiper, butcher boy "Sepp" Dietrich ordered Peiper to break out of the pocket and back to the east. Peiper was aware he could not do this; he abandoned his tanks and guns, and on the night of December 23 he and 800 of his men made their way back through the American lines and rejoined the remainder of their division on the south banks of the Ambleve River. The equipment for a battalion each of armored infantry, tanks, artillery, and reconnaissance troops was caught in the pocket. A total of thirty-nine German tanks, seventy half-tracks, thirty-three guns of all types, and thirty other vehicles were captured in this operation.

Here was a case where the fate of divisions and armies rested for a few brief moments on the shoulders of a handful of men: first, at the town of Trois Ponts; and then, only hours later, with another, smaller, handful of men at the bridge just east of Werbomont. Had either of these groups failed in their job (and the temptation to run away must have been very great), the probability that Peiper would have got to the Meuse River the next morning, behind Skorzeny's "Trojan Horse," would have been very high. And even though his was a lone panzer *Kampfgruppe*, such was the confusion of the time, the uncertainties and doubts raised by the German war of nerves, the lack of information at the higher headquarters, that it is most probable that Hodges, Bradley or Montgomery might have been thrown into a frenzy, which would have led to the forced withdrawal of all American troops behind the Meuse River. And the Germans, standing off with 2 *SS Panzer Corps*, waiting for just such a break, would have quickly followed through and exploited to the full any hole Peiper would have been able to make. But these two handfuls of American soldiers, despite the grave uncertainties as to the whereabouts of either friendly or enemy forces, chose to ride out the German attack. As a result *Kampfgruppe Peiper* was sacked in the canyons of the Ambleve River, and the second major defeat had been dealt the Germans.

By December 18, Hitler saw the first handwriting on the wall. Jodl said he knew by the 17th or 18th that they would not succeed in their plans. On the 18th, Hitler vetoed for the time being the projected attack from the north, which was to hit into the Ninth Army along its exposed flank sloping back toward the British lines from the Roer River, but he left open the attack near Arnhem. Rundstedt had pressed for this secondary attack, which would have cut off the Aachen salient if successful, but Hitler gave a final "No," and the two divisions being held in readiness for this attack, *9 Panzer* and *15 Panzer Grenadier*, were transferred to the High Command reserve pool and started on their way toward the forests of the Ardennes, where by Christmas Day they were engaged in the fight. A third division from the High Command reserve, *3 Panzer Grenadier*, was belatedly thrown into the fight raging around the Elsenborn ridge in a renewed attempt to puncture the American lines guarding the southern approaches to the ridge, but this division only shared in the failure of the others.

A second decision was made as a result of *1 SS Panzer Division's* failure to crack through to the Meuse River. Hitler, by this time back in Berlin, decided to put part of Dietrich's second wave, *2 SS Panzer Corps,* into Manteuffel's army to move south through the wide hole *Fifth Panzer Army* had created and then to strike north behind the American defenses which had grown around *Kampfgruppe Peiper,* again to open the way for a new panzer blitz toward the Meuse River. About December 19, *2 SS Panzer Division* side-slipped to the south, worked its way around the St. Vith salient and on December 22 began to come up from the south into the soft underbelly of this thin new First Army defense line. On the same day, *2 SS Panzer Division's* running mate, *9 SS Panzer Division,* jumped into the fighting in the thick forests between Malmedy and St. Vith and attacked both the north shoulder of the still standing St. Vith defenses and the river defenses of 82d Airborne Division, holding a line behind the St. Vith defenders. If we are to understand Hodges' concentration on the threat to the 30th Division, even after Peiper had been sacked, the German decision to send part of Dietrich's troops to the south and then north, and the inability of First Army to plug the gaps which Manteuffel and Dietrich had rent in its lines, we must know what was going on around St. Vith.

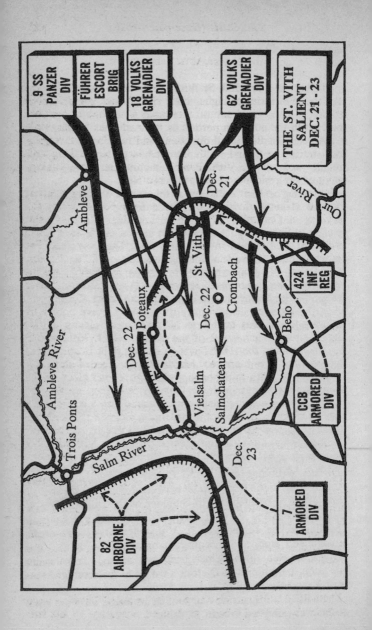

9 SS PANZER DIV

FÜHRER ESCORT BRIG

18 VOLKS GRENADIER DIV

62 VOLKS GRENADIER DIV

THE ST. VITH SALIENT DEC. 21 - 23

Ambleve

Dec. 21

Our River

St. Vith

Crombach

Dec. 22

Dec. 22

Poteaux

424 INF REG

Beho

Ambleve River

Trois Ponts

Vielsalm

Salmchateau

Dec. 23

CCB ARMORED DIV

Salm River

82 AIRBORNE DIV

7 ARMORED DIV

THE ST. VITH SALIENT

Situated on a low hill, St. Vith, Belgium, is surrounded on all sides by a series of higher hills, all excellent for defensive fighting. This town of several thousands is the hub of the best road net in the northern portion of the Ardennes forests, with major roads leading in all directions and rail lines converging from north, west, and south into the large marshalling and freight yards at St. Vith. Predominantly German-speaking, many of the residents were openly pro-Nazi.

Following up their initial successes around the Schnee Eifel, the two infantry divisions of Manteuffel's *66 Corps* on the morning of December 17 began feeling their way along the road from Schonberg, at the western base of the Schnee Eifel, toward St. Vith, seven miles to the west. They were not discovered until the assistant intelligence officer of the 7th Armored Division, Major New (who arrived in St. Vith during the early morning hours of December 17), poked his way east from St. Vith. Major New left corps headquarters at Bastogne, where he received his division's orders, with grave doubts in his mind as he was unable to obtain a clear picture of the enemy situation or extent of the attack. At St. Vith, where the green staff of the 106th Division seemed to be in confusion, these doubts were increased. Major New proceeded along the road from St. Vith to Schonberg, through a road block established by the 168th Engineer Combat Battalion, another of the VIII Corps engineer units which was to play a leading role in the unfolding drama of the Ardennes, almost to Schonberg, where he discovered that the Germans had already surrounded the Schnee Eifel. Major New scooted back to St. Vith with this information, but General Jones, 106th Division commander, still expected the early arrival of the 7th Armored Division as promised by Middleton. After once ordering the two regiments on the Schnee Eifel to withdraw and fight their way back, he rescinded his order and told them to fight it out. Middleton had previously suggested to Jones that he withdraw the troops from the Schnee Eifel, but he left the decision to the division commander who was on the scene. Jones took the opposite course, but Middleton felt that although Jones made the wrong decision, he made it in good faith, based on information then available to him.

Middleton's instructions to the 7th Armored Division were to help the 106th Division as deemed necessary by the two

commanders. General Hasbrouck, commander of the 7th
Armored Division, arrived at St. Vith around noon on December 17 after visiting Middleton at Bastogne. He, too, had
left Bastogne feeling very frustrated because he could get no
satisfactory information from the corps staff, and he decided
to go ahead on his own. Hasbrouck and Jones conferred amidst
the confusion in St. Vith and agreed upon an attack by the 7th
Armored Division toward Schonberg to re-establish contact
with the two lost regiments on the Schnee Eifel and then to
drive south to re-establish the line of the 424th Infantry, the
southern regiment of the division. There the 7th Armored
would join with Combat Command B of the 9th Armored
Division, already attacking behind the 424th Infantry. It was
a simple plan, and it looked workable, but the commanders
failed to reckon with two factors: first, the clogged roads
through which the 7th Armored Division would have to move;
and, second, the strength of the Germans.

While the Germans completed their encirclement of the
Schnee Eifel, the 7th Armored Division, alerted late on the
evening of December 16 to help out on "a little German counterattack of three or four divisions" suddenly began its seventy-mile move to St. Vith. We at the division, sitting in a
neat little Dutch town, did not have the slightest inkling of
the magnitude of the German attack. The previous day we
had read the glowing 12th Army Group summary of the German situation (see Chapter III), and everyone was feeling
in high spirits. Part of the division's men were going on leave;
one command was preparing a cavalrylike charge to swoop
down on the last remaining German stronghold west of the
Roer River. Some of us had organized a basketball league,
and we were amazing the Dutch with the complexities of
American sport; we knew we would be there for some little
time. And then the bombshell burst. All through the night of
December 16, the men readied themselves for this new uncharted move to an uncertain future. Nobody, not even General Hasbrouck, dreamed that the Germans were launching
their great attack on the Western Front. But it did not take
long to find out that something was up. No sooner had the first
tanks got on the road headed south than German reconnaissance planes were overhead dropping flares. We had four air
raids in our quiet little Dutch city, and the civilians wondered
what was going on. We did, too.

On December 17, the 7th Armored Division fought clogged
roads rather than Germans. Two routes of march were se-

lected. We have already observed how one combat command just missed *Kampfgruppe Peiper* on the eastern road; troops on the western road fought their way through the stream of traffic of small artillery and service units flowing in the opposite direction, away from the German penetrations. On the final leg of the route to St. Vith, a double-banked road, jammed with vehicles of the 14th Cavalry Group and artillery units, these troops completely stopped the tanks, until threat of their guns cleared a path. And instead of arriving at seven in the morning to attack toward Schonberg, the first tanks arrived at three in the afternoon, barely in time to meet the first Germans attacking St. Vith. Slowly, throughout the late afternoon and early evening, the troops filtered in; the attack was postponed until morning, and, in the meantime, a hurried defensive line was formed around St. Vith. When Jones saw that the attack could not be made, he canceled the attack of CCB of the 9th Armored Division to the south and ordered its withdrawal, along with his own 424th Infantry, west of the Our River, to await developments of the next day.

The quiet night of December 17 was accompanied by a terrible uneasiness. The hastily formed line east of St. Vith was expanded and improved as rapidly as possible. Intelligence officers thirsted for information of the Germans, but had nowhere to turn for it. However, the Germans soon eased this uncertainty, first, with an attack on the assembly area of the northern combat command of the division north and west of St. Vith, and then in the blooming dawn hours of December 18, with two attacks on the loose defense line around St. Vith itself. The attackers from the north were actually flank forces of *1 SS Panzer Division* feeling out the enemy strength along their southern flank, and these forces recoiled when they met sudden opposition. The attack from the east was *66 Corps,* probing toward St. Vith, which Manteuffel had planned to capture by December 17. Suddenly, and unexpectedly, the mission of mercy on which the 7th Armored Division had blithely embarked was turned into a bitter, sordid battle for survival. All plans for an attack toward Schonberg were abandoned when it became evident that the Germans were in great force on nearly all sides of St. Vith.

Manteuffel, crafty commander of the *Fifth Panzer Army,* later told me, "I wanted to have St. Vith on December 17. Although I had expected that Bastogne would be defended, I did not think that the Americans would be able to defend St. Vith." The surprise show of American strength forced a change in the German plans. Sharp probes were to be made on December 18, to be followed by an assault on the nineteenth to capture the town. It was the first of these probes which had upset the 7th Armored Division plan to relieve the surrounded forces on the Schnee Eifel. Leaving only small forces to contain the troops on the Schnee Eifel, Manteuffel rapidly closed up his *18* and *62 Volksgrenadier Divisions* with supporting armor around St. Vith, preparatory to assault. But the corps with its new *Volksgrenadier Divisions* was slow in closing around St. Vith, and by the evening of December 18 the Americans had formed a ring around three sides of St. Vith, with the 7th Armored Division on the north flank and around the town, CCB of the 9th Armored Division just south of the town, joining the 424th Infantry, and finally aided by the welcome addition of the 112th Infantry, splintered off from its parent 28th Division by the power thrust through the center of the 28th Division line. This latter regiment, wandering on its own, with no communication to division or to VIII Corps, was taken over by the 7th Armored–106th Division ring. The wide "horseshoe" defense was completed along the southern flank on December 20, when a small task force of tank destroyers, armored cavalry, miscellaneous service and lost combat troops occupied the key towns between the 112th Infantry and Vielsalm, ten miles west of St. Vith, as warning against possible attacks by other panzers flowing on to the west of St. Vith. This huge, loose line covering about twenty-five miles was completely out of touch with all friendly forces. To the south, the nearest troops were at Bastogne. Between the southern flank of the St. Vith ring and Bastogne, the Germans were pouring through an eighteen-mile-wide gap, streaking on far to the west of Vielsalm. Only isolated troops were fighting these advance German units, among them being the 7th Armored Division trains (supply forces) which had moved far to the west of the division to the "safety" of the rear. To the north, Germans of *Sixth Panzer Army* were solidly established in the fifteen-mile gap between St. Vith and Malmedy, a potent force, despite the loss of *Kampfgruppe Peiper* caught in the 30th Division sack. Not until December 20 did the 82d Airborne Division come up behind the huge "horseshoe" to connect it with the 30th Division. Thus, this huge thorn stuck deep into the German masses pouring west; it became the number one sore spot to Manteuffel, Commander of the *Fifth Panzer Army*.

Manteuffel cursed and fumed as the German attack failed

to puncture this hastily organized defensive horseshoe; his timetable had met its first serious setback. Finally, when he realized the extent of the American opposition, Manteuffel called up his army reserve, the crack *Fuehrer Escort Brigade*, sparkplugged by Generalmajor Otto Remer. The German troops piled up behind the attacking echelons, which were unable to open this key road net. So crowded did the roads become that for a time even generals were forbidden to move about. Into this jam plowed the *Escort Brigade*, ordered to the north of St. Vith to slice off the base of the horseshoe. It took Remer three days to move around into position. By December 20 all was in readiness, and on the next day, Remer jabbed from the north, while the *18* and *62 Volksgrenadier Divisions* launched a co-ordinated frontal assault on St. Vith.

During this build-up period, the American defenders of St. Vith waited with bated breath, anxiously watching the German movements. Without contact with anyone for three days, the defenders were on edge the entire time. And Generals Hasbrouck and Jones of the 7th Armored and 106th Divisions, respectively, were without command orders; they simply cooperated as best they could. They watched uneasily while German panzer units from the other corps moved by south of them. But Manteuffel, with his eyes on the distant Meuse River, kept these troops moving westward according to plan, leaving to the infantry the job of capturing St. Vith. Finally, on the 20th, a liaison officer with a pencilled note from Hasbrouck wormed his way to First Army headquarters, to break in on a meeting between Generals Hodges, Kean (Chief of Staff of First Army), Simpson, and Montgomery. In a dramatic message, Hasbrouck presented for the first time the condition of the St. Vith horseshoe. The note to General Kean read:

DEAR BILL:

I am out of touch with VIII Corps, and understand XVIII Airborne Corps is coming in. My division is defending the line St. Vith-Poteau both inclusive. CCB, 9th Armored Division, the 424th Infantry Regiment of the 106th Division, and the 112th Infantry Regiment of the 28th Division are on my right, and hold from St. Vith (exclusive) to Holdingen. Both infantry regiments are in bad shape. My right flank is wide open except for some reconnaissance elements, TDs, and stragglers we have collected and organized into defensive teams at road centers as far back as Cheram, inclusive. Two German divisions, *116 Panzer* and *560 Volksgrenadier,* are just starting to attack northwest with their right on Gouvy. I can delay them the rest of today *maybe* but will be cut off by tomorrow. VIII Corps has ordered me to hold, and I will do so, but need help. An attack from Bastogne to the northeast will relieve the situation and, in turn, cut the bastards off in rear. I also need plenty of air support. Am out of contact with VIII Corps so am sending this to you. Understand 82d Airborne Division is coming up on my north, and the north flank is not critical.

BOB HASBROUCK

In answer to this dramatic appeal for information and help, Hodges dispatched a message to Hasbrouck telling him that Ridgway's XVIII Airborne Corps was closing in behind him, and making Hasbrouck commander of all the troops in the "horseshoe." This was the first order they had received in three days. But the help was never to get as far as St. Vith. On the afternoon of December 21, the Germans attacked and overwhelmed the garrison holding St. Vith, capturing many of the defenders who were cut off in the hills east of the town. A loose defensive line was formed of stragglers who made their way out of the battle, aided by troops along the north flank, which had been unmolested, and a second stand was attempted on December 22 several miles west of St. Vith. Again the Germans attacked, not only from the east with *66 Corps*, but also from the north with the *Fuehrer Escort Brigade*, now aided by *9 SS Panzer Division*, sent south by Dietrich to help clean up the situation. All units in the horseshoe defense by this time were badly mauled, low on ammunition and supplies, and without reserves. Hodges and Ridgway, XVIII Airborne Corps Commander, had hoped to hold onto the salient, and, eventually pull their other troops up to it. On December 22, Ridgway ordered them to form a complete defensive circle, to defend until relieved, supply to be brought in by air. But the Germans made another penetration of the weak line of demoralized, poorly equipped troops. Hasbrouck sent another dramatic message to Ridgway, saying that unless the division were withdrawn immediately, "there will be no more 7th Armored Division."

This was the situation when Field Marshal Montgomery sent his personal liaison officer to visit Hasbrouck to elicit his advice regarding future action of the horseshoe defenders. Hasbrouck said he would try to defend, if so ordered, because of the tactical importance of the terrain, but he pointed out that it was difficult to supply by air in the densely wooded area he now held, and that fighting elements of the various units had lost tactical unity, were low in men, materials, and morale. Ridgway was overruled by Montgomery, who convinced the tired Hodges, much to Ridgway's disgust. Beginning early in the morning of December 23, troops in the salient began to pull back in an amazing daylight withdrawal, executed in the face of continued German attacks. By nightfall, the last of the troops were across the Salm River, through the lines of the 82d Airborne Division. On December 26, as though to add emphasis to the importance of St. Vith, the RAF, in a smashing 1,270-ton raid on the town, nearly devastated the town. Thereafter German traffic was routed around the town.

While the big battle had been going on around St. Vith, two trapped regiments of the 106th Division, still perched on the Schnee Eifel, were subjected to minor attacks by containing German forces. On December 18, the regiments were given the order to withdraw. "Mission is of gravest importance to the nation—good luck," said General Jones, division commander. Lacking supplies and, apparently, initiative, the regiments made one feeble, unsuccessful attempt on December 19 to get get back through the German lines. Then, despite the fact that many of the lower commanders and the men wanted to continue fighting, they were ordered by their regimental commander to surrender. On December 20, ten days after they had entered combat for the first time, over 7,000 men of these two regiments surrendered to the Germans in the largest mass surrender of American arms on the Western Front. Both Germans and Americans who have studied the situation since then feel that the troops could have put up a stiffer fight, but they were green, the weather was poor, no air drops were made, and communication was almost nonexistent. General Jodl expressed surprise that the two regiments were unable to hold out longer; General Middleton felt similarly.

The defense of St. Vith, recognized by German and Allied commanders alike as a turning point in the Battle of the Bulge, went almost unrecognized in the American press, being overcome by the story of the encircled troops at Bastogne. Their work did not go unrecognized, however, when on December 23, General Eisenhower addressed all of the commanders in the St. Vith horseshoe: "The magnificent job you are doing is having a great beneficial effect on our whole situation. I am personally grateful to you, and wish you would let all of your people know that if they continue to carry out their mission with the splendid spirit they have so far shown, they will have deserved well of their country."

Held up six days longer than their timetable allowed, forced to detour around this vital road net, both Manteuffel and Dietrich felt the effects of this defense. Manteuffel could have, he stated, gone to the aid of Dietrich's imperiled *1 SS Panzer Division*, and probably again opened a hole for the onrushing panzers had he been able to get through St. Vith; Dietrich, in turn, would not have been forced to detour his second wave completely around this horseshoe, and could more quickly have brought his power to bear further to the west. Neither the Ambleve River line nor the subsequent XVIII Corps line extending to the west, about which we will learn more shortly, could have been formed without this prior delaying action, which allowed the new First Army line to form up, (to draw the troops into position) at least in partial preparedness before the Germans burst into their midst. That these troops stood alone, unaided, uninformed, and unprepared is testimony enough, and added to the true importance of the stand is the fact that four of the six regiments in the ring were armored, notoriously weak in infantry troops, designed more for exploiting enemy weaknesses rather than for defense. A standard armored division has only three battalions of infantry, (the equivalent of) slightly less than a normal infantry regiment, of which there are three in an infantry division.

While this thorn pricked deep into the German right flank as they moved west, upsetting the German timetable, heavy German formations were rolling by to the south through the eighteen-mile gap between St. Vith and Bastogne. As early as December 19, First Army began to maneuver troops to block this gap, and failing that, General Hodges formed up the available units, stretching them out from Werbomont, where the 82d Airborne Division had rallied, toward the Meuse River. There they connected with British troops which, meanwhile, had taken up defensive positions along the river line and, in lesser force, east of the river. It is to this great race that we turn now.

FIRST ARMY ATTEMPTS TO PLUG THE GAP

Eisenhower, Bradley, and Hodges agreed that the most effective way of dealing with the German attack was first to seal off the several penetrations, and then to strike hard at the

German flanks and pinch off the entire German force. This was the strategy that they attempted to follow. But Hodges had to plug the gaps first. Such was his intention on the morning of December 18 when he met with Major General James M. Gavin, commander of the 82d Airborne Division and acting commander of the XVIII Airborne Corps.

The XVIII Airborne Corps, with the 82d and the 101st Airborne Divisions in France and the 17th Airborne Division in England, was a new corps born of the expansion of the First Allied Airborne Army, then formulating bold plans for a great drop on the east bank of the Rhine River. We have seen how the corps headquarters and its two tried divisions were alerted by SHAEF late on December 17 for movement to an assembly point at Bastogne. Early on the cold, dark morning of December 18, Major General James M. Gavin, senior corps officer on the continent and, therefore, acting corps commander, jumped into his jeep, and headed for Chaudfontaine, new First Army headquarters. Gavin and Hodges were immediately closeted in deep conversation; as they talked, news of the German capture of Stavelot, Ambleve River crossing, was handed to Hodges. Here was an immediate grave threat to the security of the entire First Army line, a threat which might be more than the 30th Division, just then pulling in along the Ambleve River line, could handle. It appeared from the meager information available that the Germans were at Stavelot in heavy force, and if the engineer units at the Trois Ponts bridges failed, the Germans would have a straight shot to the main Bastogne-Liége road at Werbomont, and then north to Liége, which Hodges believed to be the German objective. Hodges, in moving the 82d Airborne Division north to Werbomont, instead of around Bastogne as originally planned, recognized not only the trend of the German attack toward the north, but also indicated that he was unaware of the power of the German thrusts through the center of Middleton's Ardennes positions. Little did Hodges realize that right behind the 82d Airborne Division were the leading panzers of Manteuffel's panzer corps, driving hard for the Meuse River. Had we known the German plans and intentions, and had the 82d Airborne Division turned and fought at Houffalize, a bitter battle royal would have taken place. But we were blessed with no such divining, and the 82d Airborne went on to Werbomont.

Accordingly, Hodges ordered Gavin immediately to reroute his own 82d Airborne Division, from Bastogne to Werbomont, where they were to assemble as quickly as possible, prepared to meet the enemy wherever he might appear. Pending arrival of the XVIII Airborne Corps staff the next day, the division was temporarily placed under Gerow's V Corps, which stretched now all the way around Elsenborn ridge to Malmedy, along the Ambleve River, and then to Werbomont. The 101st Airborne Division was to continue on to Bastogne, where it would assemble under Middleton's VIII Corps.

Werbomont, Belgium, twenty miles south of Liége, dominates the intersection of the Bastogne-Liége road and the road from Malmedy to Huy. Sixteen miles due west of Stavelot, Werbomont lay directly in the path of *Kampfgruppe Peiper* of the *1 SS Panzer Division*. The high ground around the small town offered excellent defensive positions, into which the hastily assembled men of the 82d Airborne Division began pouring in the late afternoon of December 18. Unknown to them, the advance elements of *Kampfgruppe Peiper* had already been turned back shortly before their arrival, first by the engineer squad at the bridge just east of Werbomont, and later by the battalion of the 119th Infantry. General Gavin's instructions for December 19, when his division would be assembled, were to move out in all directions in an attempt to find and stop the enemy wherever he might be. His men slowly felt their way, literally, in all directions throughout the 19th and 20th, discovering to their amazement, first, the engineer company at Trois Ponts still beating off German attempts to cross the river, and, second, a reconnaissance force of the 7th Armored Division which told them for the first time of the extended St. Vith horseshoe. A third find was a strong pocket of *Kampfgruppe Peiper* south of the Ambleve River, several miles from Stoumont where the main body of the German panzers was surrounded. This group was driven across the river, but only after the loss of over a company of paratroopers. Battles between German *SS* troops and American paratroopers were prone to take on extremely violent aspects. Knives were used abundantly, prisoners were few.

By morning of December 21, the day St. Vith fell, troops of the 82d Airborne Division had successfully sealed the southern portion of the sack in which *Kampfgruppe Peiper* was to be strangled to death, and had further established defensive positions along the Salm River from Trois Ponts to Vielsalm, headquarters of the 7th Armored Division, and from there west, where they were prepared to meet any German threat from the south. Nobody knew from which direction the Germans would come in those days. In the meantime, XVIII Airborne Corps had arrived at Werbomont and, on December 19, had taken over command of the 82d Airborne Division and the 119th Infantry of the 30th Division along with CCB of the 3d Armored Division, all of which were hammering at the trapped *Kampfgruppe Peiper*. Also added to this force on the next day was a second combat command of the 3d Armored Division, which had been alerted from its reserve position in the northern portion of the First Army sector. The third combat command of the 3d Armored Division was left behind to fight the German paratroopers.

Although still primarily worried about the threat to the Ambleve River line, where the 30th Division was establishing itself, Hodges of the First Army carried on in the hope that XVIII Airborne Corps would be able to plug the gap in the VIII Corps line by re-establishing contact between V Corps on the north and VIII Corps on the south. The split in the battlefield on December 20, turning over to Montgomery all troops north of the line Prum-Givet, failed to alter this determination. Montgomery's first order to Hodges was to continue using XVIII Airborne Corps to close the gap, and to continue with plans Hodges was already laying for a strong counterattack to hit the German flanks when the gap was plugged. For this latter purpose, the sector of the northern corps of First Army, VII Corps led by Major General Collins, was turned over to the Ninth Army, and VII Corps headquarters was directed to assemble in the area west of XVIII Airborne Corps with three divisions: the 75th, new to combat and just arriving from Normandy; the 84th, a Ninth Army unit which had seen heavy fighting in the attack to the Roer River in November; and the 2d Armored, veteran of many a hard battle from Africa on, also from the Ninth Army. Loss of these last two divisions meant that the Ninth Army was deprived of four of its six divisions, having already lost the 7th Armored and 30th Divisions. The sector was strengthened by a British division, an armored brigade, and by VII Corps divisions acquired in the shift of commands. In his first report to Eisenhower late on the night of December 20, Montgomery indicated that he entirely approved of the First Army counterattack plan, and that he saw no need to give up any ground, as suggested by Eisenhower. He added that the brave work of the 7th Armored Division was slowing up enemy movement. However, new, swift, sudden German blows were to upset this entire scheme.

The great attempt to close the huge, jagged gap in the First

Army lines began on December 20, when XVIII Airborne Corps instructed the 30th, 82d Airborne, 3d Armored, and the assembling 84th Division to swing on a hinge at Malmedy in a wide southeasterly sweep to establish a line of defense through rugged hills of the Ardennes from Malmedy to Vielsalm to Houffalize, with patrols to Bastogne to contact friendly forces there. Here, in a spectacular comeback, was the wherewithal to seal the hole, and once again stabilize the shaking First Army front. The plan was imaginative and daring, and it left out of consideration only one element—the Germans. To understand what happened to this sealing force we must backtrack with Manteuffel's *Fifth Panzer Army*.

We know that Manteuffel's northern corps, *66*, was headed for St. Vith, and we have already traced its trials and tribulations as it met the unexpected American opposition. We know that Manteuffel broke through the center of the VIII Corps sector with two other panzer corps, consisting of three panzer and two infantry divisions. The southern one of these two corps headed straight for Bastogne, engulfed it, and then the panzer divisions moved around the town on either side as they sped for the Meuse River. We shall trace their activities in the next section. The middle corps, *58*, swept by the 112th Infantry of the 28th Division and pushed it north into the protecting arms of the St. Vith horseshoe as it headed without opposition for Houffalize. Arriving at Houffalize in the early morning of December 19, *58 Corps* nearly caught the tail end of the long stream of 82d Airborne Division trucks rolling slowly into Werbomont, but with barely minutes to spare the paratroopers slipped by and on to the north. The Germans then continued on through the gap between Bastogne and St. Vith and turned toward the northwest to strike for the Meuse River. Here, they collided head-on with the weak reconnaissance forces of 3d Armored Division, cautiously moving along the only three parallel roads between the Ourthe River and the Bastogne-Liége road. The resulting collision ended the immediate attack plans of both Germans and Americans, and resulting developments suddenly plunged the XVIII Airborne Corps into a grim fight for very existence. The gap-plugging mission was forgotten.

With neither force expecting the other, the colliding Germans and Americans were soon completely tangled up. One of the three American columns was cut off and, eventually, forced to abandon its equipment, and make its way back to friendly troops on foot. One German column which attempted

to seize the vital Ourthe River bridge at a little town called
Hotton was turned back by another of the unheralded small
handfuls of men so important in the ultimate Allied victory.
This fighting between the Bastogne-Liége road and the Ourthe
River went on fiercely from December 20 to 23. The weak
forces of 3d Armored Division were gradually strengthened,
first by the Division's combat command which had been on
anti-parachute duty at Eupen and then by small independent
units rushed to the crisis zone. The German panzers, *116 Panzer Division*, unable to capture Hotton, slipped back, crossed
west of the Ourthe River, and then struck northward again,
hoping to get around this new resistance. But this only brought
them head-on into the 84th Division, which was assembling just
west of the Ourthe River at the town of Marche, the first of the
VII Corps divisions to arrive preparatory to the counterattack
being planned by Hodges. The *116 Panzer Division* was once
more frustrated in its ambition to reach the Meuse, again by
only a matter of hours, as the 84th Division closed into Marche
just ahead of the striking panzers.

Meanwhile, the two Panzer divisions of Manteuffel's southern panzer corps, *47*, had left only small forces at Bastogne,
as they followed orders from Hitler to rush around the town,
if they failed initially to seize it, and continue on to the Meuse
River. On the right *2 Panzer Division* met almost no opposition as it plowed steadily closer to the river, while on the left,
Panzer Lehr Division had equally good fortune as it captured
St. Hubert and moved forward toward Givet on the Meuse.
With assurance from the High Command that he could use
the reserve divisions, *9 Panzer* and *3* and *15 Panzer Grenadier*,
released to Model when the thrust from the north through
Ninth Army was abandoned, Manteuffel drove his two loose
panzer divisions forward, regardless of the exposed north flank
caused by failure of *116 Panzer Division* to break through the
3d Armored Division and, then, as it shifted west, the 84th
Division. The northern of these two panzers, *2 Panzer Division*, pushed aside a thin screen hastily thrown up by the 84th
Division on December 23 and moved right into the assembly
area of the 2d Armored Division, just closing into position.
The 75th Division was still not closed into its assembly area
further to the north. On December 23, VII Corps took over
a sector of this rapidly forming line from Werbomont to the
Meuse River, its area being delimited by the Bastogne-Liége
highway on the east (where it took over the 3d Armored and
84th Divisions), and by the Meuse River on the west. The race

to keep ahead of the fast rolling Manteuffel panzers was reaching the critical stage. True, the British were by this time along the Meuse River from Givet to Liége, and one regiment of British tanks was arrayed east of the river in front of Dinant. But the Germans were closing fast.

Once again the offensive striking power of First Army was diverted by a fight for existence as the 2d Armored Division attempted to establish contact with the British forces and to stop *2 Panzer Division* within sight of the Meuse River on Christmas Eve. But the panzers had outstripped their supplies. The Allies, assisted with constant reconnaissance of little cub planes which kept track of enemy movements, sent the 2d Armored Division and the British Household Cavalry Regiment to strike at the Germans, cutting off the largest portion of *2 Panzer Division*. *Panzer Lehr* from the south and the *9 Panzer Division*, finally thrown into the battle, desperately attempted to free the trapped German forces, with their forward elements four miles from the Meuse. But *9 Panzer* was delayed by our air attacks, which had been in increasing frequency since December 23, when the weather turned good, and a lack of sufficient gasoline, also a direct result of the disrupting air attacks further to the rear. Of the other German reserves counted on by Manteuffel, *3 Panzer Grenadier* was diverted to the Elsenborn Ridge fight, and *15 Panzer Grenadier* was pitched into the fight for Bastogne. Huge quantities of German equipment were captured in the *2 Panzer Division* trap. An entire German regiment was destroyed on Christmas day. This victory ended the immediate threat to the Meuse River line, and Manteuffel ordered remaining troops of *47 Panzer Corps* to pull back into defensive positions running from St. Hubert to Rochefort toward Marche. There, *Panzer Lehr Division*, supported by the remains of 2 *Panzer Division* and part of *9 Panzer Division*, dug in on December 26, pending further orders from Manteuffel concerning resumption of the attack. The race for the roads to the Meuse was ended. First Army had won by a nose, thanks to rapid movement of divisions from Ninth Army, but the opportunity to launch the hopefully planned counterattack was lost.

Back to the east, other German action was renewing the earlier threat to XVIII Airborne Corps. Away from the fluid, moving battle hard by the Meuse River, the XVIII Airborne Corps was engaged in another grim battle for existence which began on December 23 at the time the St. Vith horseshoe collapsed. This fight went on concurrently with the battle just

outlined with VII Corps one step ahead of the German formations racing to the Meuse. To set the stage we must go back
to December 21.

On the night of December 21, when St. Vith was lost, the
XVIII Airborne Corps front extended some eighty miles from
Malmedy to Marche and on toward the Meuse. Although
Kampfgruppe Peiper had been bottled in the Ambleve River
sack, our intelligence officers at First Army were gravely worried about future German moves because as yet *2 SS Panzer
Corps* with two fresh panzer divisions was still unaccounted
for. And, in addition, other German reserves, including the
then unidentified *9 Panzer* and *15 Panzer Grenadier Divisions,
10 SS* and *11 Panzer Division* (neither of which ever entered
the Ardennes fighting), were still capable of entering the fray.
Colonel Dickson, First Army Intelligence Officer, believed
that the Germans were after Liége, and he, therefore, predicted that they would attack through the 30th Division to get
on the good road net leading north to Liége from Stavelot and
Malmedy. And on December 22, *9 SS Panzer Division* stuck its
nose into the German salient between Malmedy and St. Vith
and was identified and suspected of being readied for the attack to the north. Hodges rushed reinforcements behind the
30th Division and piled them up until the division had with it
an extra combat command of armor, two battalions of 90-mm.
guns for antitank defense, an extra battalion of tanks, six battalions of infantry, and four nondivisional battalions of artillery. Dickson's worries were compounded on December 21
when Skorzeny's *150 Panzer Brigade* launched an attack on
Malmedy. Skorzeny's "Trojan Horse" was assembled in the
rear when it became apparent that the *1 SS Panzer Division*
was not succeeding in its efforts to break through to the Meuse
River, and then the *Brigade* was given a sector in the forming
defense line built up by *1 SS Panzer Corps* south of the Ambleve River. This one probing attack was made on December
21. A number of Germans in American uniforms were captured and later shot. Skorzeny was unsuccessful in breaking
through into Malmedy, and after a hard day's fight, he retired
to a defensive position south of the town, where he remained
until relieved from the line on December 29. He then returned
to Germany, and the unit disbanded. Such was the ordinary
ending of the "Trojan Horse."

But Colonel Dickson's estimate failed to match German
plans. Their plan for *Sixth Panzer Army,* following failure of
1 SS Panzer Division to break out of the Ambleve River valley

and *12 SS Panzer Division* even to get started across the Elsenborn ridge, was again to open a war of movement by using
2 SS Panzer Corps to break open a new hole in the Allied lines.
With this in mind, *9 SS Panzer Division* was to attempt a
crossing of the Salm River between Trois Ponts and Vielsalm,
through the 82d Airborne Division. The *2 SS Panzer Division*
meanwhile had circled far south of the St. Vith horseshoe and
was identified as far south as Bastogne. This division was first
slated for use by Manteuffel, but instead returned to Dietrich,
who was to use it to strike north generally parallel to the
Bastogne-Liége road at the underbelly of the XVIII Airborne
Corps defense. Both of these panzer divisions were destined to
hit the 82d Airborne Division.

After carefully weighing the alternatives, Model ordered the
Sixth Panzer Army to attack in an attempt to open a hole,
rather than to move all the way around to the west to follow
Fifth Panzer Army's loose panzers near the Meuse River. But
the downfall of the St. Vith horseshoe necessitated complete
reorientation of *Sixth Panzer Army*, which was badly mixed
up with *Fifth Panzer Army's* victorious conquerors of St. Vith.
Five divisions and a brigade, representing two armies and three
corps, were mixed together in a small area with poor roads,
immediately following reduction of the St. Vith salient. At first,
Dietrich planned to drive his panzers through a hole to be
opened by Manteuffel's *Fuehrer Escort Brigade*, to capture
Werbomont from the south, and then, again, swing northwest
toward the Meuse River, but this plan was abandoned when
Manteuffel ordered the *Brigade* back into the *Fifth Panzer
Army* area in another attempt to capture Hotton.

When Remer left, Dietrich's boundary, formerly at the Bastogne-Liége road, was extended to the Ourthe River, and he
inherited the *560 Volksgrenadier Division*, which with the *116
Panzer Division* had made the initial attempt to crack through
the 3d Armored Division. The *18* and *62 Volksgrenadier Divisions*, conquerors of St. Vith, were placed in an assembly area
preparatory for their next mission, as yet undetermined. The
revised *Sixth Panzer Army* plan of attack now contemplated
a concentrated attack by *2 SS Panzer Division* to Manhay, and
then to turn northwest toward Hotton (the Ourthe River crossing which first *116 Panzer* and then *Fuehrer Escort Brigade*
had tried for, and Durbuy, another Ourthe River crossing
point, a little north of Hotton. The division mission was to
open a hole and plunge through before the First Army line to
the west had completely formed. Then, remaining elements of

1 and *12 SS Panzer Divisions,* both badly chewed up by earlier fighting, and the fresh *9 SS Panzer Division* were to follow once the break-through had been made. Again *Volksgrenadier* divisions would cover the flanks, and *66 Corps* with the *18* and *62 Volksgrenadier Divisions* was to be available to Dietrich, if a hole were opened.

As *2 SS Panzer Division* swung south around the St. Vith salient toward the 82d Airborne Division lines, it was subjected to severe artillery fire, by the small task forces of the 7th Armored Division, which observed long tank columns streaming by just to its south, and then, by the 82d Airborne Division, as the Germans approached its southern flank on December 22. Key to the southern defenses of XVIII Airborne Corps was the Bastogne-Liége highway with two vital road junctions, one at Manhay seven miles south of Werbomont and the second, an unpopulated crossroads, subsequently named Parker's Crossroads for the commanding defender of the position. The Bastogne-Liege road marked the dividing line between the 3d Armored Division and the 82d Airborne Division, and because of the head-on collision in which the 3d Armored had been involved, the junction was never thoroughly cemented. Parker's Crossroads was defended by an organization consisting of a reconnaissance company from the 7th Armored Division, an artillery company from the 106th Division, some tanks from the 3d Armored Division, a parachute company from the 82d Airborne Division, and stragglers from numerous other organizations. This strange crew had been under attack since December 21 by the *560 Volksgrenadier Division,* joined on December 23 by *2 SS Panzer Division,* which simply overwhelmed the few defenders. At the same time, Remer's *Fuehrer Escort Brigade* drove the 82d Airborne Division back out of a town just to the east of the crossroads. This was Remer's last act before leaving for Hotton. These attacks posed a new threat for the already harassed XVIII Airborne Corps which, even though relieved of part of its sector by VII Corps on its west, was still opposed by considerable German force.

First Army intelligence officer's preoccupation with the threat through the 30th Division led to a concentration of reserves behind that division and left XVIII Airborne Corps with little help to meet this new threat along the Bastogne-Liége road. Only the 7th Armored Division and attached units, still pouring out of the St. Vith salient on the night of December 23, were available to XVIII Airborne Corps. These units were completely disorganized, tired, low in men and equipment, demoralized, and without information of their own strength—no reports had been received during the seven days of the horseshoe siege. Despite this, the 7th Armored Division was ordered to prepare immediately a fighting force to take over a very narrow sector between the 82d Airborne Division and the 3d Armored Division and, specifically, to defend the crossroads center of Manhay.

The first units were in place late in the afternoon of December 24, but in the meantime, the German *2 SS Panzer Division* had pressed north from Parker's Crossroads and was punching at the 82d Airborne Division in conjunction with *9 SS Panzer Division,* which made numerous attempts to cross the Salm River to cut through the 82d Airborne Division lines from the east. Although the 82d Airborne Division occupied good defensive positions along most of its line, its front extended some eighteen miles. Known to be punching at it were the *2* and *9 SS Panzer Divisions,* from south and east, respectively, and part of *560 Volksgrenadier Division.* More alarming was the commanders' suspicion that the *1* and *12 SS Panzer Divisions* were moving to the west toward XVIII Airborne Corps. In addition, *10 SS Panzer* and *11 Panzer Divisions* were both headed for the Ardennes, according to our intelligence, and were probables for the new attack which seemed to be forming. Also the *Fuehrer Escort Brigade, 9 Panzer* and *3* and *15 Panzer Grenadier Divisions* as yet unidentified, were possible additions to the enemy attack against 82d Airborne Division.

Despite the great importance of the road from Vielsalm to Parker's Crossroads and then to Laroche, Montgomery again took over, when tired Hodges hesitated, and ordered withdrawal of the 82d Airborne Division to a series of low hills running between Manhay and Trois Ponts. Hodges subsequently concurred in the order. This withdrawal straightened out the line of First Army and drastically reduced possibility of the Germans turning the flank of the 82d Airborne Division, and thus opening a new hole through which the panzers could start again.

Withdrawal of the 82d Airborne Division caused much criticism, as we shall discuss later, but in the light of the information available, it was absolutely sound as a military expedient. Subsequent events will show that the Germans might well have turned the flank were it not for this withdrawal, because on Christmas Eve they launched their vigorous attack along the

axis of the Bastogne-Liége road toward Manhay, straight into
the new line of the shaky 7th Armored Division. What followed was a tragedy of errors by the Allies. Because 82d
Airborne Division was straightening its line, the 7th Armored
Division was ordered to withdraw to positions north of Manhay, and the 3d Armored Division's left flank was to pull
back through the 7th Armored Division and tie in with the
new line just west of Manhay. In addition, CCB of the 9th
Armored Division, temporarily with the 82d Airborne Division, was also to pull back. In the midst of this confusion, the
Germans attacked the 7th Armored Division astride the Bastogne-Liége road. The leading German tank was an American
Sherman, and the Americans thought the column was from
the 3d Armored Division.

Before the Americans could realize what had happened to
them, their forward company was completely wiped out.
A second company of tanks and infantry befell the same fate.
The Germans burst into Manhay, where CCB of the 9th Armored Division was just passing through, and the result was
complete bedlam. Already discouraged, weakened, and tired,
the 7th Armored Division troops broke, and turned north.
The Germans once again had a hole, but as they turned to the
west, and then north, they were temporarily stopped by parts
of the 3d Armored Division and a regiment of the 75th Division, also diverted from its attack role to one of fighting to
maintain the line. Three days of hard fighting ensued as
Hodges rushed troops to seal the break, fearful of the reinforcements which the Germans might throw into the battle.
With first a thin straggler line, then a small attack force, and
finally a co-ordinated attack on Manhay, and its twin town of
Grandmenil, the break was restored by December 26. The
First Army line was again intact. Thus the fourth great German threat to Hodges was frustrated. This was the last German
offensive activity in the north. To trace the further battles,
we must shift our attention to the southern portion of the battlefront. But the First Army attempt to plug the gap had been
converted to a struggle for survival, as every division sent to
First Army in a counterattacking role—first 3d Armored, then
84th, 2d Armored, and, finally the 75th—was forced into
defensive fighting to prevent a new German breakout.

BASTOGNE

To the average American, Bastogne epitomizes the Battle
of the Bulge. The heroic defense of this town, when it was

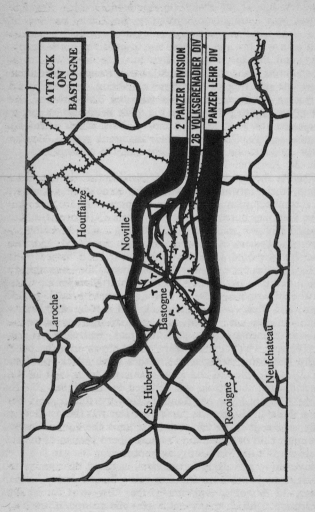

ATTACK ON BASTOGNE

2 PANZER DIVISION
26 VOLKSGRENADIER DIV
PANZER LEHR DIV

Houffalize

Noville

Laroche

Bastogne

St. Hubert

Recoigne

Neufchateau

completely surrounded by German forces, was perhaps the most spectacular event in European fighting. Line after line of newsprint came home to tell of the bravery of our boys at Bastogne. Perhaps it was because most of the picture looked so black that this ray of light was pounced upon for copy. Article after article, and book after book, has since been written.* No one has evaluated the defense of Bastogne in relation to the overall struggle. Far from detracting from the stand of the men at Bastogne, an evaluation of its relation to the rest of the fighting front serves to give Bastogne its proper perspective, to fit it into the total picture, which added up to defeat of the Germans in their last great gamble. But the Battle of the Bulge was not fought solely in Bastogne.

Alerted with the 82d Airborne Division late on December 17, the 101st Airborne Division, also near Rheims, France, was still licking its wounds from the parachute drop at Arnhem, from which it had been relieved in mid-November. Because it was less advanced in its re-equipment and reorganization than the 82d Airborne Division, the 101st Airborne Division moved out second, and, by this quirk of fate, it went to Bastogne rather than the 82d Airborne. We have already seen how the 82d Airborne Division was diverted en route to Werbomont, where General Hodges feared greatly the advances of *Kampfgruppe Peiper*. But the 101st went on to Bastogne, although not without some confusion caused by the change of direction of the 82d Airborne, and by late evening of December 19 the entire division had been assembled around Bastogne. Also descending on Bastogne were CCB of the 10th Armored Division, shifted to Bastogne while the rest of the division went to help the 4th Division at the southern hinge of the fighting, the 705th Tank Destroyer Battalion, and the remaining part of CCR of the 9th Armored Division, most of which was lost in the initial German attacks. Simultaneously descending on the town were a number of Germans, anxious to seize the town before it was occupied.

Manteuffel's *47 Panzer Corps* was assigned the mission to break through the 28th Division line with *2 Panzer, Panzer Lehr,* and *26 Volksgrenadier Divisions,* then to strike rapidly for Bastogne, which they were to seize and occupy, if possible, before American reinforcements arrived. The panzers were to continue on toward the Meuse as rapidly as they could go.

* For the best account see *Bastogne: The First Eight Days,* Col. S. L. A. Marshall, Infantry Journal Press, 1946.

We have already noted how the hole was punctured through the 28th Division; by December 18 only isolated spots of resistance appeared to hold up the panzers, and the 28th Division headquarters at Wiltz had communication with only one of its regiments. The situation was obscure, to say the least, and only stories of stragglers and small bands of beaten men relayed information about the Germans who seemed to be advancing on all sides. A futile, but valiant and important struggle was put up against the German tide at Wiltz by VIII Corps Engineers, some of the 28th Division troops, and a few tanks from CCR of the 9th Armored Division. But this force was rapidly overwhelmed, and most of the defenders either killed or captured. Only eighty-one of about 600 engineers returned. Their fight had not been in vain because every minute gave the prospective defenders of Bastogne precious time to place themselves, and to organize for the long struggle ahead.

The first troops of the 101st Airborne Division began closing into Bastogne late on December 18. The command situation was extremely confused; General Middleton experienced much difficulty in getting decisions from higher headquarters, probably because of the rapid changes in the situation. Middleton still remained in Bastogne, although his corps headquarters had been removed from there to Neufchateau. He was unaware, until after dark on the 18th when General Gavin arrived with instructions from Hodges, that the 101st Airborne Division was to be assigned to him instead of XVIII Airborne Corps. Middleton had no orders to hold Bastogne, and on December 19, General Patton's preparations to take over the southern half of the penetration did not include Bastogne. However, Middleton was strongly convinced of the ultimate necessity of keeping this road center, and as he was unable to reach First Army, he talked to General Bradley, who assented to the plan to establish a defense there. "They'll be surrounded unless they get help," Middleton told Bradley. "OK," said Bradley. The defense was on.

Bastogne, Belgium, center of an important road net is a town of only several thousand population. Like St. Vith, the town was not a defensive strongpoint, but a series of low, rolling hills around the town offered a number of excellent positions from which the town could be protected. Although forests covered the hills, there were considerable open areas, later to play a vital role in receiving the airborne supplies dropped to the besieged defenders. More important, seven road spokes radiated from Bastogne making it the hub of the southern Ardennes road net.

Bastogne was quiet on the night of December 18 because scattered remnants of the 28th Division were fighting at Wiltz, and small and ineffective road blocks of CCR of the 9th Armored Division temporarily slowed German advances on several roads. First to arrive on the scene was CCB of the 10th Armored Division, late on December 18. Three combat teams were immediately dispatched north, east, and southeast of Bastogne by Middleton with instructions to "hold these positions at all costs." To the east, one team discovered a demoralized segment of CCR of the 9th Armored Division, troops of which reported large numbers of German tanks behind them. These German troops were in fact the advance elements of *2 Panzer Division,* approaching Bastogne from the north.

The old German cavalryman, Luttwitz, commander of *47 Panzer Corps,* planned to strike with *2 Panzer Division* running north of Bastogne, *Panzer Lehr Division* to the south of the town, and the *26 Volksgrenadier Division* following, to occupy the town, if the panzers captured it in a quick coup, or capture it by siege if necessary. By the night of December 18, all three divisions were passing through the last resistance of the remaining VIII Corps troops, which had been overrun in the initial assault, and were ready for the lunge toward Bastogne. Luttwitz knew that timing was the essence of success—he had intercepted American military police instructions alerting traffic posts for the convoys which were to move the airborne divisions from the vicinity of Rheims. Luttwitz on that night of December 18 made one more appeal for permission to envelop Bastogne with his entire corps, despite all previous orders from Hitler, Jodl, Keitel, Rundstedt, and Model, to keep the panzers rolling to the Meuse, leaving areas of resistance to the following infantry. Again, Manteuffel turned down the pleas, despite the report that the Americans were closing toward Bastogne in force. Luttwitz was given permission only to engage in a limited attack, and to attempt to find a way of getting into Bastogne through a weak spot.

The cautious tentacles of the defenders of Bastogne were inched out of the town during the night of December 18 and on the nineteenth it was inevitable that these tentacles would intertwine with the German fingers pushing forward from Luttwitz's panzer corps. Some of the tentacles were chopped off, most important of these being one combat team of CCB, 10th Armored Division, which moved due east to meet a portion of CCR, 9th Armored Division, at the hamlet of Longvilly, seven miles east of Bastogne. A more southerly finger of the German probers poked in behind these American forces, and established a road block between them and Bastogne. But by a turn of fate, all three of Luttwitz's approaching divisions were concerned with this isolated, but powerful American armor-infantry team, and all three divisions devoted a part of December 19 to destroying this chopped off tentacle. Again precious hours were given the defenders of Bastogne to close in and establish their defenses.

By December 20 the defenders of Bastogne were firmly established. The engineer battalions originally established around the town, pending arrival of other troops, had performed their mission and were withdrawn. General Middleton had left to rejoin his corps. When the last stragglers drifting into town from the shattered lines to the east were tabulated, approximately 18,000 troops were in Bastogne, including artillery, engineers, tankers, and all the troops of the 101st Airborne Division. On the twentieth, three German divisions, totaling probably 45,000 men, attacked toward Bastogne from three sides. To the north, 2 Panzer Division captured the road junction of Noville, opening the route to the west. Actually, American withdrawal from Noville was forced more by attacks of 26 Volksgrenadier Division from the east which threatened to isolate the Noville garrison, but 2 Panzer Division interpreted the withdrawal as a grave weakness, and requested permission to follow the Americans toward Bastogne. Again the request to attack Bastogne directly with panzers was vetoed, and 2 Panzer Division moved on to the west, was later held up by one more road block formed to the northwest of Bastogne by defenders, and then passed off the stage at Bastogne as they struck for the Meuse River at Dinant. We have already seen how, with success nearly in its grasp, 2 Panzer Division was suddenly hit by the 2d Armored Division just moving into position with VII Corps, and by the British Household Cavalry Regiment, guarding the vital approaches to the Meuse River bridges at Dinant.

Meanwhile, back at Bastogne on December 20, Panzer Lehr and 26 Volksgrenadier Division battered at Bastogne from the east, and began to slip around to the south—by nightfall, the town was nearly surrounded. But despite heavy action, the Germans were unable to pierce the forming defensive ring completely. December 21 and 22 were days of sparring as the opposing forces felt each other out. The Germans continued to flow around Bastogne on all sides, and by morning of December 21 the town was surrounded. The night before, Brigadier General Anthony C. McAuliffe, normally artillery commander of the 101st Airborne Division, but acting divisional commander in the absence of Major General Maxwell D. Taylor, who was in Washington, held his last conversation with Middleton, who was by then at Neufchateau. Middleton jokingly said, "Now don't get yourself surrounded," and authorized McAuliffe to take the necessary steps to hold the road center. It was apparent to both that soon McAuliffe would be on his own in a besieged city, with no chance of immediate relief. By night of the twenty-first, McAuliffe was charged with command of all troops in the ring, and the siege was on.

There are rumors that the now famous American reply to the German ultimatum to surrender, delivered through four emissaries who came into the American lines on the morning of December 22, might have been the famous French answer given to the Duke of Wellington at the Battle of Waterloo, when the French, in utter contempt, sent back the crisply worded note *"merde"* to Wellington's ultimatum. Perhaps this is a piece of the folklore which has grown up around the American defense of Bastogne, or perhaps the censors changed the message to "nuts." In either event, the meaning was immediately clear to General-Lieutenant Bayerlein, colorful commander of the *Panzer Lehr Division*. Bayerlein and Luttwitz, in violation of strict orders from Manteuffel, had drafted an ultimatum to the American defenders in one last attempt to win the strongpoint effortlessly. Bayerlein and Luttwitz, both showmen with a flair for the dramatic, arrogant to the last, anxious to add this great feather to their collective cap, chanced the surrender message in the hope that McAuliffe and his defending troops would accept honorable capitulation. The puzzling, but nonetheless vehement, reply convinced the Germans that they would not win Bastogne without a struggle.

With their last hopes for a quick capture of the Bastogne garrison blasted by the American answer, Luttwitz had no alternative but to order Bayerlein's *Panzer Lehr Division* on to the west, leaving reduction of Bastogne to *26 Volksgrenadier Division*, assisted by one of Bayerlein's regiments left behind to help. This shift left the opposing forces about equal in strength. Bayerlein rapidly slid off to the west after circling south of Bastogne, slashed his way through isolated American troops, on to St. Hubert, and then northwest to Rochefort, from where he was to strike toward the Meuse River in conspiracy with *2 Panzer Division*. Bayerlein's roughriders were just slightly beyond Rochefort when he was notified of the sack in which *2 Panzer Division* was trapped. He was ordered to strike north to relieve his running mate, but too late. Before he could come to the relief of his companion division, Bayerlein bumped up against the formations of VII Corps swinging into operation. Soon he stoically received the sad news that most of *2 Panzer Division* was lost; Bayerlein immediately was instructed to assume a defensive position, pending arrival of reinforcements to continue the offensive. Another element played against Bayerlein at this time: the weather cleared, and Allied fighter-bombers began to harass his columns. Having lost nearly an entire division in Normandy to the fighter-bombers, Bayerlein had a healthy respect for their powers; he sadly decided that the offensive was ended.

Back at Bastogne, meanwhile, the siege continued through the 26th, when a relieving column of the 4th Armored Division drove into the town. Hitler, furious at his inability to take Bastogne, sent his personal aide, Major Johann-Mayer, to assess the true status of the siege. Luttwitz told Johann-Mayer that he was unable to reduce the town with the troops then available to him. Hitler, finally convinced by Johann-Mayer that an effort had in fact been made, but unsuccessfully, reluctantly ordered part of his reserve, *15 Panzer Grenadier Division*, to join in the fight on Christmas Eve. Small elements of *560 Volksgrenadier Division*, whose main body was far to the north fighting 3d Armored Division, were also thrown against Bastogne. But they arrived too late. Good flying weather beginning on December 23 allowed resupply of the depleted Allied garrison by air. In the three days before relief of the besieged garrison, 889 planes and gliders were sent over Bastogne plummeting to earth food, ammunition, desperately needed medical supplies, and gasoline to the embattled defenders. On one day, December 24, over one hundred tons of supplies were dropped into the defending lines. Of vital importance were the few medical supplies which were received; the 101st Airborne Division hospital had been captured by Germans in the first hectic days of the assembly when it had bivouacked in a field coveted by the Germans.

"The finest Christmas present the 101st could get," McAuliffe told Middleton, "would be a relief tomorrow." Unable to win on the ground, the German air force nightly pounded

Bastogne. With supplies still critically low despite resupply, with the wounded in bad shape because of the shortage of medical supplies and blankets, with troops depleted by continuous German attacks, McAuliffe was by no odds the confident general he has been painted by correspondents. When the relief failed, and German attacks continued, McAuliffe told Middleton that his troops were let down. But Patton's III Corps, since December 22 had been battering against the German *Seventh Army* to crack through to Bastogne, and in a sudden spurt late in the afternoon of December 26, one combat command of the 4th Armored Division dashed through the thinning German lines and into Bastogne where they were received with much rejoicing. The siege was ended—but the worst fighting and heaviest losses were yet to come in the days ahead.

The defenders of Bastogne carved their niche in the annals of American military exploits. In the midst of defeat and uncertainty, they held their ground, a solid rock in a German sea. The defense was epic, spectacular, but viewed in the light of the entire picture, it assumes proper perspective—an important defeat for the Germans, but not the only one in the Battle of the Bulge. The controversy concerning relative merits of the defense of St. Vith and Bastogne has since raged long and hot. Even within German ranks opinion is sharply divided. Jodl, Hitler's chief advisor in the fighting, said that Bastogne was not so important at first, but only later "as the big pocket behind our rear when you were attacking." Goering says that Bastogne was the keystone of the entire attack. Jodl, in rebuttal, pointed out that Bastogne could be by-passed while St. Vith could not. Luttwitz, the corps commander, said that if the Germans had seized Bastogne on December 18, *2 Panzer* and *Panzer Lehr Divisions* would have reached the Meuse River on December 22, and Patton would then have been forced to attack not only those divisions, but also *9 Panzer* and *3* and *15 Panzer Grenadier Divisions,* west of the Meuse.

Hitler himself personally ordered Model to forget about Bastogne, once we occupied it, and get on with their work. But the important fact about both defenses, Bastogne and St. Vith, was the physical accomplishment of occupation. The Germans wanted both without a fight and got neither. These two setbacks threw off the German timetable sufficiently to allow us time to rally our forces, regroup, and attack. Without these defenses the Germans might well have met their schedule. This was the important issue, not the relative merits of the two epic stands. Bastogne should be considered in this light.

THE SOUTHERN FLANK—THIRD ARMY ATTACKS

Like its opposite number to the north, the 4th Division, although pushed back by advances of the German *Seventh Army,* managed to hold against the tide. Brandenberger's four divisions crossing the Our River between Vianden and Echternach had been assigned the mission of fanning out to the south and west to establish a defensive line, extending roughly due west from Echternach, to protect the exposed flank of *Fifth Panzer Army.* At no time was it planned to shove this defensive line as far south as Luxembourg City; in fact, Brandenberger made strong representations to Model that the forces allotted him were even insufficient to carry out the defensive mission assigned.

German attacks across the Our River soon punched a large hole in the 28th Division, as we have previously observed. Shoved aside in the rush was the southern regiment of the division, the 109th Infantry. The 109th Infantry, along with CCA of the 9th Armored Division, fell back on the 4th Division, as that division pulled in its northern flank and reeled back to the south under German pressure. However, a good portion of the force of *Seventh Army* was diverted to the west as *5 Parachute Division* attempted to keep pace with the panzers in Manteuffel's army. The *352 Volksgrenadier Division* broke across the Our River and then attempted to close in just to the east of *5 Parachute Division.* The remaining two divisions, *276* and *212 Volksgrenadier,* pressed against the 4th Division, already reinforced by 10th Armored Division. Arrival of the 5th Division and assumption of command of the 4th Division zone by Patton's XII Corps on December 22 further increased Allied defensive power of this southern hinge, giving them two infantry divisions, the equivalent of an armored division (parts of both 9th and 10th Armored Divisions) and an extra infantry regiment, the 109th. This force was strong enough to hold the southern fringe against further German attacks, despite the heavy German pressure all along the line. A solid southern hinge, thus, had been formed, on which a new line could be anchored.

Meanwhile, to the west of the bent 4th Division line only small engineer units were available to halt the German onthrust in the first days of the attack. The *5 Parachute Division* shot through the thin Allied defenses and stretched its advance forces as far south as Martelange on the main Bastogne-Arlon road. There, the Germans mined the bridges and assumed a defensive position, the only point where Brandenberger was able to reach his designated defensive line. However, *5 Parachute Division* had outstripped its running mates, and Brandenberger was only able to fill in his defensive line by acquisition of the *Fuehrer Grenadier Brigade*, the second of the two élite brigades released by Hitler to Rundstedt at the last moment.

This *Brigade*, which further confused our intelligence officers because of its similarity to Remer's *Fuehrer Escort Brigade*, was also a powerful unit, but failed to match the striking power of Remer's favored unit. Both *Brigades*, however, further perplexed our intelligence men who were trying to figure out how the *Grossdeutschland Division*, from whom these units derived their replacements, had so rapidly moved from the Russian front.

Between the Bastogne-Arlon road and the Meuse River, some forty miles, the American defenses were practically nonexistent. Middleton's VIII Corps assumed command of this sector on December 20, when it moved to Neufchateau, but between December 20 and 25, Middleton had available to him for this long front only one provisional reconnaissance squadron, a French battalion, a tank destroyer group with one battalion of guns, and remnants of the 28th Division, amounting to only a handful of men from the 110th Infantry and some of the attached divisional units. Middleton's capability of defending during the period December 20-25, in case the enemy had broken through at Bastogne, was nil. But fortunately, the Germans did not turn south, and we have already seen how the two panzer divisions which did sweep around Bastogne, turned to the north, and subsequently were stopped by VII Corps units in First Army. Such was the situation as Patton's Third Army assumed responsibility for the southern flank of the German break-through on December 20 when the battlefield was split by Eisenhower.

General Patton's orders were to take six divisions in two corps, shift them to the north as rapidly as possible, attack as soon as ready with III Corps toward Bastogne and St. Vith, and prepare XII Corps to strike through the 4th Division lines toward Bonn. These were ambitious plans, and Patton emphasized his lack of understanding of German strength by setting an impossible target date of December 26 for arrival in St. Vith—not in Bastogne, but St. Vith. Patton's troops executed an amazing withdrawal from their front along the Saar

River, and in an unbelievably short time had turned the front
over to the new units, had prepared a logistical plan for the
movement of thousands of troops, and had begun the harrowing road march to the Ardennes forests to the north. Much of
the troop movement was accomplished at night, over unfamiliar roads and unknown conditions. Despite some German aerial
opposition and some bad road bottlenecks, Patton's armies
moved swiftly; the 4th Armored Division covered the 100-odd
miles to its new assembly area in less than 24 hours and the
80th Division in about the same time, remarkable in the face
of the many obstacles and uncertainties which confronted them
as they suddenly were diverted from their offensive mission.
Now facing North on December 22, Patton's first attack, with
III Corps, was launched seventeen miles from Bastogne. The
three divisions in III Corps, 26th, 80th and 4th Armored, immediately banged into the *Seventh Army* defenders, who were
facing south waiting for Patton.

In the stiff fighting through the hills and forests, slow but
steady progress was made. It was a straight slugging match,
with few decent roads, excellent defensive positions from which
the Germans could defend, and, consequently, with little room
for the Allies to maneuver. During all this time *Fifth Panzer
Army,* still driving westward, went about its business with
scarcely more than a glance at Patton, depending on Brandenberger's *Seventh Army* to hold back the tide. However, on the
fifth day of the attack, 4th Armored Division executed a run
to the west around the end of Brandenberger's defenses and
sent part of a combat command charging up the Neufchateau-
Bastogne road into Bastogne. This attack broke through the
5 Parachute Division, actually to catch part of *26 Volksgrenadier Division,* still attacking Bastogne, in the rear.

Now for the first time, the Germans became perturbed about
the Patton attacks, and Hitler authorized release of two additional divisions, *9* and *167 Volksgrenadier,* which were rushed
to the Brandenberger front in an attempt to stem the tide. This
was not until December 26.

Meanwhile, east of Bastogne, XII Corps closed up to the
Sure and Sauer Rivers in a series of local counterattacks which
drove the Germans back slightly, but on orders from General
Bradley the main effort was shifted to the Bastogne salient
where, despite greater distance from the base of the German
salient, he decided to concentrate his greatest striking power.
Thus, Patton abandoned his order to strike toward Bonn.

In seven days, Third Army completed its ninety degree

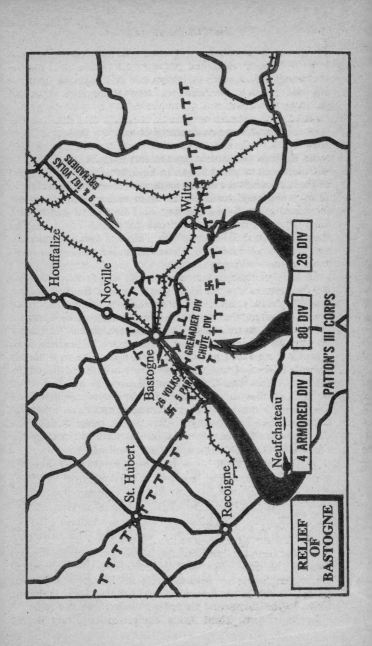

pivot, assembled two corps along the south flank of the German penetration, straightened out the line to the east, and drove a wedge through the *Seventh Army* into Bastogne itself. Patton was ready for the next great step—elimination of the entire Bulge.

THE MEUSE RIVER LINE

In the uncertain days between December 18, when the extent of the German attack began to be fully appreciated, and December 26, when the major crisis ended, almost anything could have happened—and did, for that matter. While Eisenhower hoped and believed that he would be able to stem the German advance, he was not prone to risk all by taking chances, and he early began to concern himself with protection of the Meuse River line itself. However, unlike the French in 1940, he was not willing to leave the Ardennes forests virtually undefended while he concentrated on the Meuse River line.

Late on December 19, Eisenhower warned Bradley and General J. C. H. Lee, Chief of the Service Forces in the European Theater, that under no circumstances were the Meuse River bridges to fall intact into enemy hands. "Protect them with service organizations if necessary," Eisenhower directed. But even before receiving orders to take over the northern half of the Bulge, Montgomery had directed British troops toward the Meuse should the Germans break through to the river, as they so very nearly did. On the twentieth, the British assumed control of the river bridges from Givet north, and Bradley from there south. The major strength of the Meuse River line was concentrated on the north in the direction toward which the Germans seemed pointing. From Givet to Liége, the British XXX Corps took over with two divisions, an armored brigade, and an armored cavalry regiment which screened east of the river. South of Givet to Verdun only weak forces were installed, with four engineer general service regiments, a field artillery battalion, and six French light infantry battalions with almost no equipment or training. These latter were called up at the insistence of General DeGaulle, who vividly recalled the specter of 1940. Later, the 11th Armored Division, followed by the 17th Airborne Division, and finally the 87th Division, were all at one time or other placed under VIII Corps control, but with strings prohibiting their use without Eisenhower's approval. These latter divisions were the

SHAEF reserve which had been lacking at the start of the breakthrough.

In addition to a corps along the Meuse River, Montgomery assigned part of his British troops to take the place of the four Ninth Army units shunted to the penetration area, and one British division was given to Hodges and placed just to the south of Liége, prepared to meet any German breakthrough which might occur. But the British, with limited resources, were already spread thin in their sector to the north. These were the dispositions on December 26 when the great crisis came to an end.

CHAPTER VI

The Dying Gasp (Dec. 26-Jan. 16)

THE CRISIS IS ENDED

It was a dark December for the Allied world as the great, moving drama unfolded in the Ardennes in the nine days of crisis following initial German penetrations. German colums appeared to be everywhere, heading in all directions. Sometimes, even intelligence officers, trying to post their maps showing German dispositions, threw up their hands, frankly confounded. They were days of great opportunity and great trial for the Allies.

And there is no doubt that the German plan, bold and daringly executed, might have made far greater gains—with a few extra breaks. That the Germans were stopped must be attributed to a multitude of small, but important events, many of which have been summarized here: those of Elsenborn, the Ambleve River, St. Vith, Bastogne, Marche, the south flank, and those which occurred in the shadow of the Meuse River. A brief recapitulation may serve to tie the story together.

The German *Sixth Panzer Army* to the north began meeting with setbacks on the first day when its northern panzer division was unable to crash through onto the Elsenborn Ridge. Its southern panzer division nearly broke into the open, only to end in disaster when it was trapped along the Ambleve River. Meanwhile, to the south *Fifth Panzer Army's* northern panzer corps barreled along until it reached the Ourthe River on December 21, to be finally blocked by the first of the new

First Army divisions being rushed to the east to counterattack the Germans. The southern panzer corps swept around Bastogne, after a disappointing race for the town, and one division went on to the Meuse River. It ate up more mileage than any other German division before it was hit by two more First Army divisions being rushed to the western flank. During this same time, Manteuffel's infantry corps captured St. Vith after an agonizing delay of six days. A sudden change in plans saw the *Sixth Panzer Army* shift far to the west in an attempt to open a new hole beginning December 23, when the last of the St. Vith salient was liquidated. But the German attack came too late. The small hole which had been punched was sealed. The German offensive capabilities seemed at an end.

Rundstedt now claims that by December 24, he knew he could not reach the Meuse, and that he so advised his *Fuehrer*, suggesting that the Germans go on the defensive, only to be refused by Hitler. Heinz Guderian, former Chief of Staff of the Army, told Hitler on Christmas Eve that the attack had failed and pleaded with Hitler to suspend the attack, and to give the reserves to the Eastern Front. Guderian said: "Hitler was born on the frontier of Austria and Bavaria. I am a Prussian; I was born on the Vistula. We Prussians have had to fight the eastern people for 700 years. For those of us from Prussia, it was a question of holding ground which was German since the time when America was peopled by the red men." Despite these eloquent pleas Hitler threw more reserves into the fight. On December 23, *9 Panzer* and *3* and *15 Panzer* Grenadier Divisions were released to Rundstedt. Previously, both *Fuehrer Brigades* had been turned over to the Western Front. On the twenty-sixth, the *9* and *167 Volksgrenadier Divisions* were released to Brandenberger. And *10 SS* and *11 Panzer Divisions* were released from fighting north and south of the Bulge, respectively, ordered to be immediately re-fitted, and then thrown into the fight. One division, *10 SS*, actually went into the Bulge, but arrived after the crisis had passed and was shunted south without being committed. The other, *11 Panzer*, went to Bitburg for refitting, but was delayed so long that it, too, was shunted back to the south.

Despite the complete surprise and partial success of "Operation Confusion," the Germans were unable to exploit the initial breakthrough completely. On the north flank, paratroopers were completely ineffective. Skorzeny's "Trojan Horse" did not have a chance to really gallop. And the huge tanks, which Hitler hoped would block the northern roads in the Bulge,

failed to arrive because of Allied air attacks and the weakened condition of the bridges. Early, the Germans ran into
supply trouble, partly because of the original *Wacht Am
Rhein* order which kept supplies east of the Rhine, partly because of Allied air raids which began December 23. Further
complications resulted from communication difficulties, stem-
ming from air raids which fatally affected the German telephone net in the Eifel.

Meanwhile, the Allies successfully carried out some of the
most herculean troop movements in the history of warfare. The
First Army, in the first week of the attack alone, moved 248,-
000 troops and 48,711 vehicles; the peak day was December
17, when 60,000 men were shunted into the penetration in
11,000 vehicles. These movements, which spelled disaster for
German plans, were far in excess of German estimates of our
capabilities. However, as a compensating factor, the Germans
quickly caught onto the trick of monitoring our traffic control
broadcasts to military police stations. Naturally, whenever vast
troop movements were involved, elaborate preparations and
reports were necessary. Although our security in many phases
of the battle was good, it broke down in reporting traffic
movements. The Germans were, consequently, able to determine our approximate strength (although not by division number) by monitoring these broadcasts, which were made in the
clear with no code. By simply noting the length of time it
took for a given unit to pass a given point, the Germans, with
logistics tables as accurate as ours, could early compute the
strength of the various units being moved into the Bulge. This
happened despite our security blackout, which withheld news
from home for forty-eight hours.

In addition to tremendous troop movements, ton upon ton
of supplies were moved in and out of the Bulge. Most spectacular of the moves was the removal of some 2,500,000 gallons of gasoline just north of Spa, with the loss of only 100,000
gallons poured down the road on the *1 SS Panzer Division* as
it attempted to strike north from Stavelot. We were fighting
a defensive war, however, and the troops lacked adequate supplies of mines and rockets and small arms ammunition. These
items were neglected in the huge supply movements prior to
the German attack, when we were preparing for our own
attack. The shortage of small arms ammunition became really
critical toward the end of December, with our increased ex-
penditures and losses; but the arrival of several shiploads direct
from the States eased the situation. Additional requirements

were placed on the supply system to replace 270 tanks lost by the First Army in the first weeks of fighting. By January 1, they were replaced, but only by scraping up all the tanks in repair shops, and by borrowing back a large number of tanks given to the British for use in Normandy.

On the night of December 21-22 the first snow blanketed all of the Ardennes forest. Problems of camouflage and winter equipment arose. Here, too, we were short. But winter also brought clear weather, and beginning December 23 our planes were out in force for the first time since the attack began, with a flight of over 2,000 planes. Between December 23 and 27, the Ninth Air Force alone, operating from bases on the continent, sent out an average of 447 planes a day, which also dropped a total daily average of 547.6 tons on German troops, vehicles, and lines of communication. Further to the rear of the German lines, big bombers from Eighth Air Force roared over to shatter roads, railroads, bridges and large concentrations. And from December 24, heavy attacks were made on German air fields to cut down air support of the German attack. However, the Germans averaged 600 sorties a day between December 23 and 26. This was by far the heaviest German air activity since Normandy. But even so, we did them one better. Our entire air force was thrown into the battle. Even the little cub reconnaissance planes used for liaison and artillery spotting were drafted to patrol the Meuse River and spot the roughriding Germans; much valuable information was relayed back to us by these courageous little grasshoppers.

HITLER HESITATES

A sick, tired, irrational, but stubborn man could not be convinced of the weakness of his position, as Hitler's aides found. Despite well laid plans, elaborate preparations, and complete surprise, the Germans rapidly and painfully discovered they were no longer the terror they had been in 1940. It did not take the German generals long to realize that their slim hopes for success had been shattered in the forests of the Ardennes, but Hitler was a diehard.

"After the July 20th attempt, Hitler was a sick man," Guderian summed it up. "Even before the assassination attempt, he had been very nervous, and not in complete possession of his faculties. His left side trembled. His mind was not clear enough to appreciate the real situation of Germany.

He was a man of energy and will; his will outweighed his sense. He hypnotized his entourage. He had a special picture of the world, and every fact had to fit in with that fancied picture. As he believed, so the world must be. But, in fact, it was a picture of another world."

Into the *Fuehrer's* headquarters at Berlin, a solemn delegation trooped on the day after Christmas. *"Mein Fuehrer,"* General Jodl, Chief of the Armed Forces Operations Staff, began, "we must face the facts squarely and openly; we cannot force the Meuse River." So began a review of the nine bitter days of fighting. Stopped at Elsenborn, slowed at St. Vith, trapped in the Ambleve River Valley, frustrated at Bastogne, too late to the Meuse, and now halted at Manhay, the big bulge lacked a *Schwerpunkt* (a goal). Faced with a unified attack from the south, another at the nose of the Bulge, with the possibility of one from Malmedy and Stavelot, the Germans found their *Sixth Panzer Army* with a "fluid left flank," the *Fifth Panzer Army* with advanced tentacles without flank security, and *Seventh Army* confronted with a local crisis brought about by Patton's attack. But Hitler was not yet ready to give up.

All through the day the conference dragged on; proposals and counterproposals were discussed, thrashed over, examined. As summed up in the war diary maintained by Hitler's personal historian and later reconstructed from notes: "Was it possible under these circumstances to thrust forward over the Meuse as planned? That is, was it possible to attain that objective, which in the event of an ideal course of events should have been reached within the first two days, and then the further objective of Antwerp, and thus, the rolling up of the entire enemy front from Trier to the ocean?" The answer reached, after long hours of debate, was that the thrust across the Meuse could only be considered possible if equilibrium could be restored on the south, and if the entire Allied force between the Ourthe and the Meuse Rivers could be destroyed. Translating the sometimes oblique German reasoning into blunt terms, all thought of crossing the Meuse River was abandoned in favor of a battle east of the river. The grand, swashbuckling, dramatic fight of a knight in armor, who was to smite the western Allies with one blow, was abandoned for a limited war of attrition, which the Germans were certainly ill-equipped to make.

Once the fateful decision was made, the gears of the war machine once more began grinding to put the new plans into action. To stabilize the southern front, the two reserve *Volks-grenadier* divisions were shunted to Brandenberger's *Seventh Army*. Another division, *340 Volksgrenadier*, was rushed to the Bulge. Rundstedt's projected attack at Duren in the Ninth Army sector to establish a bridgehead across the Roer River, thus further upsetting Ninth Army's plans for a crossing of the river at some future day, was abandoned in view of the probable heavy losses it would entail. To allow Dietrich greater freedom of movement, his northern corps was returned to *Fifteenth Army,* from which it had been borrowed. Replacements totalling 24,000 men were promised for the Western Front. The decree requiring a 10 per cent decrease in the strength of all theaters, intended to reduce staffs and supply units, was suspended for Model's army group until February 1, 1945. And finally, a proposal that *Seventh Army* be reinforced for a strike at Luxembourg City, for morale purposes, was vetoed in favor of an all-out attack on Bastogne, which was to be the first order of business.

THE ATTACK ON BASTOGNE

Having made his decision to fight east of the Meuse River, Hitler at once concentrated his attention on Bastogne, about which he had expressed little concern prior to the change in plans. Now, with a large battle looming east of the River, Bastogne was a huge rock jutting out of the German sea, and an ever present threat to the German line of communications. It had to be taken. With this in mind, Hitler ordered a concentrated attack on Bastogne. Suddenly, German divisions from all parts of the Bulge descended on Bastogne preparatory to a new siege of the town. During this time ensued the heaviest fighting of the battle for Bastogne; the casualties were frightfully heavy, much worse than during the actual siege.

First to be shunted south, even though in the midst of an attack on Hotton, the *Fuehrer Escort Brigade* received orders on December 26 to disengage immediately, march to the southwest of Bastogne, where it was to attack across the narrow neck opening into the town, and once again isolate the defenders of Bastogne. Then the panzer divisions of "Sepp" Dietrich's *Sixth Panzer Army* were to descend upon the town from three sides, and throttle the defenders. One by one, Dietrich's panzers shifted their weight from the XVIII Airborne Corps front, to the south. By the first of the year, *1, 9,* and *12 SS Panzer Divisions* were ringed around Bastogne, attacking from three sides. The *Fuehrer Escort Brigade*, having once failed, was again ordered to cut off the neck of the salient into Bastogne in conjunction with an attack by *1 SS Panzer Division* from the east, but the Americans were already too strongly entrenched in this narrow corridor, and the German attacks failed to break through. By the first of the year, eight German divisions were closeted around Bastogne, closing in for the kill.

To counteract the terrific German pressure being exerted on Bastogne, Patton attacked west of Bastogne. Once the threat to the Meuse River was definitely ended, Eisenhower was ready to release the divisions which had been attached to Middleton's VIII Corps; prior to this time Eisenhower had forbidden their use east of the Meuse River. On December 28, "Beetle" Smith, Eisenhower's Chief of Staff, received a message from his chief, who was touring the fronts: "Release to Bradley at once the 11th Armored and 87th Divisions, and organize a strong Bastogne-Houffalize attack." On the cold, crisp morning of December 30, the attack orders were issued, as troops of these divisions moved to the offensive through towering snow drifts. Soon joined by the 17th Airborne Division, which had also been held in reserve until this time, the divisions crawled forward in the worst of winter weather. Their progress was tediously slow, their casualties exorbitantly high: all of them new to combat, they had to fight in the severest cold, on icy roads over which tank movements were almost impossible. These new troops had been moved over long distances, and then immediately committed to action with little time for reconnaissance. But had the attack been delayed long enough for adequate reconnaissance, it is probable the Germans would have launched another attack, and surrounded Bastogne.

With Middleton's VIII Corps again reconstituted and back in the fray, the pressure on Bastogne was somewhat eased, although up through January 3 the Germans unrelentingly attacked the town. But with the III Corps divisions closing up on Bastogne along their entire front, the salient into the town was gradually widened. Further to assist the defenders, Patton diverted some of the troops assigned to his XII Corps at the east shoulder of the Third Army line. Middleton's VIII Corps attack on December 30, the diversion of troops from XII Corps to Bastogne, continuation of the III Corps attack, and brave and clever defense by the troops in Bastogne, combined to save once again the town from capture, as Germans pounded away with their best divisions: parts of four panzer, two infantry, a paratroop, and Remer's *Fuehrer Escort Bri-*

gade. During these days the conflict was intense, and casualties in the 101st Airborne Division and attached units were the greatest, as German power in force was thrown against Bastogne. But the crisis had already been met on the First Army front. The Germans, like caged lions furious at their captivity, turned on Bastogne and struck again and again with utter abandon.

On January 2, an irascible Hitler again directed Rundstedt to speed the capture of Bastogne with an attack from the southeast. But the Germans were being forced into a pocket between Bastogne and the III Corps attackers to the east, and had insufficient maneuvering space to launch their own attack. Consequently, Model ordered an attack by *1 SS Panzer Corps,* utilizing the three panzer divisions from Dietrich's army, one from the north, one from the northeast, and the third from the east. Hitler approved the plan, and on January 3 the last coordinated attack on Bastogne began. But by this time, the defenders were too well entrenched, and III Corps with 101st Airborne Division, supporting armor, and the reinforcing units which Patton had brought to the north, successfully stemmed the German attacks. This was the last of the great blows against Bastogne; on January 8, Hitler issued new directives which materially altered the war in the Bulge.

FIRST ARMY REGROUPS

Early on December 27, General Eisenhower landed at the Brussels airport. He was greeted by Field Marshal Montgomery, commander of all Allied forces in the north. Reporting on the sacking of *2 Panzer Division* at the tip of the Bulge and the subsequent frustration of the last German lunge through Manhay, Montgomery told the Supreme Commander that he was ready to pass to the offensive. Montgomery's plans were outlined to Eisenhower: relief of VII Corps by British XXX Corps which would take over east of the Meuse River as far as Marche; assembly of VII Corps, now composed of two armored and two infantry divisions (2d and 3d Armored and 83d and 84th Infantry), preparatory to launching an attack to the south to join with VIII Corps at Houffalize; and finally, the attack with the main effort by VII Corps, aided by British XXX Corps on the west and XVIII Airborne Corps on the east, both of which would make local attacks to protect VII Corps' flanks.

Throughout the last days of December, VII Corps continued

mopping up pockets of German resistance, preparatory to its relief from the line. By the end of December, all of the VII Corps divisions had been relieved by British XXX Corps and XVIII Airborne Corps. German pressure constantly fell off, as one by one the divisions of *Sixth Panzer Army* were shunted to the south for the attacks on Bastogne, to be replaced in the line by new infantry divisions, such as *340 Volksgrenadier,* and by the old infantry divisions of *66 Corps,* conquerors of St. Vith. Dietrich assumed defense of most of the northern flank of the Bulge, while Manteuffel concerned himself primarily with Bastogne. Finally, after hasty reorganization and re-equipping, the VII Corps units were grouped for the attack which began on January 3.

Some criticism has been directed against Montgomery and Hodges on two scores: first, that the attack was too slow in forming; second, that it was launched too far to the west. Say the critics: it should have burst out of the rugged area of Malmedy where it could have pinched off the entire German penetration. On the first score, we have already noted how one by one the attacking divisions were thrown into the fight to establish a line of defense, and were thus unable to launch an attack until the crisis was over by December 26. Whether they should then have been able to go immediately over to the offense is problematical. All divisions had been badly scattered and mauled in their fight for life; once a division has engaged the enemy, it is difficult to withdraw it on short notice. Not until the year's end were all German pockets of resistance liquidated; and no sooner was this done than the divisions were all relieved and prepared for the attack which began three days later. Again, the only divisions immediately prepared to attack were the British, and Hodges was reluctant to use them in his attack scheme: first, because of the co-ordination problem involved in feeding individual British divisions into an American command setup, and, second, because he thought it was an American duty to finish up the job. Since national armies have quite different methods of operating and communicating, it is no simple matter to slip a division of another nationality into an American command organization. The principle throughout the war was, wherever possible, to keep the various national army groups intact, at least within corps.

Two supporting factors governed the selection of the attack area: the snow and the road net. After thorough studies of the terrain, both Bradley to the south and Hodges to the north concluded that attacks at the base of the German penetration would be extremely difficult because of the very limited road net which ran north and south in the eastern portion of the penetration. Accordingly, Bradley and Hodges both decided to attack somewhat further to the west so that the tanks would have the best roads. Further to the east, along Hodges' line, Gerow's V Corps had been ordered to prepare plans for an offensive to cut off the base of the German salient, and General Hobbs' 30th Division was ready and anxious to cut through the German defense line south of Malmedy. Gerow felt that a mistake had been made in not attacking further to the east. Eventually, on January 13, such an attack began. Progress was slow as the Germans straddled the several usable roads in the sector. But the determining factor was the fight for Bastogne, which forced Bradley to shift his troops into the threatened area, and then attack northeast from there. Hodges, of course, had to conform to this southern attack so that the forces from north and south would meet in a pincers.

Whether Hodges' First Army attack was unduly delayed, once the crisis had been met, can be weighed by detailed analysis of the logistical condition of First Army following December 26. With two of the attack divisions badly hit by the earlier German attacks, and a third heavily engaged for several days, the problem of reorganization was great. Added to this were the very heavy and damaging losses which the First Army had suffered during the early days of the fighting. There were acute shortages: not only tanks, but many types of equipment. Units were forced to turn in all excess equipment in an attempt to procure enough rifles, ammunition, packs, and other equipment for re-equipment of the battered divisions. Old tanks with steel tracks, rather than rubber, were pressed into service, despite the difficulties of maneuvering them on icy roads. Time and again as the units moved to assemble for the attack, there were long delays when an entire tank column failed to climb a particularly slippery hill. And replacements of infantry and tankers were limited by a personnel shortage which had been felt even before the German attack began. Remember that General Bradley met with Eisenhower on December 16 to discuss that very problem. Nothing had been able to alleviate it, although shipments from the States had been immediately speeded up, and, naturally, the situation got no better as the attack progressed. Montgomery reported to Eisenhower an acute shortage of infantry in the First and Ninth Armies as early as December 23, and particularly cited V Corps which was short 7,000 riflemen. One division was understrength by 2,000 riflemen! These shortages were of major importance. Through all this, Hodges moved to prepare his attack from the north as rapidly as possible. If there was a delay, it was caused by the elements and the shortages rather than any inherent timidity on Hodges' part. And lastly, Montgomery was afraid of renewed German attacks to the north because their forces were still strong despite deflections to Bastogne. He and Eisenhower agreed to wait until January 2 to see if the Germans would attack. Then the Allied attack was to start. Cautious? Yes, another result of the war of nerves.

THE GERMANS TAKE AN INVENTORY

Model, whose battle cry on December 16 was "On to Antwerp," glibly reported to his troops on New Year's Day, "We have succeeded in disrupting the enemy's planned winter offensive against our Fatherland." This was the essence of the meeting at Hitler headquarters on New Year's Eve, when progress of the entire war was again reviewed. Having failed in their objectives, Hitler's aides now reported to *Der Fuehrer* that the primary goal of the attack was seizure of initiative on the Western Front, thereby preventing Allied penetration to the Rhine River. This, they reported, had been satisfactorily achieved. Especially noteworthy, they continued, was the employment of U. S. airborne forces in the conventional infantry role, thus eliminating for some time to come the danger of a new airborne assault on the Rhine River line. "From the information on hand," the Hitler war diary noted, "it could be seen that the enemy had employed practically all his troops available to him in the west, and that several could be regarded as unfit for battle for a long time."

Turning to other fronts, the High Command still saw nothing alarming. In Italy, the front was stabilized, while in the southeast a successful withdrawal from the Balkans had been completed, and a new front built up around Croatia. Although Hungary was in large part a lost cause, a line had been built along the Eastern Front, and the Russian attack into Courland warded off. Although new Russian offensives were expected daily, Hitler and his stooges were confident that the new defenses behind the Russian front would eventually halt any enemy drive. However, on the home front, war industries still suffered from shortages of material, labor, the air attacks, and traffic bottlenecks. Most dangerous was the gasoline shortage, which every week became more alarming. "It had now gone so far," Hitler's historian recorded, "that in any operation, even those local in nature, it first had to be inquired if adequate supplies of gasoline and diesel oil were available, and whether they could be procured at the right time." To preserve the last large oil supply, herculean efforts were being made to defend the fields in Hungary, southwest of the Platten See and the city of Komorn. And a further sword hanging over German industry was the weather, soon to improve, which would allow resumption of large scale air raids by the Allies.

With these things in mind, Hitler, the indefatigable optimist, ordered Rundstedt to destroy the western Allies by a series of repeated blows, which would knock out the Allies army by army. Hitler reserved for himself the right to name the areas of these attacks. These blows, striking suddenly, were to keep the Allies off balance, and prevent them from regrouping and organizing for another great assault on the German lines. The first of these attacks, *Nordwind* was ordered for the first week in January. Directed by Himmler in the southern sector of the Western Front, it was to pinch off Strasbourg and the surrounding territory as the Germans struck simultaneous blows from the north, and from the Colmar pocket to the south of Strasbourg. To bolster this attack, Hitler provided three extra divisions, the *6 SS Mountain* from Norway, *7 Parachute* from Holland, and *10 SS Panzer,* all of which were alerted for the Battle of the Bulge, but arrived too late to be committed. Again Rundstedt was vetoed by Hitler; the old master had wanted to attack across the Saar River toward Metz, in conjunction with a stronger *Seventh Army* attack to the south from the Bulge, to pinch off large portions of Third Army, but Hitler insisted on the more southerly attack. To make certain that his orders were carefully followed, he had Himmler report directly to his staff in Berlin rather than to Rundstedt.

Operation *Nordwind* began on January 1, as Germans attacked from north and south in a pincers closing in on the Alsatian plain. However, this time the Allied forces were not caught napping, and intelligence had predicted the exact day of the German thrust. Although the Germans succeeded in crossing the Rhine River a few miles north of Strasbourg, and gained ground toward the north from the Colmar pocket, they suffered heavy casualties, and the Allied line was stabilized without the loss of any militarily important terrain. Strasbourg, itself, was threatened, but the German drive was contained, and this political symbol, so important to the French, remained in Allied hands. Interesting to note are General Eisenhower's comments in his *Story of the War*, which relates how he considered withdrawing from Strasbourg, and the dangerous defensive ground in Alsace at the time the Germans began the Ardennes offensive. However, because of the political implications of such a move to the French, who feared the fall of the provisional De Gaulle government if a withdrawal were effected, Eisenhower rescinded his original instructions, despite the dangerous ground which added to the fear of being cut off.

Hitler, not content with a ground diversion, and worried about the Allied air assaults on his ground troops and lines of communication, ordered the Luftwaffe into its last great attack of the war on New Year's Day. Somewhere between 800 and 900 German planes swooped down on that New Year's Day in "Operation *Bodenplatte*" to blast Allied airfields in Belgium and Holland. Culminating lengthy German planning, which had considered such an attack long before the Ardennes offensive began, the Germans achieved at least partial success as they destroyed 127 Allied planes and damaged another 133, a total of 260 planes, the majority of them fighters. We claimed that about 200 German planes were lost. Hitler's war diary woefully records the success of the operation and adds, "To be sure, our own losses were so high that a continuation of such attacks had to be given up." Still, German diversions did not even achieve their purpose—to keep the Allies off balance. Though troublesome, by January 3, concentrated attacks from both sides of the Bulge spelled the beginning of the end for the Germans. The great dream was coming to an end.

WE ATTACK IN FORCE

With our air force pounding the German lines of communication and troop and supply concentrations, as well as supporting the ground troops, the return bout of the Battle of the Bulge began on January 3, nineteen days after the start of the German attack. While Third Army continued its heavy fighting around Bastogne, First Army began to press from the north, VII Corps leading the attack, accompanied

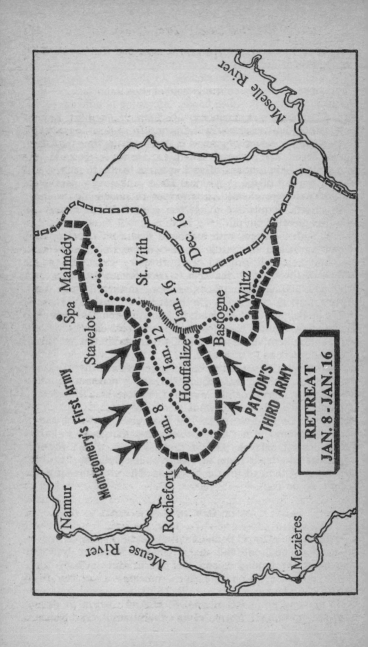

Moselle River

Dec. 16

Spa Malmédy
Stavelot
St. Vith
Jan. 12
Jan. 16
Houffalize
Jan. 8
Bastogne
Wiltz

Montgomery's First Army

Namur

Meuse River

Rochefort

PATTON'S
THIRD ARMY

Mezières

**RETREAT
JAN. 8 - JAN. 16**

by XVIII Airborne Corps on the east, and the British XXX Corps on the west.

THE DYING GASP

Of all the attacks made by Allied forces in western Europe, the conditions under which this attack was made were, by all odds, the worst. The snow in many places was waist deep, and even short infantry movements were made under the most trying conditions. The few roads were ice-coated, and often snow blanketed the ice. Most tanks were roadbound and the Germans, by carefully located antitank guns, aided by minefields to the fore, were able to halt Allied tank advances continually until the infantry could move forward to cope with the German strongpoints. It was unbelievably cold, near zero, and the battle for existence against the elements was at least as difficult as that against the enemy. But as the Third Army beat off the final attacks around Bastogne, First Army troops slowly ground their way forward through snowbound woods and fields. On January 9, Third Army finally halted the last of the German attacks around Bastogne, and Patton continued his earlier attack toward Houffalize. His army, too, was faced with equally formidable weather which made the fighting miserable.

Hilter, the eternal optimist, finally convinced that the cause in the Ardennes was lost, on January 8 ordered the withdrawal of the tip of his salient to the line Dochamps-Longchamps roughly just west of the Bastogne-Houffalize road. This was a bitter pill to swallow. His long-cherished dream of a German sweep to the sea vanished in the smoke of battle. Still far short of his original destination, he had to content himself with the thought that he had disrupted American and British plans for a winter attack—small consolation for the high hopes he had entertained. Hitler was still unwilling to forget his dream completely, and in order to prepare himself for the next moves, on January 8 he ordered the release of *Sixth Panzer Army* from the defensive line. Rundstedt was specifically enjoined against using *Sixth Panzer Army* in piecemeal fashion. The divisions were immediately to be relieved from the line and sent for refitting and re-supply preparatory to their next action—meeting the coming Allied attack.

On January 12 the bombshell fell which was to disrupt forever German offensive plans on any front. The Russians left their winter quarters and initiated their long-expected winter offensive to the east. This was the final blow to German plans in the west, and when the Russians opened wide holes in the German lines, Hitler ordered release of the entire *Sixth Panzer Army* to the Eastern Front. This was quickly followed by an order to send east the two *Fuehrer* brigades and at least three infantry divisions. Now, all the Germans could hope for was an orderly and gradual retreat back to the West Wall from which they had battered their way only a month before.

On January 16, patrols from First and Third Armies met in the town of Houffalize, their mutual goal, and the complete tip of the German penetration was eliminated. Both armies wheeled to the east, and started operations toward the West Wall. Meanwhile, on January 13, V Corps had sprung to the attack and was slowly cutting into the German flank further to the east of Houffalize. On January 23 the 7th Armored Division crashed through the German crust into St. Vith, from where they had been driven just a month before. Still fighting the weather as much as the tough German resistance, the two armies moved forward relentlessly, and by early February the Germans were back in the West Wall, along nearly the entire length of the Ardennes front.

Soon after the First and Third Armies had joined hands at Houffalize, the First returned to the control of Bradley's 12th Army Group, despite some campaigning by Montgomery for control of all ground forces. The need for a unified control on the northern flank had vanished with the end of the German threat. Although Montgomery did make capital of his role in the Battle of the Bulge to press again his demands for a ground commander for all troops, Eisenhower remained adamant, supported by Chief of Staff Marshall.

ALLES KAPUT

The greatest pitched battle for the Western Front was over. Twenty-nine German and thirty-two Allied divisions participated in the battle which raged for a little over a month. The last great German gamble had ended, not without certain successes, but far short of its ambitious goal. For all practical purposes, the war in the west was over. Early in February, the British attacked down the watershed between the Roer and Rhine Rivers. Third Army continued through the Ardennes forests, and through the West Wall toward the Rhine. In the south, the Colmar pocket was eliminated by a Franco-American attack, and back in the north, the First Army seized the vital Roer River dams, which they had been attacking on December 16 when the German attack began. On February 23, the day after one of our most paralyzing aerial attacks on Germany, in which nearly 10,000 sorties were flown over Nazi rail and transportation targets, Ninth Army with First Army support, hopped the Roer River, headed straight for the Rhine, and then in a sudden wheeling action, which threw the Germans off their guard, turned to the north to meet the British attack coming down the watershed. First Army continued straight ahead, captured what was left of Cologne on March 7, and on the same day, in a lucky stroke, seized intact the Rhine River crossing at Remagen, and immediately forced the Germans to divert their few remaining reserves to meet this grave threat to their last defense line. Meanwhile, Third Army plowed on through the Eifel, the West Wall, and then, in early March, in a series of brilliant armored movements crossed and crisscrossed the Saar region, cutting up the remaining German forces west of the Rhine. While Patton's forces in conjunction with our Seventh Army continued to mop up the trapped Germans in the Saar, his infantry forced a surprise crossing of the Rhine River on March 22, and established a second large bridgehead across the Rhine River. Now the Allies were along the entire length of the Rhine, and across it in two places.

Beginning late on March 23, Anglo-American forces under Montgomery forced a third crossing of the Rhine River north of the Ruhr Valley, with the aid of a huge airborne drop east of the River. A gigantic pincers around the Ruhr Valley developed from both sides as First and Ninth Army armor raced to meet at the eastern end of the valley, and on April 1 the enveloping forces made contact, pocketing the entire Ruhr industrial area, heart of Germany, and elements of eighteen German divisions. From there on, effective organized German resistance crumbled as armored columns ruthlessly sped across Germany, now aided by the gigantic *autobahns* (superhighways), originally constructed to move German troops rapidly from one sector to another. Only isolated German resistance was encountered in the weeks that followed. First contact with the Russian armies was made on April 25, and less than two weeks later at Rheims, Colonel General Alfred Jodl, who little more than five months previously had directed the German planning for the Battle of the Bulge, surrendered all land, sea, and air forces of the Reich on May 7, 1945.

In five short months, the pendulum had made nearly two complete swings, first as the Allies were taken from high optimism to deep pessimism as a result of the surprise German attack in the Ardennes, and then back to extreme elation, as the German forces crumbled following failure of their last great gamble.

CHAPTER VII

An Inventory

DAMAGES ASSESSED

"WHETHER IT WAS A 'CRIME' TO PROLONG THE WAR BY THIS attack in the Ardennes is a decision we leave to the Allied courts. Our own judgment is unchanged and independent of them," said Field Marshal Wilhelm Keitel and Colonel General Alfred Jodl at war's end. But in terms of Germany: "Was it worth it?"

Years will pass before an accurate appraisal can be made of the damages suffered by both sides in the Battle of the Bulge. However, tentative estimates, though admittedly rough, can be considered a fairly good guide pending the final verdict of historians. Both sides extravagantly overrated enemy losses in reports to their own commands: the Germans, for example, claimed we had suffered casualties of from 150,000 to 200,000 men and 2,000 tanks in their attack; three of our divisions had been completely destroyed, said they, and twelve others badly mauled.

"This, western warriors, was your achievement," an official German report to their soldiers, soon after the Battle of the Bulge, noted. "You have transcended all difficulties of terrain and weather to prove that you are rougher than the enemy. Your leaders and your country know that they can place their faith in you . . . The enemy was forced to commit all his reserves. Sixty-five per cent of all enemy forces on the continent were rushed to the salient. After the airborne divisions had been smashed, the intended American assault toward Cologne and the Ruhr was impossible. The danger of a western offensive, co-ordinated with the huge Bolshevist drive, was averted." Lulled by its own propaganda, the Foreign Army section of the German High Command in late January prepared an estimate of Allied potentialities on the Western Front, which reported that the Allies would not attack in force before May. The Germans underestimated our power of revival, just as we had theirs in the summer and fall of 1944.

According to Eisenhower's personnel officer, American losses in the Battle of the Bulge totalled 76,890 men, of whom 8,607 were killed, 47,139 wounded, and 21,144 missing. Over 8,000 of these casualties were in the 106th Division. Because of heavy German attacks, 733 tanks and tank destroyers were lost. Two divisions, the 28th and 106th, were nearly completely annihilated, although the 28th Division did subsequently enter combat after being rebuilt. However, the third division which the Germans claimed as destroyed, the 9th Armored Division, strikingly demonstrated that it still was hale and hearty, as CCB, which had been around St. Vith in the Battle of the Bulge, seized the Remagen bridge across the Rhine River on March 7, 1945. These were serious losses, nonetheless, and only the swelling tide of men and materials from America was able to replace the losses and quickly prepare the Allies for the steps ahead. Eisenhower was able to bargain to good advantage only after our High Command in Washington had been shaken by the suddenness and force of the German attack; he then obtained a rapid increase in supplies, individual replacements and materials from home.

Eisenhower later announced that the German attack delayed the Allied ground offensive by six weeks; in the air, where all forces were suddenly diverted to targets directly affecting the Battle of the Bulge, the relentless war on German industry was delayed by four weeks. When the attacks came, however, a weaker, more demoralized enemy was met, and, though the fighting was hard and bitter, the end was never in doubt after that. Except for isolated points of tenacious resistance, the German will-to-resist had been broken. As General Eisenhower himself pointed out to Chief of Staff Marshall, possibly more serious to the Germans than the loss of manpower and strategic reserves, was the widespread disillusionment ensuing from their failure to seize any really important objective and the realization that this offensive, on which such great hopes had been pinned, had in no sense achieved anything decisive.

What did the Germans lose besides the initiative? Nazi

casualties included their remaining strategic reserves of men, materials, and morale. We claimed nearly 200,000 men, but German High Command estimates varied between 81,834 and 98,024 casualties and 324 assault guns and tanks (to December 31 only). The accepted figure was 81,834; of these, 12,652 were killed, 38,600 wounded, and 30,582 missing. For a country which had endured five years of war, and whose manpower reserves were dwindling to the zero mark, these were serious losses. Dietrich estimated his *Sixth Panzer Army* alone lost 37,000 men killed, wounded, and frozen, and from 350 to 400 tanks, some of which were recovered. The once crack *Panzer Lehr Division*, which had fought around Bastogne, and then on to the west, limped its way back to the West Wall with ten tanks, six assault guns, and 400 combat troops. *Panzer Lehr's* running mate, *2 Panzer Division*, which had been snipped off near the Meuse River, was almost completely destroyed, and only a few troops were left of the once proud panzer division. The majority of the other divisions suffered similar fates. Without the vast reserves, such as we were immediately able to divert to the Western Front, the Germans were forced to continue on with all extra power exhausted, eaten up in the Battle of the Bulge. Even what remained of *Sixth Panzer Army* was lost when butcher boy "Sepp" Dietrich took his men to the east, where they were thrown against the crushing Russian forces pushing through Hungary. Dietrich took with him the last effective striking force in the west. With only worn-out troops to stem the Allied tide, which was loosed in February, the Germans in the west were helpless. Supplies, as well as troops, were low; shortage of spare-part supplies for tanks was so acute and the gasoline supply so low that even new tanks, as the Battle of the Bulge waned, were broken up, shipped to repair other tanks further to the front and to save the gasoline which would have been required to move the tanks forward. Many tanks which might have been saved were abandoned for lack of gas. With the last carefully hoarded reserves lost, the German war machine rapidly collapsed after the Battle of the Bulge.

In the air the story was much the same. Despite herculean efforts of the Luftwaffe, which during the Battle of the Bulge rose in force on the Western Front for the first time since the invasion began, Allied air power delivered still more crushing blows against the Germans. In spite of nonoperational flying weather between December 18 and 22, and very poor weather from January 4 to 16, 33,000 medium and heavy bomber sorties were flown against the Germans, and a total of 104,000 tons of bombs dropped on roads, railroads, bridges, marshalling yards, and other transportation facilities in a vast, hastily organized effort to isolate the battlefield. Although the Germans made remarkably quick repairs to this damage, the bombings had their repercussions in the Bulge.

Especially striking were raids on two road centers, St. Vith and Laroche. More than 1,700 tons of bombs were dropped on St. Vith, which virtually became a ghost town around which traffic was routed through the fields and pastures. At Laroche, 150 tons of bombs were equally effective, since the town was located in a deep valley around which it was almost impossible to route traffic. And with more than 30,000 sorties by the Tactical Air Forces harassing the Germans in direct support of ground operations, further heavy damage was inflicted. Unsubstantiated air claims (always found to be excessive because of the limited time for observation of bombing results) revealed that 751 German tanks and armored vehicles had been destroyed, and 509 damaged by the air attack; 6,037 motor transports destroyed, and 7,117 damaged; and 584 locomotives destroyed, and 657 damaged. Though far above probable effective destruction, these estimates by the Director of Intelligence, United States Strategic Air Forces in Europe, give some indication of the forceful Allied air attacks.

The Luftwaffe, which built its air force to 1,610 planes at offensive's peak, was whittled down to 1,290 by the close of the attack, though the Nazis tried their best to maintain this force with new replacements. Again, the Strategic Air Force reports 1,392 German planes destroyed, 129 probably destroyed, and 418 damaged during the month of the offensive, at a cost of 592 Allied aircraft. Even allowing for inflated claims, the enemy undoubtedly suffered a blow it could ill afford to take at that time. Subsequent tapering off of German air power on the Western Front indicated only too well the telling effect of Allied air attacks. Whereas the Germans did not have plane replacements, the Allied losses of 267 fighters and 325 bombers was quickly restored from the huge "Arsenal of Democracy" across the Atlantic.

Men who have studied the growth of air power in military operations report that this crushing weight of Allied air power, utilized against an enemy offensive under conditions selected

by the enemy and favorable to him, was epochal in the history
of air power. Prior to this, it had been used on a large scale
only in support of an offensive. Suddenly, the Allied air forces
were switched from their offensive mission to a new mission
dictated by the enemy. The significance of this mass diversion
of air power cannot be overemphasized.

GERMAN GENIUS GRIEVES

Several other officers and I were granted a unique opportunity, after hostilities, when we interviewed nearly all German commanders involved in the Battle of the Bulge. This
"Operation Hindsight" gave us considerable insight into the
workings of the German war machine. Especially did we learn
how wide was the chasm between the Nazi high command
and the field commanders.

Field Marshal Keitel, in effect the Minister of War, and
Colonel General Jodl, chief of a more powerful equivalent of
our War Plans Division, as chief military advisors to Hitler
were, naturally, most vehement in their justification of the
attack and its conduct. They commented: "We do not believe,
with the troops and material then at our disposal, that the
Supreme Command could have done anything better as it
saw the situation. The operation was fundamentally one of
surprise, and to this extent we believe it was a complete success." However, Rundstedt, a bitter old man, blamed these
very men for the failure of the attack when he said: "The
Ardennes offensive was planned in all details, including Order
of Battle, time schedules, objectives, and so on, by the *Fuehrer* and by the *OKW*. All counter-proposals were turned
down. Under these circumstances, there could be no belief in
success. Even during the attack, the *OKW* commanded operations by means of liaison officers and direct wireless orders
to the armies. No reports could be obtained from *Sixth Panzer
Army* at all, which sent its reports via *SS* channels direct to
the *Fuehrer*, and thus made known their difficulties to Model.
The execution of the operation was made much more difficult
also by the strict order from above that every place, including
cut off sectors, was to be held."

Generally, however, the Germans were unanimous in blam-
ing certain factors for their defeat. They were: (1) shortage
of men and materials as a result of the long war; (2) lack
of qualified leaders; (3) improper use of the *Sixth Panzer
Army;* (4) Allied air power; (5) bad roads; (6) bad weather;

(7) the Allied reaction to the attack; and (8) isolated defenses at unexpected points.

German generals rated the condition of Germany after five years of war high on the list. Not only had the Germans forfeited a large reservoir of manpower (Jodl said that 1,500,-000 men had been killed by then), but the war economy was hard pressed, despite gigantic efforts to maintain production. We have noted that in planes, artillery, and tanks the Germans had managed to maintain production levels even during the heaviest Allied air raids in the summer of 1944, but in other fields they were not so successful.

In petroleum alone, the U. S. Strategic Air Force estimated German productive capacity had been cut to 106,000 tons by September, 1944, twenty per cent of normal capacity, barely enough to keep pace with the most limited operations. Even during October, as air assaults slacked off, the production of petroleum products rose to only 171,000 tons. This was sufficient to maintain operations, even during the static period, only by resorting to horsedrawn transport from railheads to tactical supply dumps, 40 to 50 per cent reduction in the use of vehicles, a harsh system of rationing available supplies, and use of charcoal-burning transport. By these means, the Germans accumulated a small reserve, later used in the Battle of the Bulge. The Allied command was soon aware that the Germans were operating on a shoestring, although this was not so readily apparent to the troops in the field. The further they advanced into the Bulge, the more the Germans felt this fundamental weakness. Goering summed it up: "It was no longer 1940."

Equally disturbing to the Germans was the dearth of trained troops and commanders. Here the drain on manpower made a profound difference in German actions. Tank drivers were not skilled in winter driving, and no prior practice could be given because they lacked gasoline. Many of the best unit commanders had been killed off in the five years of warfare, and there had not been time to train adequate replacements.

Especially dangerous was the rapid upgrading of Hitler favorites, brave and courageous at their level, but not equipped to handle the tremendous logistical problems of larger units. Dietrich was, of course, the prime example of "an excellent division commander," as Goering later remarked, "without the military know-how necessary to run an army." Remer, the hero of the *Putsch,* was another fearless man, who was given a larger command, the *Fuehrer Escort Brigade,* because of his loyalty to Hitler. As one of the corps commanders remarked, "Remer was always having gasoline troubles"; he was unable to manage the complicated problems of moving a large body of men in the shortest possible time. Unquestionably, this lack of competent leadership loomed large among the difficulties with which the Germans were faced.

Closely related to the lack of leadership was the criticism by all except the high command in Berlin, that the *Sixth Panzer Army* had been improperly used. Rundstedt, Manteuffel, and Brandenberger agreed that because the main Allied forces were to the north, the main effort, and, consequently the major striking force, should have been with Manteuffel's *Fifth Panzer Army* to the south. Not only were Dietrich's panzers tightly jammed together on a narrow front with poor roads, but because of the early heavy Allied strength from the north Dietrich was unable to secure the hole through which he could plow. As a result, his second wave, consisting of two panzer divisions in *2 SS Panzer Corps,* remained idle behind the lines for seven crucial days of the fighting. If Manteuffel had received these two divisions at the time his panzers were eyeing the Meuse, these critics continue, he might successfully have beaten off the Allied forces along the Meuse, bridged the river, and gone on. If this had been accomplished, the *OKW* panzer reserve could have been thrown in to exploit the new gains. Dietrich, of course, failed to agree with this conclusion, and blamed his failure first, on terrible road conditions, and, secondly, on the foolishness of an attack in the Ardennes. "Only four or five tanks can fight at one time," Dietrich, the tactician, carefully explained to me after the war, "because there is no place to deploy. A big tank attack in this terrain is impossible." The consensus of army opinion about Dietrich and his leadership was summed up for me by one general in a neat, terse statement: "Dietrich is a pig."

Other contributing factors in "Operation Hindsight" included the weather, Allied air power, terrain, bad preparation, the defenses at Bastogne and St. Vith, and the quick reaction of the American command to the German attack. However, the still arrogant military élite of Germany were more prone to blame the weather or the supremacy of the Allied air force than to credit the rival Allied ground commanders with any brilliant military maneuvers. While I was interviewing various German generals, I watched the crafty build-up of this story that only through air power, which, they would hastily add, was simply material superiority, did we win any battles. Very seldom were the Germans ready to admit that our ground command acted with firmness and decisiveness to meet the German threat, as we actually did in the Ardennes during the first week of the fighting when we had no air support.

Worn thin by years of fighting, the German war machine was not the smoothly operating instrument of terror which had swept through and terrorized most of Europe in 1939 and 1940. But even in late 1944 Hitler was not yet willing to admit this fact. Despite the handicaps, the dissents, the grumblings, the weaknesses, once committed to the fight most German generals gave it their full support, and there is reason to believe that most of them, Rundstedt excepted, were temporarily carried away by this picture of another world. Only later in "Operation Hindsight" did their doubts rise to the surface. Such is the training of a good German soldier.

OLD SOLDIERS NEVER DIE

The war has long since ended, and has been forgotten by many, as our country gropes to find real peace. Of the Allies, Eisenhower is now President of the United States. Middleton is an important university official; Montgomery, Chief of the British Imperial General Staff. Patton was killed in an automobile accident. Bradley and Simpson retired for reasons of health. Aside from a small group of men in the War Department studying military history, the shadow of that dark December, 1944, is reflected only faintly in the minds of those who groped their way through the horrible uncertainty of the contest. But what of the Germans who spark-plugged this giant attack which threw the Allies into such consternation? Where are those leaders?

Hitler, we presume, vanished forever into his other world, his death still as obscure as the workings of his tortured mind. His chief conspirators, Jodl and Keitel, were tried and hanged at Nuremburg for the high crime of waging aggressive warfare; volume upon volume of testimony and papers evidenced their cruel and inhuman orders. Aged Rundstedt, far past his physical prime, still rests in a British prison camp, where he and some of his cronies talk about saving the general staff corps so they may begin to plan for the future.

They even talk of the wonderful new race which will be formed by the Russian occupation. "Imagine a man with the Russian body and spirit and the German mind," one field marshal said in prison camp. Model, the army group commander, killed himself rather than surrender to the Allies. He was an enthusiast, and he enthusiastically met his Maker. Of the three army commanders, Manteuffel and Brandenberger are still in Allied custody. Manteuffel, in England with Runstedt, complains about his treatment, staunchly maintaining that the Germans never behaved badly. The third, butcher boy "Sepp" Dietrich, was sentenced to life imprisonment at a trial with seventy-two fellow *SS* officers and men, including his Chief of Staff Kraemer, who received ten years, and Peiper, arrogant commander of *Kampfgruppe Peiper*, who was sentenced to death. Ironically enough, the butcher boy was himself sentenced at Dachau where thousands of the enemies of "Sepp" and his old friend Hitler were butchered by the Master Race. Dietrich and his cohorts were accused and convicted of killing some 900-odd American prisoners of war and Belgian civilians during the Battle of the Bulge. Seventy of these we already know about, the men who had collided with *Kampfgruppe Peiper* just south of Malmedy. Most of the civilians were slaughtered mercilessly by the rampaging Peiper men after being trapped in the Ambleve River valley. In the three little towns of Parfondruy, Ster, and Renardmont, between Stavelot and Trois Ponts, along the Ambleve River, the dead bodies of 117 men, women, and children were found, all killed by small arms fire. A platoon leader ordered his men to do away with all civilians who came in sight. So that we do not readily forget the sins of our enemies, I quote from an eyewitness account of the scene as American troops moved into the towns: "Ten or twelve completely burned bodies, charred black, were seen where a small shed had once stood . . . in the adjacent house, there was the body of a middle-aged women who had been stabbed with a knife and then shot. Bodies of two boys between the ages of six and ten were seen with bullet holes in their foreheads. . . . One old woman had been killed by a smash over the head, probably with a rifle butt. There was the body of a young man with his boots taken off; he had been killed by being shot through the back of the head. . . . Near a foxhole were bodies of a thirteen-year-old boy and a fifteen-year-old girl who had been shot, apparently, as they tried to escape."

MYTHS OF THE ARDENNES

So uncertain were those dark December days, so confusing the events, so mixed up the fighting, so erratic the reports, that it is hardly surprising that from the welter of information which emanated from both official and unofficial sources many wrong interpretations were made. These myths of the Ardennes are still being repeated by authors as varied as Eisenhower and Ralph Ingersoll. Most of them have been noted in the course of this report, but if only to clarify history they bear repeating now.

Myth—Hitler did not really want to get to Antwerp

Der Fuehrer was a stubborn, headstrong man with dreams of grandeur far exceeding his capabilities. Although opposed at every turn by his field commanders, he had made up his mind, as he lay in bed recovering from the effects of the bomb blast on July 20, 1944, that the offensive he was then dreaming about would be in the greatest tradition of German armed might. He even imagined he could drive the British off the continent. It was a great, exciting gamble for an excitable Hitler. Always uppermost in his thinking was the element of time. Deep in the heart of Germany, scientists were at work on some 137 so-called secret weapons. Two of these were already in production and were directly related to Hitler's decision to strike in the Ardennes: one was the new submarine capable of an underwater speed equivalent to the speed of an ordinary surfaced submarine and equipped with a breathing device which allowed it to remain submerged for long periods; the second was the jet-propelled plane, which Hitler firmly believed (and there are many Allied air-men prone to agree with him), temporarily at least, would have given the Germans a respite in the air. Anyone who has ever witnessed one of our jet-propelled planes in action, or who was unfortunate enough to have been the target of a German jet plane, will understand what I mean. Moving with what seemed the speed of lightning, these planes wove their way through the American fighters, literally flying rings around them. Though quantitatively inferior, Hitler believed that once in mass production, the jet planes would give him qualitative superiority with which he could once again establish a favorable balance in the air. Thus with air equality again obtained and Britain's lifeline to the

Arsenal of Democracy cut by the submarine, the Allied armies would be hard-pressed and forced to delay indefinitely their offensive plans, especially in the light of the crushing blow their armed forces were to suffer, if Hitler's battle plans succeeded. Apparently the atomic bomb did not figure in these plans; atomic scientists state that the Germans were not far advanced with their research in production of the bomb. And I, myself, discovered no evidence that the bomb was included in Hitler's gamble for time.

And so, Hitler embarked on a "holy" mission again to accomplish what his generals told him he could not do—drive to the sea. With a bold plan, the entire German army and civilian population were given a lift. And there is no doubt that German plans envisioned the shot-in-the-arm which this attack would give to both the German people and their soldiers. However, this was secondary to its main purpose—complete disruption of the Allied effort in the west.

Myth—Our attacks in November forced Hitler to launch his offensive before he was ready

Ralph Ingersoll in his book *Top Secret* confides that General Bradley forced Hitler's hand by continuing the American attacks through the late fall, and planning new attacks for the winter. Ingersoll, who twists facts to prove something that most Americans already know, that Bradley was a good commander, credits failure of the German offensive to this forced speedup in the German plans. While refraining from even commenting on whether it was Bradley or Eisenhower who decided to attack throughout the winter, I am not so constrained in pointing out that Hitler *actually delayed,* rather than speeded up, his planned offensive. And the cause of delay was his inability to mount the attack at the time desired, rather than his concern for Allied attacks. On the contrary, the *Fuehrer* welcomed our attacks in late November and early December because, he reasoned, they would weaken us sufficiently to allow him to carry out his bold plan. "It was a beautiful plan," Ingersoll admits, "and if Bradley had given Hitler and Rundstedt even another month to prepare for its execution, it might have worked."

Hitler and his staff, and even the doubting Rundstedt, were in accord that the exact opposite was true. If they had been able to attack in late November, as originally planned, there was much more likelihood of success. They said this for several reasons: first, Europe's weather is at its worst in late November and early December—as we know, the flying weather until December 23 was just about impossible.

Instead of seven days, this would have given Hitler three weeks of respite from the Allied air attacks by the *Jaboes,* which kept buzzing over the battlefield like a swarm of locusts, eating into the German supplies, manpower, and transportation facilities. Also, Hitler knew that Allied reinforcements of men and supplies were steadily flowing onto the continent, and, therefore, every delay lessened chances of success. Again, an attack in late November would have caught us when Antwerp was just beginning to go into operation, when most of our supplies were still being transported over the long truck and rail route from the beaches of Normandy, clear across the breadth of France to the fighting front. Without the huge docks at Antwerp to feed the fighting men, our ability to counteract the German attack might have been seriously limited.

Myth—It was the Rundstedt Offensive

Haughty Gerd von Rundstedt, seventy-year-old commander of the German forces in the west, called back only after von Kluge had been sacked for allegedly conspiring with the enemy, did not even take the trouble to attend the most important planning conference held at Hitler's headquarters. "They refused my advice," he gruffly said, "so I let it become their offensive, their responsibility." While he concerned himself with matters of supply for the forces, Hitler and his Berlin cronies dealt directly with the army group commander Model, who was more easily enthralled by the magic of Hitler's personality. "The German chain of command is sometimes hard to understand," Jodl's aide once told me, "but we found it easier to work directly with Model." And while the American press labeled it the "Rundstedt Offensive," the old Prussian sulked in his headquarters, and left the planning to Hitler and the work to Model.

Myth—The plot on Eisenhower's life

Yes, the rumor even spoke of a rendezvous by the notorious German saboteur Skorzeny with underground henchmen at the famed *Café de la Paix* in Paris. It was all a hoax, yet hundreds and thousands of Allied soldiers were put on guard, road blocks were hastily manned throughout the entire Allied rear area, Eisenhower was given a double, while he, himself, virtually became a prisoner in his headquarters. And all the time the blond giant whom rumor had as stealing through the Allied lines on his way to Paris was comfortably established behind the German lines, directing the attack of his brigade on the town of Malmedy, in the heart of the Bulge. No wonder that Skorzeny leaned back in his chair in his prison cell, and grinned at me as he recounted his successes: near panic in the Allied lines, a psychology of defeat which suddenly gripped large segments of the Allied command and their troops, elaborate precautions which slowed military operations. Such are the fortunes of war: an entire Allied camp transformed because of the latrine gossip of a few German soldiers.

Myth—We knew all about the Battle of the Bulge beforehand. It was merely a trap to get the Germans into the open

They fooled us, and we might as well admit it. However, the error on our part was in evaluating the information we collected, rather than in gathering the material itself. We were fooled because we were overconfident and certain that we had the Germans on the run. Intelligence officers, who were supposed to be born pessimists, were vying with each other for the honor of devastating the German war machine with words. It was a dangerous game, and the cost was high. But being a strong, resourceful country, we were able to recover from this blow as we have from others like it. However, if we do not start training our intelligence officers to overestimate rather than underestimate the enemy, we may sometime find ourselves without recuperative means. Even a strong nation of great resources needs to profit from the mistakes it has made in the past.

The Patton Myth

A great, great many people believe that the Battle of the Bulge was won by General Patton's Third Army, which did indeed liberate the now consecrated town of Bastogne. Few knew that the major German forces during the first ten days of the fighting were attacking northwest against steady, but unspectacular, Hodges' First Army. Fewer realized that the heaviest fighting around Bastogne occurred not when the town was surrounded, but about ten days later, when the Germans turned south with sudden fury, after Hitler had abandoned his grandiose scheme for the capture of Brussels and Antwerp.

As we now realize, Patton's initial fighting, though important, was conducted against the German *Seventh Army* composed of four mediocre infantry divisions sent to the south for the express purpose of blocking Patton. Meanwhile, in those nightmarish ten days, both *Fifth* and *Sixth Panzer Armies* punched, slugged, and battered their way through the First Army to the north, getting ever nearer to the Meuse River. While Patton was battling the infantry divisions of the German *Seventh Army,* four panzer corps with 1,200 tanks and 250,000 men were pounding 60,000 Americans of Hodges' First Army. Here was the great crisis of the attack. The Germans continually attempted to turn the flank of the First Army forces, who were desperately trying to build up an east-west line. But new American units, the 3d Armored, 84th and then 2nd Armored, were fed into this brittle Allied line, and they always managed to keep one road ahead of the leading German columns. Only later, on December 26, after the crisis in the north had been met and Hitler realized his great dream was going up in smoke, did the Germans turn to the south to attack Bastogne in force. Then the defenders, by this time greatly reinforced, in a magnificent stand beat off eight German divisions. The crisis had been passed, however, and the Germans were attempting to buy time by capturing Bastogne, which would have given them a more adequate defense line behind which they hoped to sit and tie down more Allied divisions. Patton's army performed well; his true glory was as part of a team, directed by Eisenhower, which was flexible enough to rebound from a completely surprising attack.

The British Myth

The most controversial figure in the Battle of the Bulge was Montgomery. Brought into the midst of the battle by Eisenhower when he made his decision to split the battlefront, Montgomery is first of all accused of recommending this split, which some Americans think was ruinous to a quick Allied recovery in the Bulge. Secondly, he is charged with poor handling of the troops which came under his command on December 20. On both these counts, the charges are not substantiated. We have already noted that Eisenhower made his decision first, told Montgomery and Churchill after. But what of the need for the split, and what of the days after that?

Eisenhower's decision has been criticized because, it is claimed, on December 20, when the split occurred, the battle was already decided, and, therefore, it was patently a one-man job to hit at both German flanks, and cut off the penetration. I leave to the reader, with no further comment necessary, the decision as to whether the German attack was under control on December 20. Competent military strategists agree that with the overwhelming German force pointed to the northwest, it was absolutely essential that a unified command in the north rally all threatened forces to shape the troop movements and strategy which could meet this threat. Bradley, separated as he was by communication and transportation difficulties, far from the scene of the crisis, and without British troops under his command, was in no position to co-ordinate the moves necessary for meeting the German attack. Montgomery was the logical person, from a military standpoint, to co-ordinate the efforts of all troops threatened with isolation and strangulation by the German attack.

Moreover, it is true that only with such a command could the efforts of British and American troops be co-ordinated. Allied troops of both nations were shunted around to best meet the attack: British troops were given to the Ninth Army when it lost most of its divisions to the First Army; British troops were along the Meuse River in force; a British division backed up the First Army line south of Liége, and a British cavalry regiment met the nose of the German penetration at the Meuse River itself. All of these troop dispositions were necessary. That the American divisions did almost all of the fighting during the crisis was due to the inherently sound tactical principle that the American First Army was meeting the brunt of the attack. Rather than feed British forces into this command, where they would have wasted precious days adjusting to American ways, and put American troops along the Meuse River, Montgomery used his troops in the reserve role where they could be directed as a unit. The question of using British forces east of the Meuse was discussed and rejected because to move them there would have entailed their crossing communication lines of both First and Ninth Armies, and the resulting tangle would have been chaotic.

Feelings ran high, and tempers short those dark December days, amid the confusion and even panic of the great

German attack. National spirit, which we have in abundance, sometimes blinds us to good sense and understanding. But viewed in retrospect, Eisenhower's decision was eminently sound and satisfactory for coping with German efficiency. This is no apology for Montgomery's action, nor is it a condemnation of Bradley. Both were doing their jobs in different ways. Both contributed to the most brilliant American strategy of the war—defeat of a strong, hard, clever German attack.

Once in control of the northern half of the Bulge, Montgomery followed Hodges' initial plan. The withdrawal from the St. Vith salient was forced by overwhelming German pressure, and the subsequent withdrawal of the 82nd Airborne Division "into the hills" was dictated by the German threat to turn the entire flank of the XVIII Airborne Corps, and to cut off the vast eighteen-mile wedge the corps held into the German line. All these movements make sense to those who have studied the fighting.

Nor did Montgomery contemplate withdrawal of all his armies to the Meuse River, as is claimed by some partisan writers. It is true, as we have already observed, that he moved his XXX Corps down to the Meuse River line, but he did not contemplate withdrawal of his entire army, nor did he suggest that General Collins' VII Corps, forming up just east of the Meuse, withdraw to the west. In those uncertain days of the crisis around Christmas, when the Germans were thrusting their armored fist into the midst of Collins' forming forces, Montgomery, through Hodges, authorized Collins to fall back to the north, if necessary, through a series of successive lines, until they were just south of Liége. At no time was it suggested by anyone that Collins' force pull west of the Meuse River.

To criticize Montgomery for not counterattacking in the midst of the hell swirling around him is only to indicate ignorance of the situation. One by one, as the American divisions of General Collins' VII Corps assembled for their counterattacking mission, they were swallowed up in the sea of battle, unable to more than assemble before being attacked. In Montgomery's typically British explanation, "It was the corps which I had formed for the offensive action which eventually took the full blow of Rundstedt's left hook. It took a knock. I said, 'Dear me, this can't go on. It's being swallowed up in the battle.' I set to work and managed to form the corps again. Once more pressure was such that it began to disappear in a defensive battle. I said, 'Come, come,' and formed it again, and it was put in offensively by General Hodges, after we had consulted together." This may be the language of an egotist, but brutal criticism of Montgomery's tactics does not square up with the facts. The Master, as he was often called, is destined to be the subject of long and bitter controversy. That he was at times cautious, I doubt any American will deny; to say he made mistakes is something which could be said of all military commanders; that he was an egotist, hardly needs repeating. But many of the mistakes he is charged with were not of his making.

The Myth in Hitler's Mind

Not all the myths were American. The greatest myth of all spurted from Hitler's imagination—a dictator's wish or hope. Hitler and his advisors were never convinced that Eisenhower had real command of this troops. Herr Adolf, the Chief of State, who, himself, reviewed the most minute movements of German troops, would not, could not, believe that Eisenhower could decide for himself to abandon two gigantic attacks without first getting approval from his masters, Churchill and Roosevelt. Hitler reasoned that before Eisenhower could divert troops to the attack area, he would first have to comprehend the seriousness of the German attack, then be obliged to wrangle with his bosses for several days before getting permission to switch to the defensive. And by that time, Adolf gleefully told his confidants, the Germans would be comfortably across the Meuse River, well on their way to Antwerp. The most surprised man was Hitler when the democracies could and did act with firmness and resolution during this crisis.

WAS IT A DARK DECEMBER?

There are many who would answer a sharp unequivocal "yes" to the proposition that December, 1944, was truly a dark December. First, they would point to the tragic destruction, the shattered bodies and minds, the arms and legs which lay crumpled on snowcovered hills and forests of the Ardennes, the total misery of the infantrymen wading waist deep in snow, the dead tankers in burning hulks, the pilots in falling planes. They would tell you of things difficult to recount —of chaotic days when for the first time in Europe the Allied invasion forces were sent reeling by German blows. To the victorious peoples and their armies on the march, the effect was almost unbelievable: curfew in Paris; prayers in New York; wonder in London; frantic preparations for withdrawal in Maastricht, Holland, headquarters of Ninth Army; dazed amazement in Spa, Chaudfontaine, and Tongres, successive headquarters of a fleeing First Army; stark fright on faces of Belgian and Luxembourg citizens left behind by retreating armies; the punchdrunk look of lost soldiers; the utter despair of French liaison officers remembering only too vividly the tragic summer days of 1940; and then, as the bitter truth dawned on the at first uncomprehending mind, grim determination and bitter hatred as reports were received about the slaughter of American soldiers at Malmedy.

They would point to the 76,890 American men who were casualties in that great struggle, of their youth and vigor, of stricken parents and wives and sweethearts who received the form telegrams which began "The War Department regrets . . ." They would conclude the battle was stupid and senseless because we should have predicted the German attack, and should have been ready for it. But was the picture so dark?

Granting that we should not have been caught in the Ardennes, we are still faced with the undisputed fact that once the surprise was over, our reaction was magnificent. History will prove that the team led by Eisenhower put on one of the greatest performances of the entire war when it faced the German attack. The 90-degree turn by Patton, rapid redeployment of most of the First and Ninth Army, the movement of two British corps, rearrangement of supplies, an entire new air plan developed overnight, the complicated logistical rearrangements, which have barely been touched upon in this book, all are military feats of which we may rightly be proud. They are feats which surprised the Germans. That the Battle of the Bulge, and its irreparable damage to the German war machine and morale, hastened the day's end, stands as an inescapable fact. Caught in the open, away from their fortifications and their river defenses, the Germans were hit and hit again. It was a stroke of luck for which we have only Hitler to thank. As he had done at Stalingrad before, the *Fuehrer* gambled heavily on his intuition, and lost.

Perhaps even more catastrophic to the Germans was the complete collapse of home-front morale. From the dizzying emotional heights of those pre-Christmas days, when for the first time in two years the German armies were on the march, German civilians were suddenly jarred back to their senses by the hard realities of impending national defeat. For two joyous weeks the years of suffering seemed meaningful, as hopes for the western armies pyramided. But just as rapidly, these hopes were shattered, not only by Allied advances in the west, but also by stupendous Russian advances in the east. Once more the faces in the villages grew long, smiles vanished. To most, only despair and an uncertain future lay ahead.

Although the unexpected fury of the German attack threw the Allied team off balance, and upset the timetable of advance, the blow inflicted only temporary damage, which was quickly repaired. The jolt of even temporary defeat shocked many overconfident Americans, military and civilian, into realization of the serious nature of the fight; the laughing and joking about the German armies ceased. And our intelligence officers at last began to overestimate German power, too late, I grant you, to prevent the nearly fatal attack, but nonetheless a healthy sign. And from the overseas Arsenal came men and materials, which soon replaced the damage wrought by the unpredictable Hitler. The *Fuehrer* had gambled and lost; our top military men in the battle, Eisenhower, Bradley, and Hodges, all believe that Hitler made one of the greatest mistakes of his career when he ordered the Ardennes attack. It was in the tradition of this fanatic to risk all in one great gamble. His only regret, shared by many Germans today, was that he lost the gamble.

Nor should we ever forget that the Battle of the Bulge was only a part of a larger struggle which we won, a struggle against one particular form of selfishness and greed called Fascism. This struggle, of which the Battle of the Bulge was only a small segment, was important because it gave us the opportunity to create a better world in which we all could live. We triumphed over one form of social malignancy, and gained that chance. If we throw away that opportunity, we will have only ourselves to blame.

Choose From These Outstanding Ballantine War Books